saltwater people
of the broken bays

saltwater people

SYDNEY'S NORTHERN BEACHES

of the broken bays

John Ogden

CYCLOPS PRESS

Publications by Cyclops Press
can be purchased online at:
www.cyclopspress.com.au

Dedicated to Louise Whelan
who has shown me the beauty,
power and dignity of love.

In Honour of the Rights of Indigenous People

With deep respect we acknowledge the Guringai (Ku-ring-gai), the Gai-mariagal and the Cammeray (Cammeraygal) clan people of the Eora nation who, over tens of thousands of years, cared for the land and shore where we live and play. We also acknowledge the contemporary Aboriginal custodians of this land.

"I am forever walking upon these shores, Betwixt the sand and the foam, The high tide will erase my foot-prints, And the wind will blow away the foam." Khalil Gibran (1883–1931)

Mortuary warning and spelling discrepancies
It is customary for some Indigenous communities not to mention names or reproduce images associated with the recently deceased. Members of these communities are respectfully advised that a number of people mentioned in writing or depicted in images in the following pages have passed away.

Users are warned that there may be words and descriptions that might be culturally sensitive and not normally used in certain public or community contexts. In some circumstances, terms and annotations of the period in which a text was written may be considered inappropriate today.

A note on the text
The spelling of Aboriginal words in historical documents is inconsistent, depending on how they were heard, interpreted and recorded by Europeans. As per standard academic practice, original spelling has been retained in quoted texts, while names and place names have been standardised, based on the most common contemporary usage and ability to best assist with the correct pronunciation of these names. The word 'lore' is used to describe a set of customary practices, ways of living, storytelling and tradition.

Photographs shown on pages 28, 30, 31, 42, 304 & 307 are for illustrative purposes only. Photography did not arrive on Australian shores for almost six decades after the traditional life of Sydney's coastal clans had been interrupted and changed forever.

Title page *Photo Oceaneye.*
Previous spread *Photo Jon Frank.*
Right Fishman rock carving, Beacon Hill.
Opposite Rock carving of two fish. *Photo oggy.*
Next page *Photo Oceaneye.*

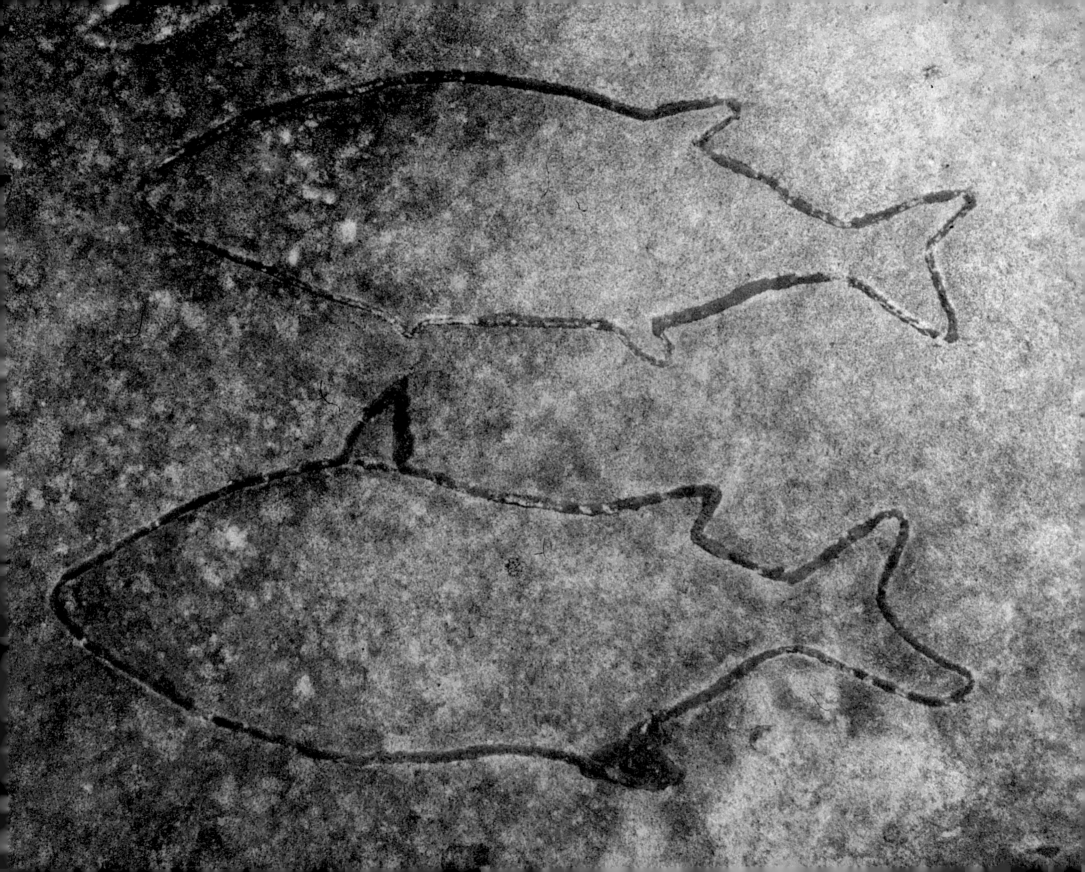

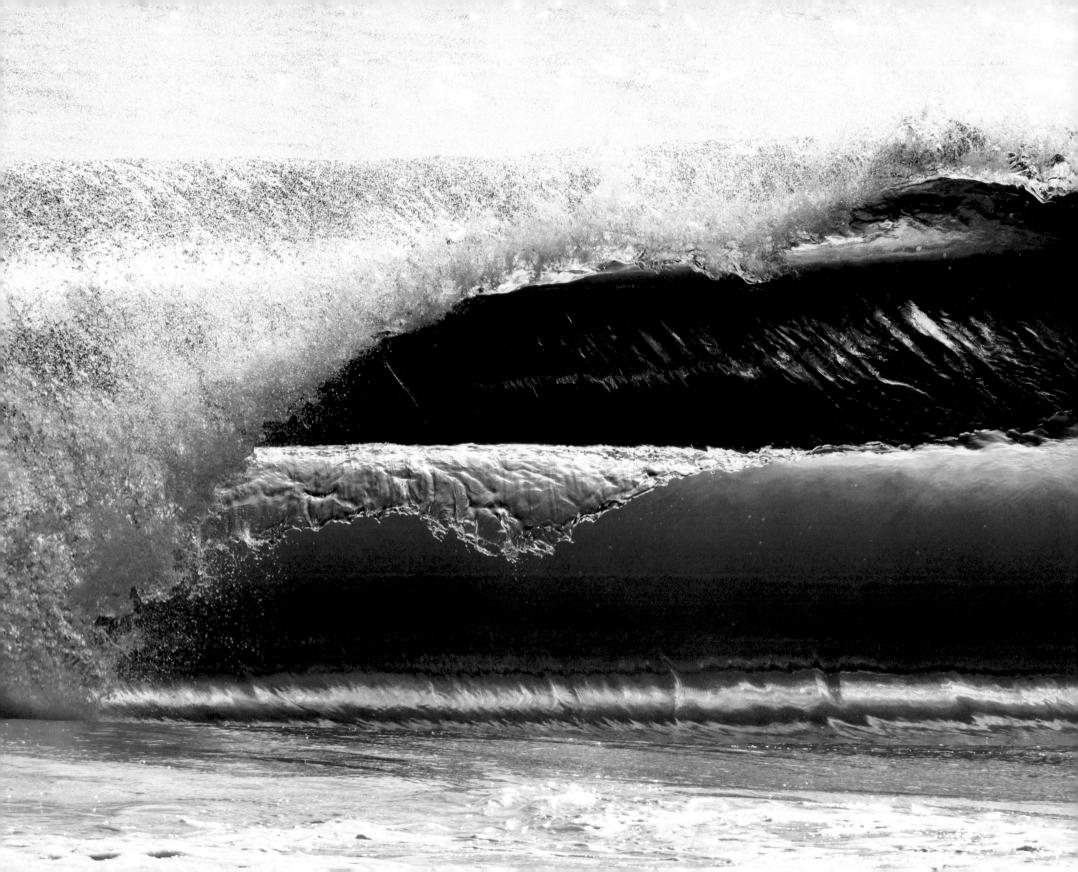

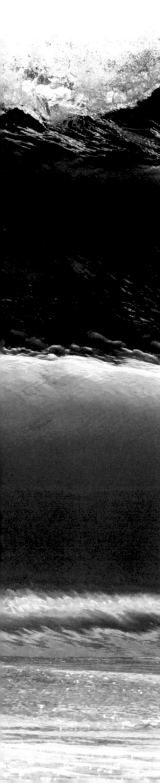

foreword

Who are the Saltwater People? For tens of thousands of years, longer than anyone really knows, the clans of the *Eora* have been the Traditional Owners and Custodians of this glorious coastal land.

Their name, derived from *ee* (yes) and *ora* (here, or this place) conveys the complex animist connection, the sense that they are *of this land*.

Before Sydney Harbour existed it was a river valley, and the ancient coastline was much further towards the sunrise. The Saltwater People fished from canoes and hunted on land that is now deep beneath the sea.

At the end of the last Ice Age, the ocean left the Barrenjoey Headland only thinly connected to one of the most dramatic peninsulas on earth.

Wander the bushland, the mangrove creeks and tidal lagoons, along the sandstone cliffs and rock platforms, sit and listen to the sea in the hidden coves, on the sandy dunes or high on the rocky headlands covered with grass trees, angophoras and wind-blown scrub, and this country will speak to you.

All of us who love this meeting place of land and sea are aware that we walk in the footsteps of the Ancestors. Around Broken Bay and much of the Sydney basin are

Previous page Bilgola.
Photo Murray Vanderveer.

Above The last break, c.1912.
Photo Frank Hurley.
Carbon photograph.
National Gallery of Australia,
Canberra.

hundreds of Australia's most stunning galleries of rock art. Aboriginal people will tell you the stories in oral history fashion, and the totemic figures carved into the sandstone will detail the lizards, birds, kangaroos, echidnas, sharks, fish and whales that are part of this natural world.

After you look out at Lion Island and the sweeping beauty from West Head, study closely the engravings of the mythic sky heroes and other symbols on the thousand-year-old rock galleries in the Ku-ring-gai National Park. Astronomers and Aboriginal people say that here is further indication that the sophisticated Indigenous knowledge system included an awareness of the planets and an ability to use the stars for navigation.

John Romer, one of the greatest archaeologists of our age, warns us to focus on what we do know about the past and admit what is uncertain or has been erased. The impact of invasion, dispossession, violence and disease most certainly obliterated so much life and Culture here.

The foundational work of Aboriginal historians, such as Professor Dennis Foley's book, *Repossession of our Spirit*, with its striking photographs by Ricky Maynard, gives us a new way of seeing the *Eora*, far more expansive than the colonial views of naturalists, amateur botanists, sailors and new settlers.

The late Burnum Burnum's *Aboriginal Australia* explains how Aboriginal art and storytelling has many layers of knowledge and deeper levels of meaning, sometimes veiled but always expressing the connectedness to the land and the life force.

John Ogden has a particular gift to enrich the story of *what we do know* about the Saltwater People of the Broken Bays.

More than three decades spent photographing Aboriginal life has given him a wonderful appreciation of the *Eora* way of seeing. His archival research in completing his landmark photographic book, *Portraits from a Land Without People,* opened up a treasure trove of knowledge.

Living on this coastline he has experienced the way the environment calls and shapes us all, the Aborigines, the artists, the architects inspired by the drama of the natural beauty, and the surfers entranced by the endless waves.

My son, Will, who was born here, has a particular way of expressing the gleam of the water on a day when all of life seems in balance. *"These are the dolphin days."*

When the humpbacks are passing on their migrations and sometimes breach in extraordinary shows of their majesty and power we are all reminded of our place in the eternal scheme of Nature.

This book reminds us of our responsibility.

The most important word missing today from the Australian Constitution is *Custodianship*. It is a word of strength and beauty that can unite us and bind us to the ideal of what it means to be Australian.

Custodianship is a central concept of both Aboriginal and Torres Strait Islander knowledge and gives everyone who lives in this land a responsibility to contribute to the balance of life. Custodians will look after this land and all its people for generations to come. This valuing of life, respect for all creatures, connects past, present and future. It unifies the descendants of the world's oldest continuous Cultures with the newer arrivals from more than 230 other places. The land owns us all.

Australia is our home.

Jeff McMullen
Whale Beach 2011

North Head. *Photo oggy.*

Right *Photo Alex Marks.*

"... they are far more happier than we Europeans, being wholy unacquainted not only with the Superfluous, but with the necessary Conveniences so much sought after in Europe; they are happy in not knowing the use of them. They live in a Tranquility which is not disturbed by the Inequality of Condition. The earth and Sea of their own accord furnishes them with all things necessary for Life. They covet not Magnificient Houses, Household-stuff, etc.; they live in a Warm and fine Climate, and enjoy every wholesome Air, so that they have very little need of Cloathing; and this they seem to be fully sencible of, for many to whom we gave Cloth, etc., left it carelessly upon the Sea beach and in the Woods, as a thing they had no manner of use for; in short, they seem'd to set no Value upon anything we gave them, nor would they ever part with anything of their own for any one Article we could offer them. This, in my opinion, Argues that they think themselves provided with all the necessarys of Life, and that they have no Superfluities." JAMES COOK, 1770

introduction

The east coast of Australia was the last piece of the puzzle for the European explorers mapping the 'newly discovered' Great Southern Land. After the Dutch had completed much of the hard work charting the continent's immense coastline, HMS Endeavour arrived at arguably the most attractive and fertile shore of *Terra Australis*, and Lieutenant Commander James Cook promptly claimed all he surveyed in the name of the King of England. Cook apparently did not feel a need to consult with the Indigenous people about this development, although he had been requested to do so by the British Crown. Even if the esteemed mariner had taken the time to communicate with the locals, the Aborigines would have had difficulty comprehending the colonial concept of land ownership, as: *"No two people could have been more different in their concepts of the world and the meaning of human life than Europeans and Aborigines."*[1]

On Monday 7 May 1770, while navigating the coastline, James Cook wrote in the log of HMS *Endeavour*:

> Little wind, Southerly, and Serene pleasant Weather. In the P.M. found the Variation by several Azimuths to be 8 degrees East; at sunset the Northermost land in sight bore North 26 degrees East; and some broken land that appear'd to form a bay bore North 40 degrees West, distant 4 Leagues. This Bay I named Broken bay ...[2]

Native Family. *Artist Joseph Lycett c.1819.*
National Library of Australia, Canberra.
pic-an2962715-s13

Cook is recognised as an extraordinary hydrographer and explorer, not prone to making mistakes, but locating the present site of the Narrabeen Beach Surf Life Saving Club clubhouse in Broken Bay is regarded as one of his small errors.[3] This was later corrected by Governor Arthur Phillip, and later again by Matthew Flinders … but perhaps Cook can be excused.

Broken Bay is now usually only referred to as the area around the mouth of the Hawkesbury River, but at the time of first settlement by Europeans the whole region between North Harbour (Balgowlah) and Pittwater was known as Broken Bay. It is this broader sense of the name that I wish to employ when discussing the geography covered by the title of this book. Bookended by two impressive rock monoliths that are actually the tops of hills flooded at the end of the last ice age, these islands are now linked to the mainland by sand spits. With Car-rang-gel (North Head) guarding the entrance to Sydney Harbour and Barrenjoey (meaning 'young kangaroo') standing sentinel to the mouth of the Hawkesbury River to the north, this coastline forms a string of broken bays.

The focus of *Saltwater People of the Broken Bays* is on the shoreline, that high-energy intersection between sea and land where waves, whipped up by wind and storms sometimes thousands of kilometres out to sea, pound the coast in a final dramatic explosion … or caress it with a gentle cascade or surge. This constant, hypnotic dance with the shore is repetitive but always changing. It can be calming, and it can be confronting. When a new swell arrives, excitement grows. The ocean becomes energised and the surf zone challenges us with its power and sense of danger. Like the Saltwater People—the coastal Aboriginal people before us—we are drawn to the ocean and its shoreline. It influences our lives, and in turn our presence affects this playground on the edge of the vast Pacific.

When asked, few living in Sydney know about the Aboriginal people of the Eora nation who lived along the coast near what is now Sydney Harbour for many millennia before the coming of the Europeans. There are also many misconceptions when asked about the culture of the first people. One common belief is that they were all somehow frightened of the ocean, but this is far from the truth. The Aboriginal clans along the northern beaches were true Saltwater People, at home not only in the sparkling estuaries and rivers, but also in the ocean waves. Theirs was a canoe culture, and they were known to take these craft out in large surf. They fished with spears, or lines and hooks, and would dive off rock ledges into the surf, re-emerge with lobster and abalone, and then ride a wave surge back onto the rock shelf. This part of our history has remained largely hidden, and it is important to reveal here the influence of our Aboriginal heritage, not only on the people of Sydney, but also on our national psyche.

Considered to be one of the world's most magnificent stretches of coastline, Sydney's northern beaches were the birthplace of modern Australian beach culture. It is here that Australians witnessed the first ocean bathing, the development of swimsuits, the genesis of the surf life saving movement and the beginning of wave riding. Because of the quality of the surf beaches, many world surfing champions were either raised here or chose to make the area their home at some stage of their career. Some of the world's best recognised painters, potters, writers, poets, photographers, filmmakers, musicians and architects also call the northern beaches home. Despite the perceived conservative image of many of its current citizens, the area was once a refuge for outlaws—escaped convicts, bushrangers, smugglers and illicit breweries. These broken bays have produced some truly unique individuals and some incredible stories.

The European occupation of Australia began on the country's edges, determined by the ships that connected us to the world, and 90 percent of the population has remained near the coast—the first point of contact. Ironically, Britannia may have ruled the waves and Britain considered a great maritime nation, but immersion in the ocean was a frightening thought to the early British mariners and colonists. As commander of the *Nautilus*, Captain Nemo said in Jules Verne's *Twenty Thousand Leagues Under the Sea*:

> The sea does not belong to despots. On its surface they can still exercise their iniquitous claims, battle each other there, devour each other there, transport every earthly horror. But thirty feet below the surface, their power ceases, their influence fades, their power vanishes.[4]

The sea was perceived as vexatious, even perilous, concealing monsters and predators.[5] Shipwrecks and drownings were common. It would take many generations of waterpeople to turn the tide until we were as comfortable as the Aboriginal coastal people had been at play in the ocean.

If we had listened, the Saltwater People could have taught us much about protecting these valuable resources. The British sense of destiny and belief in the supremacy of science subverted all else, blinding the colonialists to the environmental sustainability practised by the original custodians of the land. There is now a growing awareness that something is wrong, and that the modern world is out of balance. The natural beauty of the coast is under threat. It is obvious that the first people protected this country, and, as they did for many millennia before us, we need to think from the heart and preserve our shoreline for future generations.

Hollandia Nova detecta 1644: Terre Austrandale decouverte l'an 1644.
Map by Melchisedech Thevenot.
State Library of New South Wales.
Call number: MRB/ F910.8/T V. 1

the first people,

the saltwater people

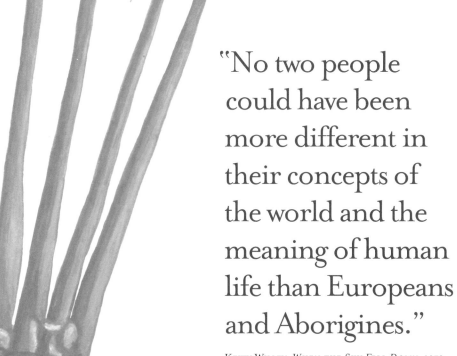

"No two people could have been more different in their concepts of the world and the meaning of human life than Europeans and Aborigines."

KEITH WILLEY, *WHEN THE SKY FELL DOWN*, 1979

Left *Photo Nathan Smith.*
Right *Illustration Ian Faulkner.*

The vast area of land stretching between Deerubbun (now known as the Hawkesbury River) through to Tuhbowgule (the deep harbour named 'Port Jackson' by the European settlers) was home to many Aborigines living in harmony with the coastal environment as they had for at least 20,000 years before the arrival of Europeans. Their history predates the harbour itself, transformed from a deep river valley into a harbour when it was flooded at the end of the last ice age over 6,500 years ago. They moved through a landscape steeped in spiritual significance, in a land that was close to paradise with plenty of game, lagoons alive with fish and wildfowl, and deep ocean waters filled with bounty.

Due to the rapid and devastating impact of European colonisation on traditional life, and a lack of records, there is an ongoing discussion about the correct boundaries, spelling, and even names of the various groups of Aborigines and clans. The word *Koori* means 'man' or 'people' in numerous languages of southeastern Australia and is a general term signifying people from New South Wales and Victoria. The people of the Greater Sydney Basin have collectively become known as the Eora nation, with *Eora* basically translating into 'people of this place', or 'ours'. This book concerns itself only with the coastal clans that inhabited the northern beaches, and so a more specific nomenclature is required.

The beaches between the Hawkesbury River and Bongin Bongin (Mona Vale) were the territory of the Gur-ing-gah and, specifically, the Garigal clan. The name 'Kuringai' (Gur-ing-gah) is made up from the word *Koori,* meaning people, and *(n)g-gai,* perhaps meaning 'belonging'.[1] According to oral histories, the coastline between Bongin Bongin and Kay-e-my (Manly) was the territory of the Gai-mariagal, and in particular the Gaimai (Kayimai) and Gatlay (Cannaigal) clans, with the Cammeray (Cammeraygal) clan living further up the harbour.[2] Many of the clan names end with *-gal,* which means 'group of people'.[3] Clans (incorrectly referred to as 'tribes' by the Europeans) within Sydney belonged to several major language groups, often with coastal and inland dialects.[4]

Port Jackson, New South Wales. Aborigines fishing in canoe, North Head in background. *Artist Augustus Earle c.1825. Watercolour, 10.7x35.21 cm. Rex Nan Kivell Collection, National Library of Australia, Canberra. pic-an2818282*

Fishing, 1813.
Artist M. Dubourg. Rex Nan Kivell Collection,
National Library of Australia, Canberra
nla. pic 8936126

"We have sometimes, in fine weather, seen a man lying across a canoe, with his face in the water, and his fish-gig immersed, ready for the darting." JOHN HUNTER, 1787

WEAPONS, IMPLEMENTS AND ORNAMENTS
NEW HOLLAND, NEW SOUTH WALES

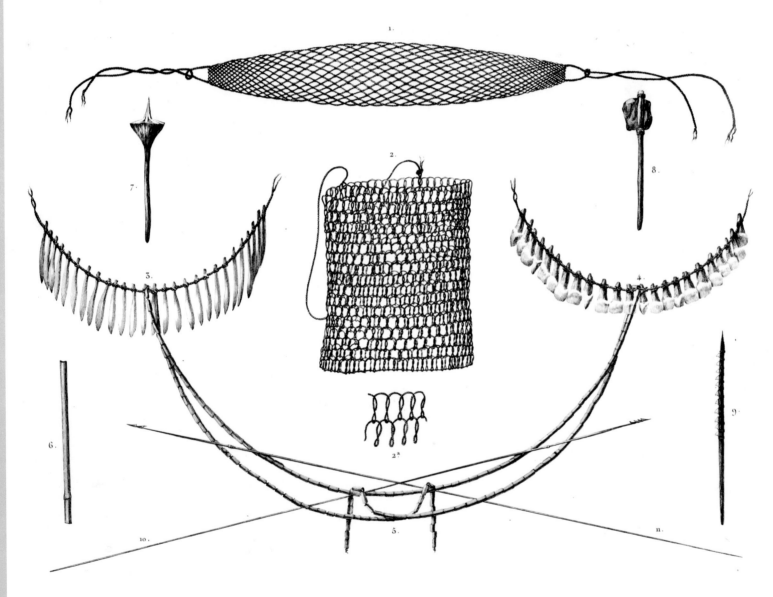

1   Net band that Aboriginal people wear on their foreheads.

2   Net bag, in which they put their provisions.

2a Details of the mesh of the previous bag.

3, 4 Necklace of kangaroo teeth.

5   Necklace made with pieces of threaded reed.

6   A piece of reed, natural size.

7   Club, made from a single piece of gnarled wood.

8   Club, made of stone fixed in a wooden handle.

9   Tip of a war spear, barbed with shark's teeth.

10, 11 Two barbed war spears.

Péron, F. [and de Freycinet, L.], *Voyage de découvertes aux Terres Australes, fait par ordre du gouvernement, sur les corvettes le Géographe, le Naturaliste et la goëlette le Casuarina, pendant les années 1800, 1801, 1802, 1803 et 1804, 4 vols and atlas*, Paris, 1824.

Palawa historian Emma Lee gives voice to the view of some Indigenous academics: *"The use of individual clan names is a personal history, not open access like a town name on a map."*[5] In Aboriginal culture, information is restricted to those with the appropriate level of initiation. 'Linguistic correctness' may in fact be a fanciful idea, since our knowledge of traditional life is a mixture of both fragments of Aboriginal oral history and European interpretation through scant records.[6] There is evidence that the term 'Kuring-gai' was coined by linguist the Reverend John Fraser in 1892, but local Aboriginal groups still prefer to use the name 'Kuringai' for the Aboriginal people of the coastal areas of Manly, Warringah and Pittwater. In this book, I will respect the decision of these groups, but will also defer to another accepted practice of referring to coastal Aboriginal clans as Saltwater People. This term suggests a relationship with the ocean and the beaches, and serves well to separate the coastal dwellers and those who roamed further inland.

There is a tendency to think that there was a single Aboriginal culture, but it would be more accurate to describe Aboriginal Australia as a collection of First Nations. While many aspects of culture were shared across the continent, the clans along Sydney's northern beaches were influenced by the local environment and seasonal food supply. The Saltwater People were heavily dependent on the ocean and waterways for the bulk of their diet, but they also enjoyed a variety of game meat, native fruits and vegetables. This was in stark contrast to the commoner in Europe at the time who had little choice at the dinner table. The sustainability of food supply for the Saltwater People was such that they would gather food for three to five hours per day, leaving time for rest, socialising and ritual. That traditional lifestyle was interrupted with the arrival of the Europeans, and the effects were devastating. Many believe all that remains of the Saltwater People is the shellfish middens (pits of empty shells left over from centuries of seafood barbecues

"... altho' they do not use outriggers, I have seen them paddle through a large surf without over-setting or taking in more water than if rowing in smooth water."

Lieutenant William Bradley, 1789

Weapons, implements and ornaments by C.A. Lesueur, 1824. *Australian Museum Research Library. Depiction of Aboriginal weapons and implements, c.1790.*

on the beach), rock paintings and engravings left behind. The truth is that their powerful legacy only now being recognised.

This area was rich in food, allowing time for ceremony and cultural practice. As was common in traditional Aboriginal Australia, the Saltwater People moved about in a totemic landscape steeped in meaning and shaped by ancestral beings. Creation stories were passed down in dance and song, *"spelling out the relationship between man and nature"*.[7] Every person was given a totem name, taken from nature, that became part of their identity. This also brought a responsibility to protect that totem, whether it be a bird, fish, insect or object. Ceremonies for initiation and burial were supervised by *kooringals* (elders) and *koradgee* (clever men), who were known for being healers and great warriors. These men had to pass through many initiations, including ritual circumcision, scarification, septum piercing and incisor removal to achieve their status, and were respected as *"men of high degree"*.[8]

The Saltwater People were admired for their fine physique, confidence and humour, remarked upon by Captain Arthur Phillip after his encounter with Kayimai people when entering Middle Harbour for the first time. The Cammeragal clan, whose country is usually regarded as being further inland and adjoining the north side of Sydney Harbour, were said to be *"very powerful People"*, more numerous than other groups and the *"most robust and muscular"* of the Sydney people.[9] Some historians believe that the clan names 'Cammera' and 'Kayimai' (the place name for Manly Cove) were derived from *ka-mai*, *cammi* or *camey*, meaning 'spear'. During his survey of the Greater Sydney Harbour at the end of January 1787, John Hunter noted that the Eora people *"always appeared cheerful and in good humour"*.[10] To settlers coming from eighteenth century Britain where endemic diseases were rife, the state of Aboriginal health looked very good. Surgeon George Worgan commented on how they *"seemingly enjoy uninterrupted Health, and live to a great Age"*.[11]

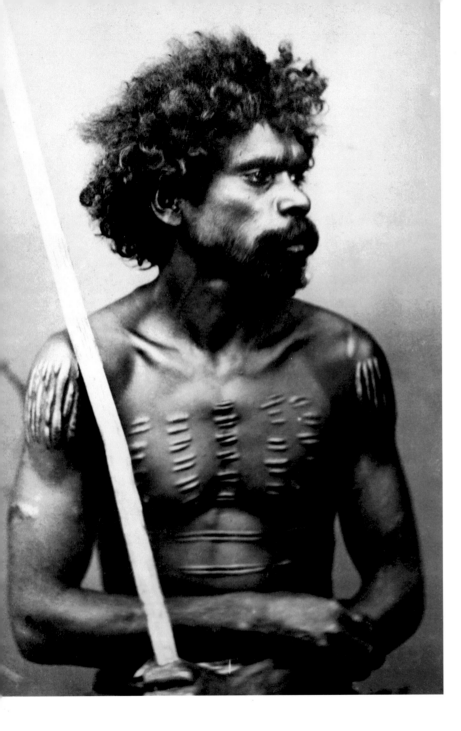

Whether their muscular build and longevity were due to their canoe culture and seafood diet can only be guessed at, but their skills as waterpeople, at ease fishing either the estuaries or surf beaches, were well recognised. Both men and women could dive to considerable depths in the search for such delights as crayfish and abalone.

> Getting onto the rocks that projected into the sea, they plunged from them to the bottom in search of shell-fish. When they had been down some time, we became very uneasy on their account … At length however, they appeared, and convinced us that they were capable of remaining underwater twice as long as our ablest divers. An instant was sufficient for them to take breath, and then they dived again. They did this repeatedly until their baskets were nearly full.[12]

William Govett wrote in the 1830s that *"the natives are not … Cowards of the Deep; on the contrary, they are bold and surprisingly expert, both in swimming and diving"*.[13] Govett went on to relate how he borrowed a fishing line from an Aborigine in an attempt to emulate his success catching snapper from a rock ledge (believed to be Newport Reef), but had only managed to snag the line on rocks below the water. In an attempt to reclaim his line, an Aborigine *"stood upon the verge of a rock"* and in an instant *"plunged through a rising wave, and disappeared"*. He stayed under the water *"full a minute"* before he emerged with the line and the hook intact and rode a *"heaving surge"* back onto the rock.[14] There are similar stories told during the early days of white settlement in Sydney, and it is hoped that more diaries and letters will be unearthed to shed light on the lives of the Saltwater People.

It is estimated that the fruits of the sea provided up to

VIEW of PORT JACKSON in NEW SUOTH WALES.

80 percent of the Saltwater People's diet. Settler accounts in New South Wales noted that women generally fished with hook and line, and men fished with spears.[15] Saltwater People were seen fishing in canoes outside the heads of the estuaries between Port Jackson and Broken Bay as well as inside the harbours. These craft were a source of great interest for early British settlers, and there are many comments on them in their diaries. Among these early records are reports of canoes going out in 'large surf', suggesting that the Saltwater People of Sydney may well have been the first surfers.

Research of archaeological evidence by Sandra Bowdler suggests that Aboriginal women became increasingly involved in fishing after the introduction of the shell hook some 600–900 years ago.[16] Lieutenant William Bradley described the way these shiny crescent-shaped lures or hooks were made in Broken Bay in the late 1700s:

> **One of the women made a fishing hook while we were by her, from the inside of what is commonly called the pearl oyster shell, by rubbing it down on the rocks until thin enough and then cut it circular with another, shape the hook with a sharp point rather bent it and not bearded or barbed.[17]**

These mother-of-pearl shell fish-hooks, known as *bara*, were most commonly made from the large turban shell (*Turbo torquata*), and remains found along the New South Wales coastline indicate that they varied in length from about 13 to 50 millimetres, most of them having *"small notches on the shank end for securing the line"*.[18] Fishing lines consisted of *"two strands evenly laid and twisted hard; made with a grassy substance dark in colour, and nearly as fine as raw silk"*.[19] Writing in 1929, William Scott described how the Aboriginal women of Port Stephens made their fishing lines from young kurrajong trees:

> **The bark would be stripped carefully from the tree and soaked in water until the outer portions could be readily scraped off with a shell. This left a white, flax-like fibre, very tough and strong. The women twisted this fibre to the required thickness and length by rolling it on the front part of the thigh with the hands.[20]**

According to Scott, these fishing lines were incredibly strong, *"capable of landing the heaviest of edible fish"*.[21]

In January 1788, the sailing ships of the First Fleet entered the world of the Eora nation, causing fear and fascination. The Saltwater

Above Hunting—man climbing palm Port Macquarie, c.1910-1923.
Photo Thomas Dick. Australian Museum.
097vV7722

People wondered if the ships were giant birds, floating islands, sea monsters, or even devils. Mahroot, an Aborigine from Botany Bay, recalled that when the old people saw figures *"going up the masts they thought they was opossums"*.[22] They quickly accommodated the presence of these new and gigantic 'canoes', but the arrival of the ships changed their lives forever.[23] Within a few years of the appearance of these invaders, the traditional life that the Saltwater People had lived for thousands of years had been virtually destroyed by the impact of disease and disruption to sustainable food harvesting.

Traditional Aboriginal culture lives on in local place names and half-forgotten stories, but perhaps the main legacy is the way modern Australians view life. The fact that Aboriginal society did not tolerate despots and kings but sought decisions by council is reflected in the broader Australian sense of 'fair go' and egalitarianism. The cult of celebrity is making inroads, but Australians are still wary of 'big noters', preferring a sense of quiet achievement and self-deprecating humour. The Saltwater People were remarked on for their lightheartedness, even in the face of adversity (a 'black' or 'gallows' humour the convicts shared), in much the same way many contemporary Australians display stoicism and humour when confronted by fire and flood.

Fortunately, Aboriginal history and culture is now studied in schools and universities, and a sense of pride in this heritage has developed. The post-modern revisionism of empirical history, and the nodding acceptance of Aboriginal oral histories, has revived the discussion about our nation's mythology. This new and informed educational drive helps bridge the new waves of migration with our nation's Aboriginal heritage. With technology continuing to shrink the world, Indigenous values may gradually become homogenised into a world view, but it must be remembered that these are the values that have helped define Australians as a people with a distinct culture and view of life.

Mother and child, New South Wales, 1898.
Photographer unknown.
Museum Victoria.
NSW180. 017NSW180-co

"Upon the edges of flat rocks which jut out into the sea from beneath the headlands of the coast between Port Jackson and Broken Bay, the natives were accustomed to fish for snappers. They are often seen to great advantage when employed in these occupations ..." WILLIAM GOVETT, 1829

Aborigines spearing fish, others diving for crayfish; a party seated beside a fire cooking fish. *Artist Joseph Lycett c. 1820. National Library of Australia, Canberra. nla.pic-an2962715-s17*

Top right Different stages of mother-of-pearl fish hooks' production from turban shell. *Photo oggy (with thanks to Val Attenbrow and Australian Museum).*

MALGUN

The Aboriginal custom of finger tip removal—malgun, observed in coastal New South Wales, especially in the Sydney region—was a source of curiosity for colonial observers. Initially the British were unsure why some women and girls in coastal areas were missing the first two joints of the little finger on the left hand. In the absence of an obvious explanation, some colonists misinterpreted the custom and created their own explanations for the practice …

Although [Arthur] Phillip and [Watkin] Tench both inquisitive enough to realise that their assumption was ill-founded …

By the time John Turnbull visited Sydney in 1800, most white settlers realised that malgun was related to fishing. Turnbull describes the practice:

Whilst the female child is in its infancy, they deprive it of the two first joints of the little finger of the right hand; the operation being effected by obstructing the circulation by means of a tight ligature; the dismembered part is thrown into the sea, that the child may be hereafter fortunate in fishing.[1]

This custom of amputating a small portion of the little finger of young girls to mark them out as fishers was also practiced further north in the Port Stephens region, and was observed into the 1860s. William Scott, who grew up in Port Stephens and counted the 'lads of the tribe' as his 'playfellows',[2] explains how this practice was related to fishing:

An Aboriginal woman, Fanny, who was a servant of our family for many years, was in her girlhood days dedicated to the art of fishing. When quite young, a ligature was tied about the first joint of her left finger very tightly, and being left there for a considerable time, the top portion mortified and, in time, fell off. This was carefully secured, taken out into the bay, and, with great solemnity, committed to the deep. The belief was that the fish would eat this part of the girl's finger, and would ever, thereafter, be attracted to the rest of the hand from which it had come.[3]

According to Scott, at least one woman from each tribe was usually dedicated to fishing through the malgun operation. These women were not only defined as fishers, but also as the makers of fishing lines so that "the virtue accruing from her innate powers over fish" were "communicated to the lines she made".[4] Scott had no doubts that the malgun operation was effective, saying that Fanny "was indeed a wonderfully lucky fisher".[5]

Turnbull and Scott's accounts of malgun demonstrate that women were in fact the designated fishers in Aboriginal societies in coastal New South Wales in the eighteenth and nineteenth centuries. This directly challenges the stereotypical notion that men with spears were primarily responsible for fishing. Women were largely responsible for fishing in coastal New South Wales, and were designated as such both symbolically through the absence of two joints of their little finger, and practically, as this joint removal was said to aid fishing ability.

Reprinted courtesy of the Department of Environment, Climate Change & Water. Alex Roberts, with Kath Schilling, Aboriginal Women's Fishing in New South Wales: A thematic history, Department of Environment, Climate Change & Water NSW, Sydney, 2010, pp. 9–10. www.environment.nsw.gov.au/resources/cultureheritage/10131abwfish.pdf

the arrival
of the first
boat people

"The new lands were treated as if they were empty lands, Terra Nullius, and devoid of human habitants, Terra Nullius." Oren R. Lyons, Faithkeeper, 2010

In 1766, James Cook journeyed to Tahiti in the Pacific Ocean aboard HMS *Endeavour* to observe and record the transit of Venus across the sun, and to then search for the fabled 'Great Southern Continent'. After leaving Tahiti he sailed west, reaching the southeastern coast of the Australian mainland on 19 April 1770. In doing so, the men on his expedition became the first recorded Europeans to have encountered the eastern coastline of *Terra Australis.* Before departing the shores of this 'new land' Cook stopped at Possession Island off the Far North Queensland coast, and just before sunset on Wednesday, 22 August, he declared the coast a British possession:

> Notwithstand[ing] I had in the Name of His Majesty taken possession of several places upon this coast, I now once more hoisted English Coulers and in the Name of His Majesty King George the Third took possession of the whole Eastern Coast ... by the name New South Wales, together with all the Bays, Harbours Rivers and Islands situate upon the said coast, after which we fired three Volleys of small Arms which were Answerd by the like number from the Ship.[1]

Although famed for his seafaring accomplishments, Cook made scant reference to the water skills of the Indigenous people he found along the Australian coast, but perhaps this should come as no surprise. The normally inquisitive mariner also seemed to take little interest in recording the curious activities that the locals were getting up to with their small craft in the surf when he visited the Big Island, Hawaii, on his third and final voyage in 1778. It was on this ill-fated voyage that Captain Cook and his crew became the first Europeans to visit the Hawaiian Islands and to sight the Hawaiian sport of surfboard riding.

The recording of these exploits in the surf was left to the commander of the *Discovery*, First Lieutenant James King, who enthused about the islanders' amazing dexterity guiding their planks of wood onto *"the greatest Swell that sets on Shore"* sending them in *"with a most astonishing Velocity"* and avoiding being *"dashed to mummy against the sharp rocks"*.[2] It must be pointed out, however, that King wrote these words when completing the journals of the voyage, adding to Cook's own account, after Cook's death in 1779.

Cook and his men had managed to get into a confrontation with the Hawaiians and unwisely attempted to take hostage the King of Hawai'i, Kalani'ōpu'u. Angry villagers prevented this and attacked Cook's party. Cook was struck on the head while retreating and then stabbed to death as he fell face-forward into the surf. His demise in the surf zone was prescient in that this son of a Yorkshire farmhand, like virtually all British mariners of his generation, viewed the ocean as a dangerous force that needed to be conquered. *"Those who would go to sea for pleasure,"* a British adage went, *"would go to hell for pastime."*

Hawaiians have long held the bragging rights for being the world's first surfers, and who is brave enough to argue the point? Surfing had previously been observed by crew-members of the *Dolphin* in Tahiti in 1767, and the sport appeared to be a central part of ancient Polynesian culture. References to surf riding on planks and single canoe hulls have also been verified in pre-contact Samoa, where surfing was called *fa'ase'e* or *se'egalu*.[3] The 'Peruvian Theory' of surfing's origins promoted by former World Surfing Champion Felipe Pomar in a 1988 issue of *Surfer* magazine claims that fishermen on the Peruvian coast surfed on their reed-built fishing craft, known as *caballitos*, anywhere from two to three thousand years ago. The Aborigines along Sydney's northern beaches lived in a canoe culture for many millennia, and were observed taking these craft out in big surf. In 1789 Lieutenant William Bradley witnessed

Aborigines landing their canoes *"which they did with ease altho' a very great surf was running"*.[4] This report refers to landing on the open surf beach now known as Manly Beach.

When discussing this theory in his book *The History of Surfing*, Matt Warshaw questions the accepted accounts of how long humans have been riding the waves for fun in any number of diverse locations scattered around the globe:

> For any society living on a temperate coastline, riding waves would likely be a natural, if not intuitive act. Dolphins and pelicans and other animals seem to do it purely out of enjoyment, after all. When did the first human wade into the shorebreak and try to imitate a dolphin?[5]

Fishermen in Peru, and here in Australia, may well have ridden waves before the Polynesians, enjoying their free ride to the beach, but those endeavours are regarded as *"a self-contained prelude to surf history, not the starting point"*.[6]

The missionaries nearly killed off surfing in Hawaii, but the impact of European diseases also helped reshape Hawaii's native customs and culture. It had a similar effect in Australia. The Aboriginal population around Sydney Harbour was profoundly changed by the impact of European epidemics, and traditional life was irreversibly altered within a few years of the arrival of the First Fleet. Dispossessed of their lands and cut off from traditional food sources, there was little alternative for the remnants of the Saltwater People than to disperse or become fringe dwellers. The change was so swift that very little of their traditional culture, especially in the remote bays to the north of the harbour, had been documented. You have to wonder if the traditional fishermen and women of Sydney may have been recognised for their prowess in the ocean if they had

been observed by the likes of King and given better coverage. Fortunately, several references to the Saltwater People's fishing skills and ability in the surf do exist.

The First Fleet arrived at Botany Bay on 18 January 1788, but the original site proved unsuited to settlement. While undertaking a reconnaissance of Port Jackson as an alternative site, Arthur Phillip and a small party encountered the men of Kay-ye-my (the Manly area), and the meeting was recorded in May that year:

> The boats, in passing near a point of land in this harbour, were seen by a number of men, and twenty of them waded into the water unarmed, received what was offered to them and examined the boats with a curiosity that gave me a much higher opinion of them ... And their confidence and manly behaviour made me give the name of Manly Cove to this place.[7]

It would be the following year before the first known reference of the watercraft used by the Aborigines near Sydney appeared in a London report attributed to 'An officer'. Although he described their canoes as *"despicable"*, he praised the Aborigines for *"their dexterous management of them, added to the swiftness with which they paddle, and the boldness that leads them several miles into the open sea"*.[8] Lieutenant Bradley later wrote about the water skills of the Aborigines around the area now referred to as Manly, and although he too was not a great admirer of the craftsmanship of the local canoes he enthused about the way the Aborigines handled their craft: *"altho' they do not use outriggers, I have seen them paddle through a large surf without over-setting or taking in more water than if rowing in smooth water."*[9]

There appear to be no surviving original bark canoes of the Eora, but there do exist numerous drawings and accounts of how the canoes were made, and the State Library of New South Wales reconstructed a canoe for their 2010 'Mari Nawi: Aboriginal Odysseys 1790–1850' exhibition using traditional techniques. What is striking about this craft is how the design would have suited negotiating the surf. The substantially curved bow and stern of traditional canoes would have helped the fishermen as they paddled over waves or caught a ride to shore. William Bradley's account of canoes going out in large surf suggests that the Saltwater People had a remarkable level of skill in handling their craft in the surf. Their training began early, with very young children and even babies carried in canoes when fishing or travelling, and these skills would have been become second nature.

As Cook had done before him, Governor Arthur Phillip took possession of the land in the name of King George without consultation with the Indigenous people. His dispatches told the British Government that Sydney Aborigines had a strong attachment to the land, but no policy came in reply. In his instructions Phillip had been ordered to establish contact and maintain friendly relations with the Aboriginals, and he took these humanitarian injunctions seriously. At first he seems to have succeeded, as the Eora remained peaceful and showed no desire to drive the whites out. In fact, they showed little interest at all in the invaders:

Although the newcomers' belief in their own superiority was impregnable, there is little doubt that the Aborigines failed to share this conviction. During the first years of contact they showed a decided preference for their own way of life.[10]

In a letter to Lord Sydney, Phillip suggested that one possible explanation of why the Aborigines treated him with respect was the fortuitous fact that he was missing an incisor: the same tooth

"The tossing waves, the foam, the ships in the distance, The wild unrest, the snowy, curling caps —that inbound urge and urge of waves, Seeking the shores forever."

WALT WHITMAN (1819–1892), *FROM MONTAUK POINT*

that the Aboriginal men of the district had removed as part of *Yoo-long Erah-ba-diang*, an initiation ceremony.[11] According to Kuringai belief, the sky god Daramallan would preside over these initiation ceremonies conducted at sacred sites. Young men were instructed in the lore and had the right upper incisor tooth knocked out to mark their initiation. Of course, it would have helped that Phillip's expeditions to meet the locals were backed by armed men, who on occasion demonstrated the effectiveness of their muskets:

Our first object was to win their affections, and our next to convince them of the superiority we possessed: for without the latter, the former would be of little importance.[12]

When it became clear that the visitors were there to stay, the initial tentative welcome towards the British settlers shown by the Aboriginal people soon turned to misunderstanding and hostility as *"the colonists invaded their territory and competed for food and land"*.[13] The two groups had totally different world views, compounded by difficult language barriers. The Saltwater People considered *"their land to be communal territory, whereas the British concept of land bestowed individual ownership"*.[14] Phillip was astute enough to note: *"Certain it is that wherever our colonists fix themselves, the natives are obliged to leave that part of the country."*[15]

The relationship between the two cultures became even more strained in December 1788 when Governor Phillip resorted to kidnapping a Kayimai man in an attempt to learn about Aboriginal culture. Following the death of this man, known as Arabanoo, after about six months of captivity, there seemed little hope of rapprochement. Watkin Tench, a Captain with the marine corps, described how the *"same suspicious dread of our approach, and the same scenes of vengeance acted on unfortunate stragglers, continued to prevail"*.[16]

The 'Discovery'.
Photo Frank Hurley, 1929.
Mawson Collection, Adelaide University.

Native Child and Puppy, 1914.
Photo Frank Hurley.
Carbon photograph 35.5x45.5 cm.
National Gallery of Australia,
Canberra.

"… we have taken possession of their country; their very existence has been overlooked, their natural rights have been denied, their lands have been sold by the state, and their children disinherited …"[35]

THE REV. SAMUEL LEIGH (1785–1852)

It was a strange way to try and forge a relationship with the locals.

In April and May of 1789, the smallpox (*gal-gal-la*) that had claimed Arabanoo had reached epidemic proportions and devastated the Koori population around Sydney. Bradley wrote:

> **It was truly shocking to go around the coves of this harbour, which were much frequented by the natives; where in the caves of the rocks, which used to shelter whole families in bad weather, were now to be seen men, women and children, lying dead.**[17]

Bodies thickly scarred with pustules began to wash up on the shores of the harbour. On a journey to Broken Bay, David Collins recorded that "*in many places our path was covered with skeletons, and the same spectacles were to be met with in the hollows of most of the rocks of that harbour.*"[18]

The once-healthy Eora people had no immunity to European diseases, and the epidemic is estimated to have killed more half the Aboriginal population, with that figure climbing as high as 90 percent in some clans. The Saltwater People suffered both physically and psychologically from the trauma of invasion. Within two years of settlement, occupation had dispossessed them not only of their traditional food and water supplies, but had also severed spiritual bonds to their country, shattered kinship ties in the area and destabilised their society.

By May 1789 the epidemic had abated, but the governor had not learnt from his failed experiment with Arabanoo. In a misguided attempt to promote his goodwill, Phillip sent William Bradley down the harbour to the 'North Arm' on 25 November 1789 to take another native by force.[19] Aboriginal warriors Bennelong and Coleby (also known as Colebee, meaning 'white-breasted sea eagle') were captured, but Coleby, a *koradgee* man, soon escaped. Bennelong was

held captive for several more months, but when released from his shackles he too soon left, having "*stripped himself of his very decent cloathing, left them behind and walked off.*"[20] Watkin Tench made the prophetic comment about Bennelong:

> **Had he penetrated our state, perhaps he might have given his countrymen such a description of our diminishing numbers and diminished strength as would have emboldened them to become more troublesome.**[21]

The fledgling colony was experiencing food shortages, as most of the food brought from Britain had been consumed or had fouled in the warm climate. They had little luck with agriculture and turned to the sea, descending onto the Saltwater People's own fishing places, depleting the supplies with the use of purse seine nets. It is thought that Aboriginal numbers around Sydney had perhaps halved following the epidemic, and because of the rapaciousness of the newcomers' fishing the Saltwater People were now also experiencing food shortages: "*The fish stocks, plant foods, animals and their habitats had been systematically destroyed by the colonists and the Saltwater People were starving.*"[22] When the Second Fleet arrived, replenishing food supplies for the settlers and bringing more people, the First People began to consider if this was perhaps their last opportunity to take action. Just at that point they received a sign from an old friend.

On 23 July 1790, a whale entered Sydney Harbour for "*the first time since we have been here.*"[23] On that same day, the whale capsized a boat near Middle Head, drowning the crew and leaving only one survivor. Another boat witnessed these events and chased the whale, but only succeeded in wounding it with a few harpoons. It would be another five weeks before the whale was seen again, this time washed up on a beach at North Head. Tench's words, written after the event, understate the significance of these events: *"The tremendous monster, who had occasioned the unhappy catastrophe just recorded, was fated to be the cause of farther mischief to us."* [24] Emma Lee argues: *"The Saltwater People were aware of the state of the colony, and had plans to rid themselves of it and restore the lands to the traditional owners."* [25] It would seem that the kidnapping of Bennelong may have worked against the settlers. During his captivity he had not only gained knowledge of their language but some important intelligence regarding the perilous state of the colony as well. He had also established an alliance with Coleby, and both would have known that time was running out for their people to take action. In the same month that Bennelong returned from captivity, the whale arrived with an act of defiance by drowning the settlers. The symbolism was powerful.

North Head holds special significance for Saltwater People. It had always been known as *"a special purpose place, or island, where burial ceremonies took place."* [26] Bungaree's widow, Kaaro (known as 'Old Queen Gooseberry'), told George Angus in 1840 that the land around North Head was *"koradjee ground"*, or *"priests ground"*, a place that she could not visit. [27] It was also known as *"the place of the whale"*. Emma Lee observes that if a line is drawn linking all the locations of saltwater heritage sites, the outline of a whale begins to take shape around North Head, which was an important viewing platform for watching migrating whales. [28] It was near here, at Kay-e-may (Manly Cove), where Bennelong and Coleby were kidnapped. It was also Manly Cove where the tides had brought the whale to rest, providing a feast that would replenish the hungry Saltwater People. And it was here that a plan to assassinate or 'pay back' the highest British authority in the land, the colonial Governor, was launched. It seemed a perfect opportunity for the Saltwater warriors.

On 7 September 1790 a British exploration party pulled into Manly Cove to start an overland trip to Broken Bay, but their plans soon changed when they came across about two hundred Aborigines, including Coleby and Bennelong, who had gathered to feast on the beached whale. After learning that Governor Phillip was at South Head, Bennelong asked that the British take four chunks of whale meat to him, with an invitation for the Governor to join them. Invitations to visit the Saltwater People were rare, so Phillip readily complied. The atmosphere appeared friendly at first, but armed warriors that had been hidden began to crowd around him. [29] One of these warriors, said to be Willemering, a *koradgee* man from Broken Bay, threw a spear at Phillip with *"great violence"*. Henry Waterhouse reported that the spear *"struck the Governor, entered the right shoulder and went through about 3 inches just behind the shoulder blade close to the back bone."* [30] More spears followed as Phillip and his men retreated to their boat to get their muskets, but there were no further serious injuries. Phillip survived his wound and expressly ordered that the Aborigines should not be fired on, [31] believing the attack to be the result of a misunderstanding—or perhaps he understood the reason behind the assault.

In his book *The Commonwealth of Thieves*, Thomas Keneally supports the view that this was an orchestrated payback, or ritual punishment, on the leader of the invaders for the devastation inflicted on the Eora by shootings, disease and the plundering of food supplies. [32] It is ironic that it was this attack and Phillip's subsequent reconciliatory reaction that led to communication between the two groups, with negotiations made through Bennelong. Emma Lee regards these events to be a turning point, where *"the dynamic shifted and Saltwater People came into the Sydney camp and never really left"*. [33] Other warriors away from the coast such as Pemulwuy and Windradyne took up where Willemering left off, waging resistance, organising war parties and instilling fear in the colonies, [34] but for the Saltwater People traditional life had changed forever.

Aborigines cooking and eating beached whales,
Newcastle, New South Wales, c.1820.
Artist J. Lycett.
Thought to be Nobby's beach, Newcastle
National Library of Australia, Canberra.
nla.pic-an2962715-s11.

cetaceans

"Large marine animals feature at this site, whose rock surface undulates, making whale or wave shapes. There are distant ocean views. Of the several whales one has teeth like structures, perhaps indicating that it is a sperm whale. A dolphin can be clearly identified... One man appears to be standing on or in a whale. The usual interpretation for this is that he is performing some rite to entice the whale to become beached."

PETER STANBURY & JOHN CLEGG, *ABORIGINAL ROCK CARVINGS*, SYDNEY UNIVERSITY PRESS, 1990.

Background Gumbooya, Allambie Heights.
Courtesy Peter Stanbury & John Clegg,
Sydney University Press.
Right Rock carving, Gumbooya Reserve,
Allambie Heights. *Photo Peter Solness.*

Passing Whales. *Linocut by Jacqui Williams.*

"So is this great and wide sea, wherein … there is that leviathan, whom thou hast made to play therein."

PSALMS 104:25—26

The order Cetacea includes whales, dolphins, and porpoises.
It has just over eighty living species, divided into the suborders
Odontocetia (the toothed whales, including dolphins and
porpoises) and Mysticeti (the filter-feeding baleen whales).
Cetaceans are the mammals most fully adapted to aquatic life.

> "Ancient, unknown mammals left the land
> In search of food or sanctuary,
> And walked into the water.
>
> Their arms and hands changed into water wings;
> Their tails turned into boomerang-shaped
> tail-flukes,
> Enabling them to fly, almost weightless,
> through the oceans ..."[1]
>
> HEATHCOTE WILLIAMS, *WHALE NATION*, 1988

Nearly everyone who lives along the northern beaches coastline
has a story to tell about sighting dolphins and whales at play.
People are uplifted by the sight of these magnificent creatures
enjoying themselves. Whales and dolphins play three times
longer than they spend searching for food. They swim in herds
and crave intimacy, are the perfect models of parental care and
training, and appear to be impressive and enthusiastic lovers.
In total, about forty species of whales and dolphins have been
recorded in Australian waters.

In the southern winter, humpback whales journey from
the Antarctic feeding grounds to Australia's coastal waters on
the way to the Coral Sea to mate and give birth, before returning
to the Antarctic with their newborn at the end of each spring.
Dolphins can be seen all year round, and, unlike the large whales,
some species may spend their whole lives in the one region.

These creatures have become so efficient at protecting and feeding
themselves that they have more time to play, riding the waves with
an ease and skill that we can only admire.

It is not unreasonable to suggest a connection between humans
and these mammals of the sea. We too were conceived into a watery
world, cocooned in amniotic fluid until ready to emerge and breathe
oxygen. Our bodies average about 70 percent water, corresponding
to the amount of the planet's surface covered with water. We are
drawn to the ocean and the warm-blooded dolphins and whales
who leave the water to breathe air as we do. Whales and humans
have also mutually evolved with large and elaborately structured
brains, with the whale having the largest brain and cerebral
cortex that has ever existed.

Every Saltwater Person had a totem name, usually that of
a fish or bird, adopted from nature as personal emblem at birth.
Aboriginal people along the Australian coast have a long association
with whales, and the whale is an important totem for numerous
Aboriginal groups. As evidenced by the enormous number of rock
carving sites in the Sydney area featuring whales and dolphins, these
creatures held immense spiritual significance. The Saltwater People
had a special affinity with the humpback whale in particular, and
would have watched from the cliffs surrounding sheltered coves as
humpback whales gave birth and suckled their young. Pilot whales
also ventured close to shore and may have swum with the Saltwater
People in the shallows.[2] There are numerous rock carvings of whales
along the Sydney coastline, some believed to be part of ritual magic.
As far inland as Muogamarra, the site of an ancient volcano near
Mooney Mooney Bridge on the Hawkesbury River, is a carving
of an orca whale.

While they were not hunted by the Saltwater People, stranded
whales and dolphins were an opportunistic source of food, medicine,
and utilitarian goods. The fat was used to varnish weapons and tools,

and whale bones were used to manufacture shelters as well as a variety of utensils and weapons. Professor Dennis Foley writes: *"When they were sick, they were sung and attracted to shore where they were swiftly put out of their misery and readily eaten, not only because they were of immense importance to our diet, it was also out of respect for them."*[3] Women would sing, and twist their feet in the sand to make high-pitched noises to attract the whales.[4]

Singing to whales and dolphins was known among various indigenous people around the world. Credo Mutwa, African living legend and *songoma* (shaman) once told me how the Zulu people sang to these creatures. There are Eora stories about whales swimming up the Parramatta River to what is now Homebush Bay to sing songs to Aborigines when they met,[5] and clans along the east coast of Australia called on porpoises to herd schools of fish into the shallows so that they could be speared or netted.[6]

Seeing the large numbers of whales, early settlers soon began to exploit them commercially, and shore-based whaling stations were established on the northern side of Sydney Harbour. Commercial whaling began as early as 1791, when whaleboats hunted sperm whales for their valuable oil and baleen whales for whalebone. It would not be until the 1970s when people realised that some species of whales had been hunted to near-extinction and began to protect the cetaceans. These efforts were rewarded with an apparent about-turn in the Japanese whaling fleet in February 2011, putting a hold on large-scale whaling.

Like the traditional indigenous people of the world, Cetaceans have no need for the tons upon tons of artifacts that we have become dependent on, all destined to become rubbish. Their sophistication has become internal and their skills are all perceptive. They breed with ecological consideration, in precise relation to the amount of food available.[7] Whales once walked the land but returned to the ocean where they remain our marine brothers and sisters.

MUSICAL FOOTNOTE:

The first sound a whale calf hears is singing. The grey whale's large penis is affectionately referred to as 'Pink Floyd'.

> "From space, the planet is blue.
> From space, the planet is the territory
> Not of humans, but of the whale."
> HEATHCOTE WILLIAMS, *WHALE NATION*, 1988

North Head.
Photo Ian Bird.

Humpback whales.
Photo Wayne Osborn.

"How inappropriate to call this planet Earth
when it is quite clearly Ocean." ARTHUR C. CLARKE (1917–2008)

WHITE-HEADED DOLPHIN

Illustration Ian Faulkner.

Opposite Dolphins, Manly.
Photo Scott Needham.

When the earth was younger there lived a Gatlay man who was once a great fisherman. He fished in the coves of the open sea, rarely venturing into the sheltered waters of Tuhbowgule. He was taught by the spirits how to fish with the thighbone of the wallaby sharpened to a razor point at both ends, and a strong line fixed to the middle of the bone. When attached to a small bait-fish and placed in the 'blue' water with chopped up cunje and fish gut he caught the oil-fish with great skill, swimming them onto the rocks and then spearing them. When the larger fish swallowed the free-swimming bait-fish (originally netted in the rock pools), it pulled on the line, causing the bone to catch in both sides of the mouth or gullet that was impossible for the oil-fish to toss or spit out. (The oil-fish is the tuna, highly regarded by our special people and old people.)

This man also knew the ways of the white-breasted sea eagle, and it was said that his mother was of these people. He could talk to the eagle and find out where the schools of fish were. With the eagle's help, they could be herded towards a cove or a deep hole in the surf line where he would wait with scoop net or spear. On catching fish he would always give the best to the eagle in payment for its help.

Over the years he came into contact with many of the shark people and the dolphin families. He showed kindness to them and always shared his catch with them too, especially if they presented themselves to him in shallow water. (It is our belief that our sister clan to the north is related to the ocean whaler shark, and likewise a related clan to the south is of the dolphin.) In time he became very close to the dolphin and shark and they became close friends, often seen talking to each other in the shallows and the calm bays where when they were not catching fish. He never married, and as he grew older his hair changed to

snow white. He only mixed with his family at night, when he returned with enough fish for the evening meal.

The day came when he did not return to his people's campfires. On looking for him they heard a strange noise, a cry like someone in distress. As they came closer to the shore they saw his body, motionless in the shallows of the surf. He had died of old age doing what he loved best, fishing. Here were the dolphins pushing his body back towards shore, the noise that was heard was the dolphins crying for they had lost their dear friend. The men carried his body back to camp, they wrapped him in a possum rug and placed him gently into the branches of a high tree so that Biame could talk to his spirit.

That night around the campfire few could sleep, such was the clan's grief at the loss of this wonderful man who was so generous in his life towards the young, the old and the women in child. He would always ensure that they had an evening meal of fresh fish. What were they to do? His brothers and sisters had long since passed on; he had never married and had no children. The dolphin seemed to be his only family. Their cries could be heard on the morning breeze as the sun painted the dawn of another day. The old ones decided. They cut a large canoe for him and worked through the day without rest.

In the cool of the afternoon they returned to the bay where the dolphins had gathered, still crying for their loss.

The fisherman was placed in the canoe, wrapped tightly in many possum-skin rugs, his white hair garnished with sweet fruits of the forest and his body wrapped in bark, painted with ochre and washed in oil. He was smoked and his loved ones bade him farewell. They placed him in the canoe and pushed him away from the shore with the receding tide. Many minutes of silence followed. To the clan's amazement the dolphins surrounded the canoe and with gently nudged pushed him far out to sea. As the night's shadows settled on the water, the canoe vanished on the horizon and so left our land. The dolphins also left the waters for many cycles of the moon.

When the wattle next bloomed, the children came running back to the

camp of the elders; "the dolphins, the dolphins are back", they yelled in unison. When the clan came to the beach, there were the dolphins with a large school of mullet cornered in the bay and there was the white-headed dolphin, splashing as if telling the other dolphins what to do, and the people realised that this was the old man. From that day in a certain place now called the Collaroy Basin, the members of this clan have spoken to the dolphin and they have helped them to fish, and the white-headed dolphin can still be seen with the pod.

Reproduced with kind permission of Dennis Foley and Aboriginal History Inc. from Repossession of Our Spirit, *pp. 78–79.*

saltwater seafarers

Following the smallpox epidemic and the breakdown of traditional life, remnants of various clans of Saltwater People began to amalgamate into a group known as the 'Broken Bay tribe.'[1] They retreated to 'Blacks' camps' close to freshwater creeks and estuaries in less-populated parts of the northern beaches such as Narrabeen. Coming from a canoe culture, with salt water as part of their natural habitat, many Aboriginal men reacted to dispossession by seeking work on sailing ships. Ironically, these were often the very ships that brought the settlers and disease that had devastated their traditional life.

Saltwater People embarked on voyages across the globe and played a significant role in Australia's early maritime history. *"With remarkable resilience, they became guides, go-betweens, boatmen, sailors, sealers, steersmen, whalers, pilots and trackers, valued for their skills and knowledge."*[2] By the end of the eighteenth century Aboriginal seafarers had journeyed to England, North America, Hawaii and India. There were many of these Aboriginal mariners, but I will concentrate here on the stories of three voyagers: a father and his son from Broken Bay, and an Eora man who was the first Australian to visit Hawaiian shores and witness the noble art of surfing.

Photo oggy.

"He turns his head, but in his ear
The shady trade winds run,
And in his eye the endless waves
Ride on into the sun."

LAURENCE BINYON (1869–1943), *JOHN WINTER*

three seafaring tales

Surf Swimming by Sandwich Islanders.
Illustration of surf riding in Hawaii, 1878.
Etching, artist unknown.
Courtesy Bishop Museum, Hawaii.

one

gnung-a gnung-a murremurgan (?–1809)

Gnung-a Gnung-a Murremurgan ventured into the English settlement at Sydney Cove in November 1790, and less than three years later embarked on an epic voyage across the Pacific to Nootka Sound (now Vancouver, Canada), California and Hawaii as part of an expedition to the Pacific coast of North America under the command of Captain George Vancouver. Working on board the supply ship HMS *Daedalus*, Gnung-a Gnung-a sailed to Owyhee (Hawaii) in 1793 on the way to Nootka Sound and then on to the Spanish colonies of Santa Barbara and San Diego.

On the return voyage, Vancouver's ships reached the east coast of Hawaii in January 1794 and took safe anchorage at Kealakekua Bay. Hawaiian nobles were traditionally buried in the cliffs surrounding this bay, and the ships were greeted warmly by

Nouvelle-Hollande. Gnoung-a- Gnoung-a, mour-re-mour-ga (dit Collins).
Engraving by Barthelemy Roger (after Nicolas-Martin Petit).
Engraving Plate 21, Atlas, François Péron, Voyage
de découvertes aux terres australes, Paris, De l'Imprimerie Imperiale, 1811.
Mitchell Library, State Library of NSW.

King Kamehameha. The good-natured and handsome Gnung-a Gnung-a so impressed Kamehameha that the Hawaiian king wanted to buy him, offering in exchange canoes, weapons and curiosities, but Gnung-a Gnung-a was keen to return to his wife and people back in Sydney.[3]

During his one-month stay in Hawaii Gnung-a Gnung-a often went ashore, where he *"readily adopted the manners of those around him"* and was known to have been *"'well received' by the Hawaiian women"*.[4] Being a good swimmer and waterman, he must have also admired the young men riding the waves in Kealakekua Bay on their long wooden boards described by King aboard the *Discovery* as *"an oval piece of plank above their Size and breadth"*.[5] James Hanson's journal and log books of the *Daedalus* have not been found and probably went down with him in his last command when all hands were lost. Therefore, there are no accounts telling us if Gnung-a Gnung-a ever ventured onto the waves with the Hawaiians—but if he was tempted to try he would have been the first Australian to ride a surfboard. He was certainly the first Australian to witness the noble art of Hawaiian surfing.

Gnung-a Gnung-a was married to Warreeweer, the younger sister of the Wangal leader Woollarawarre Bennelong. He was given the adopted name 'Collins' from the Acting Judge Advocate David Collins. After his voyage to the Pacific Gnung-a Gnung-a was involved in several other adventures, including the early exploration of New South Wales, and he survived being speared by the famous resistance fighter and *koradgee* Pemulwuy during a ritual revenge combat in 1795. In January 1809 the body of Gnung-a Gnung-a Murremurgan, a man held in high esteem by both the settlers and his own people, was found at the site of the present Macquarie Place in Bridge Street, Sydney.[6]

bungaree (c.1772–1830)

It is unclear in which year exactly Bungaree (Boongarie, Boungaree) was born, but it is thought that it was shortly after Captain Cook's brief visit to the east coast of Australia in 1770. We do know that by the time the First Fleet appeared in 1788 Bungaree bore most of the marks of an initiated man. Early records state that Bungaree was born in the Broken Bay area, which would indicate that he belonged to the Guringai clan based around the Hawkesbury River (known to the Guringai as 'Deerubbun'). Bungaree's place in history has often been demeaned, but many are now beginning to recognise his importance.

Bungaree was a natural waterman, and by 1799 was employed on voyages to Norfolk Island and Hervey Bay in the company of Matthew Flinders. In 1801–03 he accompanied Flinders aboard HMS *Investigator*, becoming not only the first Aborigine, but also the first Australian, to circumnavigate the continent. All the others on the ship were British. Then, in a survey of the west and north Australia coast in 1817, he sailed on the *Mermaid*, commanded by Phillip Parker King, helping make contact with tribes in the Kimberley. During this voyage the ship visited Timor for supplies, and the French explorer Jules Dumont d'Urville recalled a droll anecdote about Bungaree, who had gone ashore and demanded the change that was owed him for a glass of gin on his previous visit fifteen years before, when he had to quickly rejoin the *Investigator* as the ship set sail.[7]

Bungaree's skills in bushcraft, finding water, fishing and hunting kangaroos were invaluable. His knowledge of Aboriginal protocol and his advice and assistance as a guide helped avoid conflict when

Opposite Bungaree, A Native of New South Wales.
Artist Augustus Earle, 1826. *Oil. Rex Nan Kivell
Collection. National Library of Australia, Canberra.
NK 118, nla.an-2256865*

BUNGAREE.

This singular Countenance is an authentic Likeness from an original Drawing of the Chief of the Broka Bay Tribe, New South Wales, well known at Sidney

Drawn on Stone by C. Pye.

probing new frontiers, often saving lives in the process. When called on to liaise with the local Aborigines in the Gulf of Carpentaria and elsewhere, Bungaree would remove his clothes, allowing the strangers to see his initiation scarification (cicatrices) and thus put them at ease even if their language was not understood. This willingness to go ashore empty-handed and attempt to negotiate with unknown and hostile tribes demonstrated great bravery. Matthew Flinders described him as *"a worthy and brave fellow"*.[8]

In the new histories about how our nation was founded, important work is being done by the likes of Henry Reynolds and Dr Keith Vincent Smith to uncover the stories of the clash of cultures. This research reveals the impact on Bungaree's own family. In 1801, Bungaree was asked to help in the establishment of a penal settlement on the Hunter River, Newcastle, but according to a report by Surgeon John Harris *"Bonjary ran off … and has since not returned."*[9]

Like many Aborigines, Bungaree may have been appalled by the treatment of the convicts, but it is interesting that several years later he assisted the commandant at Newcastle, Lieutenant Charles Menzies, in capturing runaway convicts. Menzies described Bungaree as *"the most intelligent of that race I have as yet Seen."*[10] Unfortunately for Bungaree, the convicts took revenge by killing his father *"in the most brutal manner."*[11]

Bungaree had several wives. His first wife was named Matora (or Madora), whose totem name, *muttaura*, means 'small snapper' in the language of the Hunter River and Lake Macquarie, where it is likely she was born.[12] Kaaro, known as Cora Gooseberry, became his principal wife. Kaaro was the daughter of Moorooboora, headman of the Murro-ore (Pathway Place) clan and half-brother of Daringa, who had married Colebee (Coleby, Colby) the Cadigal. Moorooboora took his own name from his clan's camping place, named from *muru* (pathway) and *Boora* (Long Bay), and now the seaside suburb of Maroubra. Bungaree had several children, including Bowen, Boio (Long Dick), and Toúbi (Toby).

Admired for his intelligence, bravery, and acute sense of humour and mimicry, Bungaree became well known around the streets of Sydney. In 1815, Governor Lachlan Macquarie, recognising Bungaree's importance and popularity, set up the fifteen members of his group on a farm at George's Head with huts, implements, stock and convict instructors. The Governor bestowed Bungaree with the dubious honour of a brass gorget inscribed *"Bungaree: Chief of the Broken Bay Tribe"*. Aborigines did not recognise 'chiefs',

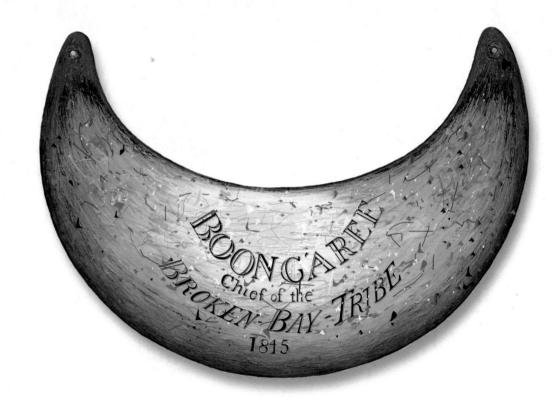

but Bungaree was influential within his own Aboriginal community, taking part in corroborees and ritual battles. His later years were marred by a fondness for alcohol.

Bungaree died on 24 November 1830, *"in the midst of his own tribe"*,[13] and was buried at Rose Bay in an unmarked grave. The story should end here, but recent research by historian Dr Keith Vincent Smith has revealed that grave robbers may have disturbed Bungaree's last resting place to gather his skull for the 'scientific' trade in Aboriginal skulls. In notices of donations made to the Australian Museum in Sydney during November 1857 was listed: *"… skull of 'King Bungaree', an Aboriginal of New South Wales"*,[14] although there

Above Bungaree's gorget.
Illustration by Ian Faulkner based on the 1820 sketch by Pavel Nikolaevich Mikhailov.

Opposite His Majesty's Cutter Mermaid.
Etching by Phillip Parker King, 1817.
Mitchell Library, State Library of NSW.
Original PXC 767, No.85,

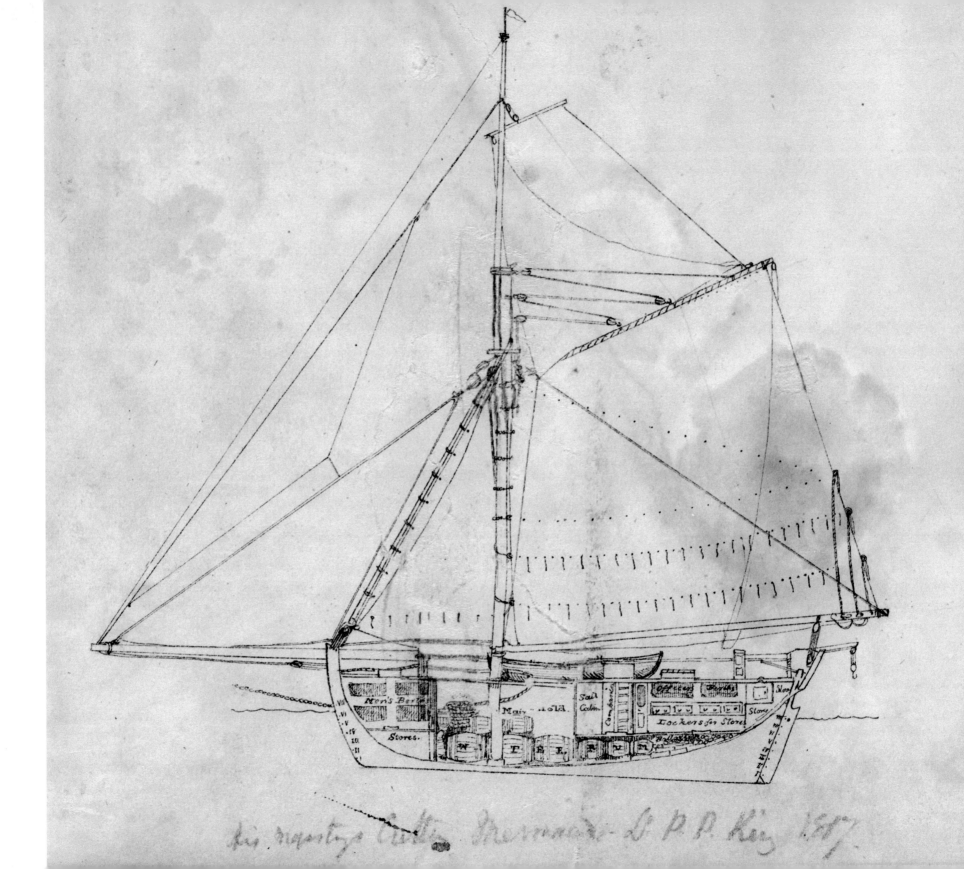

His Majesty's Cutter Mermaid — D. P. P. King 1817.

appears to be no museum record of that item. As this notice was placed some twenty-seven years after Bungaree's death, Dr Keith Vincent Smith suspects that this 'donated' skull *"might have been that of Bungaree's eldest son Bowen Bungaree of Pittwater, who succeeded his father and wore his gorget."*[15] Bowen died in 1853, closer to the time of the notice of donation.

three

bowen bungaree
(c.1797–1853)

Bowen (or Boin) was the eldest son of Bungaree and his first wife Matora. He was born in Broken Bay around 1802, and after spending some time at Bungaree's camp at George's Head shifted back to his clan territory of Broken Bay with his four children. This may have been an attempt to escape the ravages of alcohol besetting the town camp. It is not known if his wife Maria (Man Naney, sometimes called 'Queen Maria') joined them. Bowen was employed as a tracker on the northern beaches and Pittwater, detecting illegal stills and helping capture bushrangers and escaped convicts. He was also a skilled fisherman, and caught and traded fish with the assistance of a boat arranged for him by Howard, the Customs Officer at Barrenjoey, as a reward for his work.

Being a proficient waterman, Bowen was employed as an interpreter and mediator on John Oxley's exploration of Moreton Bay in 1832. Later he was one of the 'black' crew on the 1849 voyage to San Francisco on the brig *William Hill*. Bowen and five other Broken Bay men were taken to San Francisco by Sydney merchant

Richard Hill, bound for the California Gold Rush. According to historian Maybanke Anderson, Mr Hill took the blackfellows with him because they were used to boating, and could be employed to row the boats which were needed to carry the crowds who were flocking to the Eldorado. Black Bowen was the only one of the six who survived. The others all died far from their native home. Black Bowen always spoke with scorn of: *"That country!! No wood for fire, but plenty cold wind, and plenty, plenty water. No good for me! No good for blackfellow!"*[16]

Bowen returned to Sydney and resumed his police duties in the Pittwater area. He was trusted to carry a rifle, said to have had been given to him by the Governor. John Farrell, Jr, said: *"This he ever afterwards carried about with him as a trophy … for few white men, let alone blacks, possessed a gun in those days."*[17] Like his father before him, Bowen had a penchant for uniforms, and often sported a military jacket and cocked hat, but wore his hair *"knotted up behind, and three feathers stuck in it."*[18]

Bowen was murdered at the reported age of 56, with his friend Farrell claiming that he had been ambushed and shot in the back by bushrangers while sitting at a campfire near Bushrangers Hill, Newport, in 1853. Bowen was buried at St Lawrence Presbyterian Church cemetery in Sydney as befitting the high regard in which he was held. When the church was demolished to make way for Central Railway Station, Bowen's gravestone was moved to Pioneer Park, Botany.

boin (Bowen Bungaree).
Artist Pavel Mikhailov, 1820. Image courtesy AIATSIS.
In 1820, the artist Pavel Mikhailov (1786-1840), from the Russian scientific expedition led by Captain Fabian von Bellingshausen, sketched watercolour portraits of 'Boìn' (Bowen, then aged about 18), his father Boongaree (Bungaree), his mother 'Madora' (Matora), brother 'Toubi' (Toby) and other members of Bungaree's family who were camped at Kirribilli on the north shore of Sydney Harbour. The original artwork, pencil and sanguine on brown paper, is held at the State Russian Museum, St Petersburg, Russia. (Dr Keith V. Smith)

65

"A ship in harbor is safe,
but that is not what ships
are built for." JOHN A. SHEDD, 1928

Photo oggy.

N. Petit del.   J. Milbert direx.   B. Roger sculp.

saltwater resistance

The Saltwater People did not passively accept the destruction of their way of life. Land was not simply real estate. It provided food and sustained their spiritual beliefs. Along *"the Upper and Lower Hawkesbury there were many recorded cases of Aboriginal resistance and murder up to the 1840's."*[1] Collins wrote that from the mid-1790s to the early nineteenth century there was open warfare, especially in fertile parts of the colony such as the Hawkesbury River, where farmers tried to establish themselves in small acreages.[2] A large detachment of New South Wales Corps sent to the Hawkesbury in 1795 to protect the settlers *"fired upon a large party of Aborigines, killing seven or eight of them."*[3] Sporadic conflict occurred around Broken Bay, and in 1805 a party of settlers pursued an Aboriginal force estimated at more than three hundred men.[4]

Grewin, a Guringai man, was a known pirate of the Pittwater. He began by befriending the crews of the coasters that travelled up the river to the farms to collect produce for Sydney[5] and recovering supplies of rope, ceramics, nails and bottles from wrecked ships. Grewin gradually turned his attention to piracy. In 1805 he *"organised a canoe attack on the* William and Mary *in Pittwater"*,[6] followed by later attacks on other coasters using his flotilla of canoes.

Up until 1876 *"evidence given by Aboriginal witnesses was not admitted in criminal trials in New South Wales because their oath sworn on the bible was not viewed as valid"*.[7] In July 1805, Judge Advocate Richard Atkins gave a legal 'Opinion on the Treatment to be Adopted towards the Natives'. Finding that Aboriginal people could not present evidence in a criminal court, he suggested the only course was to *"pursue them and inflict such punishment as they merit"*.[8] On this basis, resistance leaders such as Bulldog, Musquito and Dual were exiled to Norfolk Island or Van Diemen's Land (Tasmania), thus becoming unwilling voyagers transported as convicts.

Musquito (c.1780–1825), also known as Mosquito, Musquetta, Bush Muschetta and Muskito, was the brother of Phillip, who said he was also the brother of Gnung-a Gnung-a Murremurgan. All three were from Broken Bay or the mouth of the Hawkesbury. The Reverend Samuel Marsden described Musquito as an Aboriginal resistance leader against settlers *"on the banks of the Hawkesbury River"* around 1805.[9] After the *Sydney Gazette* reported that, in good English, he had expressed his determination to continue his *"rapacities"*, General Orders issued on 9 June 1805 authorised his arrest to prevent further mischief. Governor King exiled Musquito and 'Bull Dog', *"principals in the recent outrages"*, to Norfolk Island, where Musquito remained for eight years.[10]

Opposite Portrait of Musquito. Nouvelle-Hollande-Y-Erran-Gou-La-Ga, sauvage des environs du Port Jackson (New Holland-y-Erran-Gou-La-Ga, savage of the Port Jackson area).
Artist Barthelemy Roger after Nicolas-Martin Petit.
Engraving Plate 24, Atlas, Voyage de découvertes aux terres australes, Paris, 1811.
Mitchell Library, State Library of NSW.
Call No. MRB/ F980/ P Atlas [1811] part 2

Musquito eventually joined the 'Tame Mob', a group of Palawa (Aboriginal Tasmanians) and coordinated attacks on settlers. The Reverend William Horton (1800–1867) said that the Palawa were "*governed by a Native of Port Jackson named Muskitoo*", who had been made leader because of his "*superior skill and muscular strength.*"[11] Musquito was captured and convicted of murder. He was hanged in Hobart Town in 1825, along with a Tasmanian Aborigine called Black Jack and six bushrangers.[12]

bushrangers

smugglers, illicit stills and murder most foul

The northern beaches were a solitary place in the early 1800s, and they attracted an increasing number of escaping convicts. In 1801 Lieutenant James Grant's account of a journey to Pittwater recounts finding a half-starved escaped convict who had absconded with others, taking with them the *Norfolk* sloop (the same boat used by Bass and Flinders to circumnavigate Tasmania).[13] Acts of piracy on the Hawkesbury were becoming so common that restrictions were placed on shipping. Local Aboriginal men, such as Grewin, were also known to be pirates. The area was gaining a reputation for lawlessness, with judicial officials stating: "*That part of the country is well known to bushrangers and other bad characters.*"[14]

Local legend and a story in the *Town and Country Journal* claims that in 1818 a family of settlers at Narrabeen were murdered by a band of roving convicts led by an Irish convict known as 'Big Mick'. In 1820 the home of James McCarr was broken into and his boat stolen. The "*Most Notorious Bushranger*", Newcombe, having escaped

from Coal River for the second time, was apprehended for the crime and sentenced to fourteen years' transportation. In 1823, three bushrangers broke into the house of Third Fleeter John Fincham,[15] then aged 82, and stole a box containing his certificate of freedom.

In 1827, local farmer David Foley performed a citizen's arrest when a man hiding on his property "*confessed himself to be a bushranger*". While waiting for a boat to take the 'bushranger' into police custody, there was an altercation on Manly Beach and the bushranger escaped with a flesh wound to his head from a musket ball.[16] David Foley was murdered near his home in Bungin Bungin in 1849 following an ongoing feud with his neighbours, the Collins clan, but no one was ever convicted. Guns were very much part of frontier culture, and: "*Such was the isolated nature of the district that many felonies undoubtedly went unreported, while those that were investigated often failed to be resolved.*"[17]

Bowen Bungaree was employed to track escaped convicts and bushrangers in the Pittwater area near the mouth of the Hawkesbury River. Writing in the *Sydney Mail* in 1861, journalist Charles de Boos quoted John Farrell II (John Farrell, Jr) of Newport, who said that in about 1829 Bowen had shot and killed a bushranger named Casey. On 17 April 1837, the *Sydney Morning Herald* reported that Bowen had helped in the capture of three bushrangers holed up in the Mooney Mooney area, and there are several more accounts of Bowen's success in finding illicit stills and uncovering smuggling operations. After an adventurous life (see page 62), Bowen was murdered by bushrangers in 1853 in the Newport area.

The first John Farrell, patriarch of the Farrell clan, had been transported to the colony in 1813 for the crime of being in possession of a forged banknote,[18] and his family were to be associated with cattle duffing, smuggling and other illegal activities over three generations. Historian Shelagh Champion reveals that "*his eldest son, Daniel Farrell, after being implicated in smuggling*

(see page 62)

and attempted arson, left for San Francisco in March 1851, and was not heard of again.[19] Daniel's younger brother, John Farrell, Jr, and his wife Mary Ann were caught and tried for a series of cattle-stealing offences in 1864 and 1865. In 1870 John Jr obtained the licence to operate the New Steyne Hotel in the Corso at Manly. His son, Johnny, was also convicted of cattle stealing and was sentenced to three years' gaol at Port Macquarie.[20] It has been conservatively estimated that around this time about 80 percent of the adult population were either convicts or had a convict background, so it comes as little surprise that the district also had a reputation for being a *wild place*.[21] The law-abiding small-time farmers who began to settle on the northern beaches had to coexist with a disreputable element not afraid to use violence to get their way.

The first reported case of attempted smuggling in the Pittwater area occurred in 1808, and by the 1830s and early 1840s smuggling had become rife, with barrels of rum bound for the South Seas often offloaded at Broken Bay.[22] The collector of Customs posted a notice in 1841 offering a reward for information relating to smugglers who were often *"persons residing on the shore, who in other respects are considered respectable."*[23] The following year, Daniel Farrell and James Tooney found a large amount of contraband in a cave, but the prime suspect, a Newport resident named Robert Henderson, could not be convicted. Governor Gipps suggested that smuggling was the chief industry at Pittwater, and in 1843 he ordered a Customs House to be established near the base of Barrenjoey.

In September 1863 Frederick Ward, alias Captain Thunderbolt, escaped from Cockatoo Island gaol where he was serving a sentence for stealing horses. He is said to have gone into hiding near Narrabeen before plying his bushranging trade around the Windsor area and northern New South Wales. His daring and flamboyant style had attracted grudging admiration, and he is acknowledged as being the *"most successful and last of the 'professional' bushrangers"* until he

was shot dead on 25 May 1870 near Uralla.[24] The *"Captain's lady"* was an Aboriginal woman known as Mary Anne, or 'Black Mary', who rode with Thunderbolt, defying the police between 1863 and 1867.

There have been more than a few modern-day scoundrels and scandals on the northern beaches. Perhaps inspired by the Farrell clan, Tim Bristow, one of the hard men of Sydney, lived in Newport for many years. Big Tim, the one-time police cadet turned legendary private eye and notorious standover man, made his name in the 1950s and '60s in divorce work, when he would crash through bedroom doors, photographer close behind, to catch adulterous couples in the act. According to legend, and his own mythologising, Bristow was the original model for Chesty Bond. Disgraced former New South Wales police officer Roger Rogerson recalled that Bristow in his heyday cut an impressive figure, and: *"When he was in charge of security at the Newport Arms, blokes would come from all over the state to try him out. They never beat him."*[25]

Bristow would later be associated with the likes of underworld figures Lennie McPherson and Chris Flannery, or so it is said. According to those who knew him, anything this larger-than-life character said needed to be taken with more than a grain of salt, but there is no doubt he knew an awful lot of influential people. Tim Bristow died at his Newport home in 2003 at the age of seventy-two.

In recent times the scoundrels have been less colourful. Instead of rum smugglers and illicit distilleries there are now drug importers and illicit labs. The bushranger has given way to the corporate criminal, with the characteristics required to be a successful CEO said to be the same as those required to be a classifiable sociopath. Usury was once considered by the world's major religions as unworthy profiting from no substantial labour or work but from mere avarice, greed, trickery and manipulation. In the modern world, usury and avarice have become acceptable, even admired, and the bountiful rewards for the high rollers include not only extreme wealth, but also high social status and political power. As Tim Bristow once declared: *"I found that the higher I went in society the lower the morals became."* Roger Rogerson, as part of *"the best police force that money could buy"*,[26] would have probably agreed.

"Traditionally, the violence of the sea was a warning of God's anger and a reminder of the Biblical deluge. Once that fear was conquered, people learned to enjoy the coastal waters."

JORGE CALADO, *WATERPROOF*, 1998

the ocean's outlaws

swimming, surfing and breaking the law

Australian society has always been split into two broad camps: wowsers and larrikins. John Norton, editor of *Truth*, claimed to have invented the term 'wowser' to express healthy contempt for those who attempt to force their own morality on everyone. Or as C.J. Dennis defined the term: *"Wowser: an ineffably pious person who mistakes this world for a penitentiary and himself for a warder."* Victorian-era morality with its arcane bathing rituals would initially separate us from the *"naked pleasures of our climate."*[27]

The Saltwater People were not concerned about nakedness, but then the Europeans came along and complicated everything. It began with the settlers bathing—actually washing themselves—in the ocean. Since swimsuits had not yet been imagined, rules were enacted so as not to offend early colonial standards of public decency. At the turn of the nineteenth century most men wore

Bodysurfer, c.1960.
Photo David Moore.

only that long-forgotten wisp of bathing wear, the cloth 'V', and for much of the century beachgoing along the northern beaches was governed by curfews for "*sea bathing*", with dress codes enforced by city-employed "*Inspectors of Public Nuisances*". By the late 1860s English-style bathing boxes had appeared on the beach at Manly, and within two decades visitors to the beach had moved from wading in the shallows to donning swimming costumes and venturing out into slightly deeper waters—even up to the waistline!

Although not banned outright, bathing in the surf was confined to the southern corner of South Steyne and only allowed between the hours of dawn and 7am. The wowsers petitioned council about "*these creatures without shame*",[28] but Sydneysiders resisted attempts by officials to limit their freedoms and continued to seek the cool ocean waves during the heat of the day. During the 1880s Tommy Tanner began to 'shoot' the waves, inspiring Freddie Williams and other body surfers who found it hard to leave the water as the law directed. In 1902 William Gotcher, editor of the *Manly and North-Sydney News*, led an early campaign against the restrictions on bathing and the following year Manly Council "*reluctantly*" allowed all-day bathing. The surfer's fight for freedom on the beaches had by and large been won.

For the sake of decency, however, women bathers moved to the isolation of North Steyne, but this was a long way for any rescuer to "*run from the men's corner at South Steyne.*"[29] Common sense prevailed and the women moved closer in, and mixed bathing in ocean water finally became accepted practice. The somewhat rebellious attitude that many Australians held towards authority helped encourage participation in this new "*culture of pleasure*", but it was the Surf Bathing Association of New South Wales, formed in 1907, that gained control of the beaches. In 1920 these surf bathing clubs reinforced their move to promoting life saving in the surf with a name change to the Surf Life Saving Association of New South Wales.

Concern over bathing costumes continued into the 1930s, but although bathing regulations demanded that neck-to-knee costumes should be worn, these had already disappeared from Manly beaches where the scene was described as "*free and easy.*"[30] In 1935, a concerned government minister introduced legislation that would ban men from wearing trunks, and bar women from wearing "*brassiere type*" costumes.[31] Although Mayor Hanson-Norman declared that Manly was not Sodom or Gomorrah and that aldermen would have to change with the times, in 1945 the Manly Council voted to ban "*abbreviated French type*" swimming costumes for women. By the early 1950s these costumes, now known as bikinis, were still considered "*unacceptable*"—but not for much longer. The beach provided a cheap recreational reserve, especially in those lean years around the two world wars. Stripped down to your togs and freed from blatant displays of wealth, the beach proved to be a great social leveller, and this form of recreational egalitarianism would become a dominant part of the cultural landscape.

Women had to fight for their place on the beach on several fronts. Arguing that women were not strong enough to operate the equipment or swim in heavy surf, the Surf Life Saving Association (SLSA) banned them from qualifying for the surf bronze medallion and therefore from patrolling. One of the most insightful early publications on Australian beach culture was a book titled *Surf: Australians Against the Sea*, written by C. Bede (Violet) Maxwell and published in 1949. Extensive research and personal interviews were the basis of Maxwell's account of the early days of surfriding in the first, and officially sanctioned, history of surf life saving. The brilliant writing displayed obvious skill, but it is said that she had to disguise the fact that she was a woman when corresponding with the various officials of the time.

Women's participation in surf sports was generally not encouraged, and the SLSA only allowed clubs to admit women as full members in 1980. Palm Beach continued to oppose the

Background Rexona—The Surfers' Friend.
From The Surf, *12 January, 1918.*
Mitchell Library, State Library of NSW.

Hand-coloured postcard. *Courtesy MLSC.*

admission of women, referring to *"problems"* associated with its residential facilities. Many active members were concerned that women surf life savers would destroy the 'mateship' and character of the club. It would not be until 1985–86 that the first active women members walked into the Palm Beach club. Opponents vowed to make life hell for new female members, and the first women full members confronted ostracism and verbal abuse. Their detractors coined a new moniker, 'pog' (a combination of the words pig and dog), which they used unashamedly. Today women make up 35 percent of active members and 41 percent of total members of the SLSA, hold official positions in club administration and serve as patrol captains. The surf life saving movement may not have survived into the modern era without the contribution of female members.

The tradition of small acts of civil disobedience and rebellion leading to liberation on the beaches continued with the growing popularity of surfing. In the early 1950s only a handful of 'rebel' surfers existed outside the SLSA. By the early sixties, when fibreglass Malibus had popularised surfing, the regimented and authoritarian stance of the surf life saving movement faced open acts of rebellion.[32] Ken Brown, an Honorary Beach Inspector, apparently took his appointment very seriously and gained notoriety during the 1960s when the local council introduced a registration fee for surfboards. Any surfboard that did not have the required registration sticker was diligently confiscated, and police had to be called to resolve confrontations with the surfers on several occasions.

The introduction of the lighter Malibu surfboards and the increase in the number of cars allowed many more people to travel to the beaches for a surf, thereby joining a growing counterculture that symbolised freedom and the pursuit of pleasure. After all the belt-tightening of the war years the hedonism of surfing was often viewed as subversive, but the floodgates were well and truly open by the late sixties.

Andrew 'Boy' Charlton wearing the swimming costume of the day. *Courtesy North Steyne SLSC.*

LADIES' COSTUMES,
with Skirts,
3/6, 4/6, 6/-, and 8/6

GENTS,

Ask for JARVIE'S

(England's
Champion)

THE AUSTRALIAN CRAWL

2/6 and 3/6

LASKER'S

THE POPULAR

SPORT
DEPOT,

George Street

Near King Street.

Advertisement for Canadian costumes.
Manly Surf Club 2nd grand carnival,
30 January, 1909, souvenir programme.
Mitchell Library, State Library of NSW.

References to swimming can be found as far back as 2000 BC in various literature, including *Gilgamesh*, the *Iliad* and the Bible. The front crawl swimming style first came to the attention of the western world during a swimming race in London in 1844, when Native American swimmers easily defeated the British breaststroke swimmers.

The English may have been a little miffed by being outclassed by 'natives', because they decreed the style 'un-European' and continued to use the breaststroke in competition.[1] During a trip to Argentina around 1873, John Arthur Trudgen witnessed native South

Americans swimming the front crawl style, and reintroduced it to Great Britain. Trudgen adopted the sidestroke (scissor) kick, but it is believed that the native South Americans had used a flutter kick. This time the speed of the stroke was appreciated, probably because an Englishman introduced it.

The stroke usually referred to as the Australian crawl came about when two brothers from Sydney's Cavill family, arguably Australia's most important swimming dynasty, improved the trudgen swimming technique by using the flutter kick. Arthur Cavill, known as 'Tums', is acknowledged for developing

the crawl stroke after observing a young boy from the Solomon Islands, Alick Wickham. The 'crawl', as it was afterwards named, was apparently used by all Rubiana natives, whose name for it was the 'Tuppa Ta Pala'. Tums' younger brother Richmond, better known as Dick, is said to be the first person to use it in competition, in 1899, and is also credited for introducing it to England, New Zealand and America.

At his peak Dick Cavill had no peer in the world at all distances from 50 yards to a mile, and he was classed as one of the three best Australian swimmers along with Freddy Lane and 'Boy' Charlton. 'Playboy Dick' claimed to have been first to break a minute for the 100 yards freestyle, but in an official match race in July 1902 he lost this

honour in England to fellow Australian Freddy Lane. Lane's victory was considered *"just dessert for Cavill who horrified sportsmen with his training diet of ginger beer, ice cream and brandy snaps"*.[2]

The American swimmer Charles Daniels and Duke Kahanamoku from Hawaii made modifications to a six-beat kick, thus creating the American crawl. Duke learned the crawl stroke from Australian swimmers who visited the Hawaiian Islands in 1910, and adapted the kick from Hawaiian Elders to win the 100 metres freestyle event at the 1912 Olympic Games in Stockholm. In 1922 Johnny 'Tarzan' Weissmuller became the first person to swim the 100 metres in less than a minute, and the front crawl became acknowledged as the fastest stroke in swimming.

"We speak of course of that narrow strip of land over which the ocean waves and moon-powered tides are masters —

that margin of territory that remains wild despite the proximity of cities or of land surfaces modified by industry."

WILLIAM J. DAKIN (1883–1950), *Australian Seashores*

the broken bays

Sydney's northern beaches enjoy a rich history and can rightfully claim to be the place where beach culture, surf life saving and board-riding all began in Australia. They can also claim to be the birthplace of commercial surfboard manufacturing and the fledgling surf media. As discussed previously, these beaches may even have an earlier claim to surfing with the canoe culture of the ocean-loving Saltwater People. Working hard to enjoy our moments on the beach, we can only envy their lifestyle, enjoying daily fresh seafood cooked on a beach barbecue.

Until the early 1900s, this area was mainly a holiday destination, with camping areas in Collaroy and Narrabeen, and on the dunes at the north end of Palm Beach. The completion of the Spit Bridge and Roseville Bridge in 1924, followed by the Sydney Harbour Bridge in 1932 and the rapid rise in car ownership, accelerated residential development on the northern beaches. Following the carnage of the two world wars it seemed that that *"the entire country went to the beach for healing and reconciliation."*[1] By the 1950s and 1960s the northern beaches had become a very desirable place to live.

Along this 30 kilometres of coastline there are over a dozen bays, big and small, strung together like blue sapphires on a golden necklace, or seated in line like the Apostles in Leonardo da Vinci's *Last Supper*. Each of the beaches found within these bays abounds with stories, some lost in time and some recounted here. These broken bays with their beaches and reefs represent one of the finest sections of surf coastline to be found anywhere in the world. They have also been the training ground for many of Australia's international surfing

Previous spread Broken Bays aerial *by oggy.*

champions,[2] from Midget Farrelly's win in 1964 through to Avalon girl Chelsea Georgenson's 2005 championship.

Initially, surfing was dominated by the Surf Life Saving Association, but nothing was going to contain the joys of board riding for very long. The rise in the popularity of surfing in the 1950s and '60s would in turn lead to the development of the surfboard manufacturing industry, with the hub of production at Brookvale, not far from Manly–Freshwater, the home of surfing. Inspired by developments in California, a surf media was born to cover the rising popularity of surfing in Australia. In 1962 Manly's Bob Evans not only released the first issue of *Surfing World*, but would also become Australia's first surf-filmmaker with the release of *Surf Trek Hawaii*. Before long, surfing was everywhere. Australia's own band, The Atlantics, had a hit with 'Bombora',

and surf music swamped the local charts. Barry Crocker recorded 'I Can't Do The Stomp' in 1964, followed by Little Pattie's 'My Blonde-Headed Stompie Wompie, Real Gone Surfer Boy', and the stomp became a dance craze held at most surf clubs every weekend.

There are plenty of surf guides, atlases and websites dedicated to telling anyone interested where to find good surf on any given day or in any conditions, so I do not intend to repeat their work. Neither do I wish to discuss the northern beaches as though they were part of a marketing drive for the surfing industry, fawning on rising surf stars and what they wear. My aim is to look at each of the individual scalloped bays that make up the northern beaches and use the looking glass of history to discover what makes them so special, and how we can protect them for future generations.

Wamberal

Terrigal

Brisbane
Water

TASMAN

SEA

WAKELOA

Marramarra Creek

Bar Island

Patonga

Broken Bay

GARIGAL

Palm Beach

Whale Beach

Careel
Bay

Avalon Beach

Bilgola Beach

Newport Beach

Bungan Beach

Hornsby

Mona Vale Beach

Narrabeen
Lagoon

Warriewood

CAMERAIGAL

Narrabeen

Collaroy Beach

GAIMAI

Long Reef

Dee Why

DARRAMURRAGAL

Curl Curl

GATLAY

Freshwater

Lane Cove River

Balgowlah

Manly Beach

WALLUMEDEGAL

Manly
Cove

BOREGAGAL

CANNALGAL

GAMARAGAL

Cammeray

BIRRABIRRAGAL

WANGAL

Sydney CBD

DARUG

GADIGAL

0   10

KILOMETRES

"The string of gold-gleaming surf beaches that Sydney, alone amongst the world's great cities, displays bazaar-fashion about her doorstep, came truly into their own in the years preceding the outbreak of war in 1914. A generation grew up with the newly formed habit of beach-going."

C. Bede Maxwell, *Surf: Australians Against the Sea*, 1949

manly
and queenscliff

Manly Point.
Photo Ray Leighton.
Courtesy Manly Gallery

Previous spread, left Language map
for northern beaches.
Illustratiom by Ian Faulkner.
Previous spread, right *Photo
Mandy Zeiren.*

"Their confidence and manly behaviour made me give the name of Manly Cove to this place." GOVERNOR ARTHUR PHILLIP, 1788

Governor Arthur Phillip's 1788 encounter with the Kay-ye-my (Camaraigal) men had impressed him with *"their confidence and manly behaviour"* and made him *"give the name of Manly Cove to this place."*[1] The area around the present site of the town of Manly was inhabited by the Cannalgal and Kay-ye-my clans, and was named Eve's Cove by Hunter on the earliest known map of Port Jackson, apparently to commemorate the first meeting with Aboriginal women.[2] It was then renamed Ellensville in 1855, then Brighton, and finally Manly. The name 'Manly' had originally been given to Middle Harbour where Governor Phillip's men kidnapped a local native in 1789. They called him 'Manly' until they found out his real name: Arabanoo.

The sickle-sweep of Manly's ocean beach lies guarded between North Head and Queenscliff. North Head, on the northern side of the entrance to Sydney Harbour, was a site of much significance to the Camaraigal Aborigines as a burial and ceremony place.[3] It also impressed visitors. William Govett, who mapped the north shore in the 1820s, wrote that North Head

appears as a peninsula; and all that mighty mass of rock … stands out at sea, a vast and impregnable barrier, forming a grand and magnificent entrance to the principal harbour and city of the southern world.[4]

North Head is a giant sandstone promontory connected to the mainland by an isthmus of sand where Manly's town centre now sits. This ti-tree covered sand flat was occasionally breached by waves and king tides near where The Corso now stands, revealing North Head's true identity as an island. Over time it became a unique environment for the long-nosed bandicoot, brush-tailed and ring-tailed possums, water rats, echidnas and reptiles that inhabit the area. All are now listed as endangered species. On the southwest edge of this headland lies Blue Fish Point, a favourite fishing spot for the Camaraigal, *"as were many of the exposed rock areas where lobster and abalone could be found with ease in a calm sea."*[5]

Fairy Bower, a legendary big-wave spot for surfers, sits at the

Above 'Appy eyre'. *Postcard courtesy MLSC.*

Right *Photo Oceaneye.*

3 Children—Georgie and Margaret Cameron with Pat Walker, 1907.
Courtesy Manly Library.

southern edge of the headland and takes its name from the fairy-like beauty of the bushland. The Bower turns on a great point surf when big southerly swells wrap themselves around the headland into Cabbage Tree Bay. The cabbage tree palm (*Livistona australis*) is a native Australian palm found in the lowland forests and swamps of eastern Australia and was once thick in this part of the headland. The 'cabbage' is the palm's growing tip, a traditional food for Aboriginal people and thought to have become popular with the first settlers. In those early days of white settlement, the trees were cut down for building materials in the development of Sydney Town, and in the nineteenth century cabbage tree fibres were used to make the popular cabbage tree hats. Manly Council has recently begun replanting them along the pathway that meanders along the shoreline between Shelly Beach and South Steyne, past good snorkelling grounds and waterside restaurants.

South Steyne was the common name given to Manly Beach by the increasing numbers of holiday-makers. The name 'Steyne' is taken from a thoroughfare in Brighton, England. It set the tone for many other seaside resorts in New South Wales, and from the 1850s the affordable Manly Ferry helped Manly become "*the favourite resort of many Sydneysiders, who travelled from Redfern, Waterloo, Woolloomooloo and the Rocks with their picnic hampers and fishing tackle in search of amusement.*"[6] In the days before World War I when Bondi Beach was just being discovered, Manly was already an established resort. By the end of the 1940s more than 10.5 million people were travelling on the ferries annually—twice the number currently carried, despite rising petrol prices.[7]

South Steyne remains the business end of the beach, home to Manly Life Saving Club and The Corso (named after a street in Rome), with its surf culture megastores, fast food, bargain stores,

Above left The Fairy Bower corner of the Ocean Beach, Manly,
National Library of Australia, Canberra.
c.1885. nla.pic-vn3993363.

Above right Manly view from Fairlight, 1888.
National Library of Australia, Canberra.

Group portrait of members of Manly
    Ladies Swimming Club at Manly Baths,
Manly Cove c.1900-1922.
Photo Frank Bell.
Courtesy Manly Art Gallery and Museum.

Above Snowy McAlister.
    Courtesy MLSC.

Queenscliff Beach, 1975.
Photo Roger Scott.
Courtesy Josef Lebovic Gallery.

pubs, restaurants, ice cream parlours, buskers and tourists. People decant from the ferry, stroll down The Corso, and stand on the promenade to look out to sea. North Steyne Surf Life Saving Club lies roughly half way between South Steyne and Queenscliff. Queenscliff, at the southern end of Manly, was named in honour of Queen Victoria. About a kilometre offshore from Queenscliff Headland is a bombora, or reef, where monster waves break on a big south to southwest swell. The locals know it as the Bombie and, along with the Bower, the break is famous as one of the few really big wave sites in Sydney.

Manly Lagoon was originally called Curl Curl Lagoon, and the name Curl Curl appears to be the original Aboriginal name for the Queenscliff–Manly Vale area. Manly Creek was originally Curl Curl Creek, and Queenscliff Headland was originally Curl Curl Headland. Inland from Manly, overlooking it from the plateau, lies Balgowlah, also referred to as 'Bulgowla', or 'Bilgowla'. There have been many variations in the translation, from 'middle harbour' to 'white devil', but the accepted version comes from the Aboriginal word *bulgoola* meaning 'harbour view'. Another translation is from the word *bulagoola*, meaning 'two harbours' (*bula*—two) and (*googla*—harbour) named after the separation of Sydney Harbour from Middle Head.

On 1 January 1810, Lachlan Macquarie took up the governorship, marking a new era for the young colony with the illegal Rum Rebellion government. He soon signed two land grants in the Manly area: 100 acres to Richard Cheers, occupying most of the land west from the present Corso to North Head, and 30 acres to Gilbert Baker, bounded by The Corso and extending west to Ashburner Street. In 1818 both grants were sold to D'Arcy Wentworth, who was also granted another 380 acres in the area to supplement his salary as a medical officer. The restrictions on Wentworth's considerable estate imposed by his will meant that most of Manly would remain virgin bush for the next 60 years.[8]

Opposite Dave Thomas, Fairy Bower.
Photo Ron Perrott.

Above Manly Ladies March Past team.
Photo Ray Leighton. Courtesy MLSC.

swimming
& surf-shooting

One of the earliest settlers in the area was John Whaley, who received permission to buy 20 acres near Manly Lagoon in 1836–37, but the door to the 'development' of Manly was opened by Henry Gilbert Smith, the so-called 'Father of Manly'. Smith had an entrepreneurial spirit, and in 1852 began to convert Manly into a coastal resort. By the 1860s the first English-style bathing boxes on wheels made their appearance on Ocean Beach, allowing bathing between 6am and 7am. On 1 January 1858, businessman Charles Hemington leased eight acres (3.2 hectares) along the cliffs for £60 a year, and established the Fairy Bower picnic, entertainment and refreshment area. Before long the bushland reserve surrounding Cabbage Tree Bay's Shelly Beach was an established picnicking and bathing place attracting up to fifty bathers a day.

The notion that there *"was no native surfing tradition to encourage or restrict either body or craft-based surfing"*[10] is incorrect. If the traditional culture of the Saltwater People had survived on the northern beaches, the European settlers may have learnt the Aboriginal skills in the surf both with bodysurfing and canoe craft, but it would not be until the 1880s that the art of 'bodysurfing' would be appreciated. A South Pacific Islander known as Tommy Tanner was observed 'shooting the waves' and credited with introducing bodysurfing to Manly, and hence Australia. 'Tommy Tanner' was a common nickname for Kanaka males at that time because many of the indentured labourers in Australia came from the island of Tanna in the South Hebrides, now part of Vanuatu. No feet-on-the-sand *"cautious vertical motion"* for Tommy Tanna.

SHOOTING THE BREAKERS, MANLY. HALL, PHOTO.

"... unconsciously, I found myself plunging with the wave as it rolled to the shore ... I was following a certain course set for me ... to recover man's greatest, most thrilling and cheapest sport ever, requiring no clubs, bats or balls, next to no garments ... just one's body and health and strength."

Arthur Lowe, c. 1958

Opposite Ray and Betty Leighton, Manly, c.1946. *Courtesy Betty Leighton.*

Top Surf-shooting, Manly. *Courtesy Manly Library.*
Above Manly Women's Team Surf Lifesaving. *Gallery Manly Gallery.*

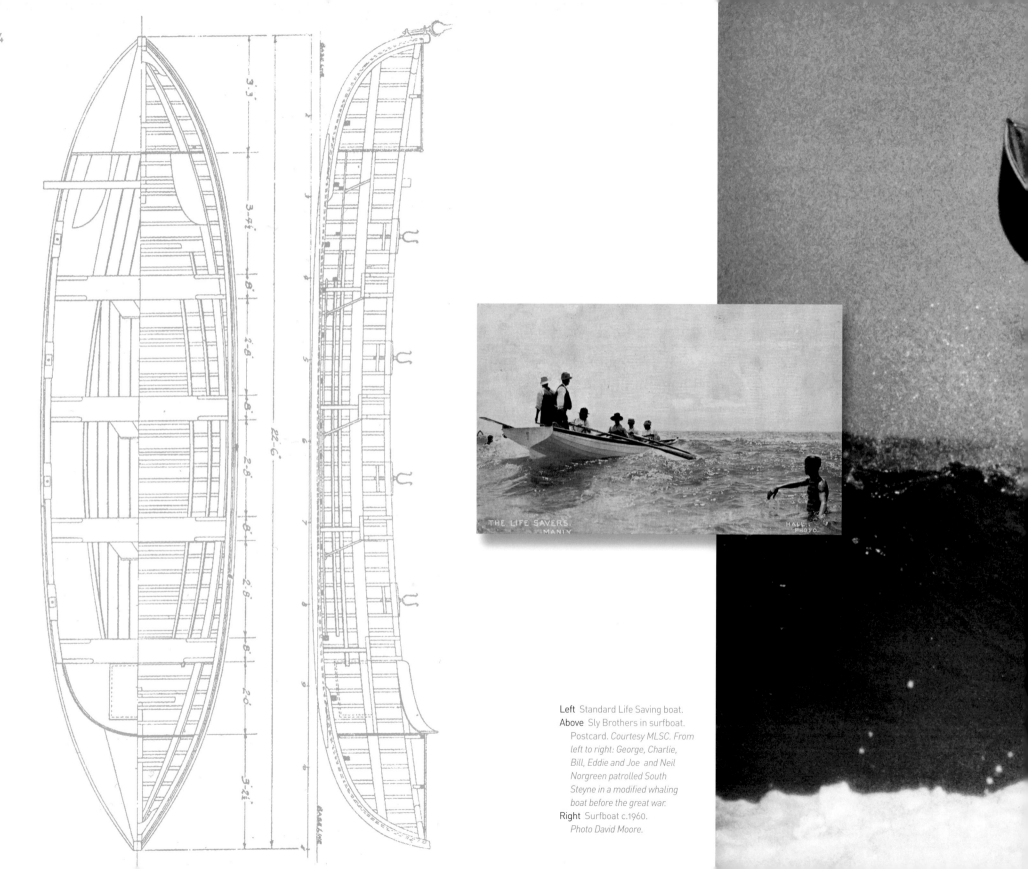

3'.3'

3'.4½'

2'.8'

8'

2'.8'

8'

2'.8'

8'

2'.0'

3'.2½'

22'-6'

THE LIFE SAVERS.
MANLY

HALL.
PHOTO.

Left Standard Life Saving boat.
Above Sly Brothers in surfboat.
    Postcard. *Courtesy MLSC. From
    left to right: George, Charlie,
    Bill, Eddie and Joe and Neil
    Norgreen patrolled South
    Steyne in a modified whaling
    boat before the great war.*
Right Surfboat c.1960.
    Photo David Moore.

Thrusting past those who bobbed and splashed
and laughed at the water's bubbly edge, he made
his way out to the break, threw himself in the
path of a wave, and was carried inshore at speed,
howling and yelling for the joy he had in his
progress. He was with the sea, not against it.[11]

Arthur Lowe and other locals like Freddie Williams were soon
inspired by Tommy's feats. Lowe, from Manly Beach, recalled his
"discovery" in 1886, as a lad aged seven, of the joys what the locals
began to call 'surf-shooting'.

Unconsciously, I found myself plunging with
the wave as it rolled to the shore ... I was following
a certain course set for me ... to recover man's
greatest, most thrilling and cheapest sport ever,
requiring no clubs, bats or balls, next to
no garments ... just one's body and health
and strength.[12]

Another Manly youth, Freddie Williams, was constantly being
hounded from the water by the law, but soon *"mastered the Islander's
skills, then refined them to the point that he was venturing further
and further from shore to 'shoot' bigger and better breakers."*[13]

Gradually a distinction grew up between the 'dippers' and
the 'shooters'. These pioneer surf-shooters had to learn the hard way
which waves gave the best ride and which were 'dumpers'. They learnt
that the rips used wisely could be employed to give a good run out to
the waves. Knowing the right waves to catch and the best time to kick
yourself onto one, hands extended in the familiar trudgen stroke, all
became part of the bodysurfer's skills. This form of surfing, in the
days before swim fins, remains the purest form of wave riding.

At Manly Beach more and more people were enjoying the
simple pleasures of ocean swimming. This growth in popularity
was accompanied by an increase in deaths by drowning. In 1902,
a number of people drowned at Manly Beach and the need for some
organisation to assist in rescues became obvious. Manly Council
considered the use of buoys chained together and moored beyond
the breakers, but settled for life-buoys with lifelines attached housed
on the beach.[14] The first *"demonstration of life-saving"* was a rescue
made by the Sly brothers—Eddie and Joe—that took place on Manly
Beach on Boxing Day in 1903, the same year they began to use their
four-oar clinker-style fishing boat to run an informal rescue service.
This family of fishermen from Fairy Bower is credited with being
the first lifesavers in Manly, if not the first in Australia, and in 1907
were acknowledged for saving approximately one hundred people.
Another brother, 'Tod' Sly, is said to be the first man to use a belt
and line on a Sydney beach,[15] but this claim cannot be confirmed.

Between 1904 and 1907 Edward 'Happy' Eyre, Manly's first
professional life saver, enacted many rescues while employed by
the Life Saving Society and then the council. In January 1907 Happy
Eyre's lone lifesaver status was augmented with the formation of
the Manly Surf Club (this private club still exists on South Steyne).
It was also decided to construct a purpose-built surfboat, designed
by Charles Sly and launched at Manly's first surf carnival on
23 March 1907. Some lifesavers left Manly Surf Club in 1911 to
form a new club: the Manly Life Saving Club. In 1914, Warringah
Shire Council purchased five 18-foot surfboats made from Huon
pine and gave them to Freshwater, Dee Why, Collaroy, North
Narrabeen and Newport.[16]

Duke Kahanamoku from Hawaii is credited with introducing
surfboard riding to Australia in 1914–1915 (see pages 118–123),
but there are even earlier claims. Snowy McAlister credited Tommy
Walker with being *"first man to ride a surfboard at Manly Beach"*,

Tommy Walker (left) and Snowy McAlister.
Courtesy Manly Library.

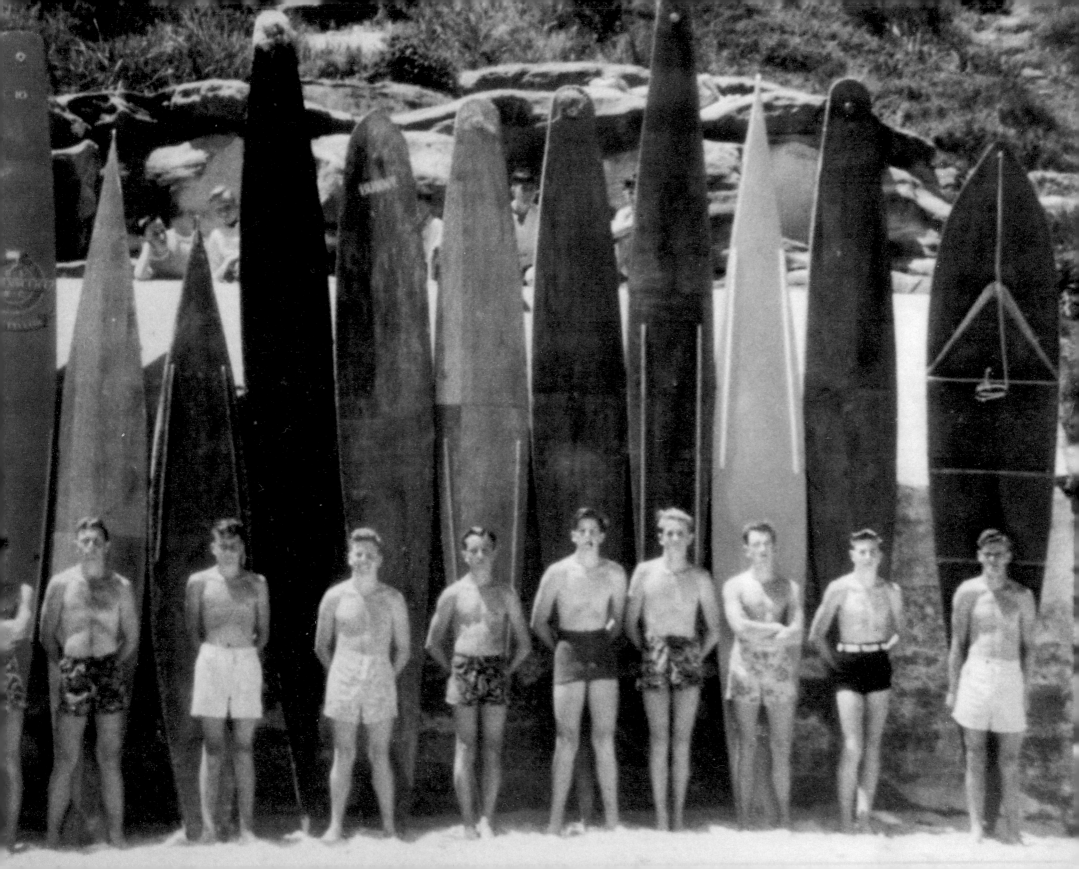

and a 1909 *Walkabout* photograph shows Tommy on the beach holding his board. In a 1939 letter to a sports newspaper, the *Referee*, Tommy himself explains that he bought the board at Waikiki Beach for two dollars during a ship stopover in 1909. Photographs taken by Olleric Notteley demonstrate Walker riding the board and doing his trademark headstand at Yamba as early as 1911. North Steyne surf club records show that its first president, Charles Paterson, brought a solid timber 'Aiala' surfboard back from Hawaii several years before Duke's visit, and that the first locals to ride the board successfully were the Walker brothers (William, Tommy and Russell), Jack Reynolds, Norman Roberts, and Charlie and Frank Bell.[17] Duke, however, rode with a style and skill not seen before, and his demonstration of board riding is covered in more detail in the following section, 'Freshwater and Curl Curl'.

These were troubled times in Australia. In 1914, the country was in the grip of a three-year drought and the year's wheat crop had failed. Men were beginning to be slaughtered in the Great War, yet on the surface Australia seemed *"a nation of optimism, energy, and good scallope edged beaches [that] filled the gaps between headlands and points."*[18] While Duke rode at Freshwater, Jack Reynolds was camped at the base of the Great Pyramid at Mena Camp in Egypt, just prior to landing on another beach that would define the Australian spirit— Gallipoli. Reynolds and another digger from Manly named Richardson are said to have gone surfing in South Africa on the way to the Middle East, and may have introduced surfing to that part of the world. Cecil Healy, Olympic swimmer and one of North Steyne surf club's truly legendary members, would die fighting in France in 1918. In all, 600,000 Australians would perish on the killing fields of Europe during the First World War.

Following the end of World War I, the Royal Life Saving Society continued with its calm-water activities, and in 1922 the Surf Life Saving Association of Australia (SLSA) was formed to concentrate on surf rescue. Its early members were returned servicemen, and the regimented parade ground drills and teamwork of the all-male environment gave a home to the mateship forged on the battlefields. Charles Justin 'Snowy' McAlister (1904–1988) was a real stalwart of the SLSA and board-riding organisation. McAlister was just 11 when he witnessed Duke Kahanamoku surfing at Freshwater in 1915, and it proved a defining moment in his life. A champion surfer from the 1920s, Snowy won three Australian titles and was a common sight at Manly's Fairy Bower, where he continued riding his toothpick until the mid-1970s.[19] The Queenscliff Surf Life Saving Club was formed in 1924, the same year Andrew 'Boy' Charlton, Manly's modest swimming champion, won the gold medal for the 1500-metre event at the Games of the VIII Olympiad in Paris.

During the Second World War, many life saving club members joined the services (Manly Club placed 271 members), and, to fill the void, women were recruited into surf life saving.[20] At the end of the war, the surf life saving clubs became the hub of Australia's swimming and surfing sportsmen and women. In the early 1950s, only a handful of 'rebel' surfers existed outside SLSA, and in 1951 the surf life saving clubs even introduced a law prohibiting riding a surfboard unless you were a member of a life saving club. This created a backlash from the surfers and a schism in the ranks of life savers. Ironically, surfing in Australia was helped to progress beyond this rigid, regimented structure by the 1956 visit of a group of visiting American lifeguards who demonstrated their style of surfing on shorter balsa Malibu surfboards. Australian surfers had been riding 14–18 foot (4–5 metre) hollow paddleboards, and the agility of the Americans witnessed in surfing displays in Manly and Avalon created a demand for these new boards. American surf movies began to appear around the same time, adding to the surge of interest in surfing.

By the early sixties, when fibreglass Malibus had become popular, the authoritarian world of the surf life saving movement

Previous spread Line of surfers at Queenscliff with their wood boards, 1953. Bob Evans on extreme left.
Courtesy Manly Library.

Right The Bower.
Photo Ray Leighton.
Courtesy MLSC.

"The sea becomes the shore, the shore becomes the sea." INDONESIAN PROVERB

Above Surfboards along South
Steyne wall, early 1960s.
Photo Douglas Baglin.
Courtesy Manly Library.

Left Midget Farrelly winning
the 1964 world crown.
Photo Jack Eden.

Far left Phyllis O'Donnell, Manly
World Championships, 1963.
Photo Ron Perrott.

Right Midget Farrelly, Manly
World Championships, 1963.
Photo Ron Perrott.

Far right The Stomp, 1963.
Photo Ron Perrott.

Group of girls in swimwear lying
on long wooden boards of
Manly Life Saving Club 1940s.
Photo Ray Leighton.
Courtesy Betty Leighton.

1st. WORLD SURFBOARD TITLES

Manly, New South Wales, Australia
May, 1964

Sponsored by Ampol Petroleum Limited in conjunction with the Australian Surfriders Association.

Courtesy MLSC.

"No one forgets the old Manly crew like Bob Pike, Graeme Bennett, Flacky, Peter Cornish, Warwick Smith, Nipper Williams, 'Doc' Spence and of course mad Morrie Lee."[24] KEN GRAY

experienced even greater acts of rebellion. Ken Brown, an Honorary Beach Inspector, apparently took his appointments very seriously and gained notoriety during the 1960s when the local council introduced a registration fee for surfboards. Brown would diligently confiscate any surfboard that did not have the required registration sticker, and police had to be called to resolve confrontations with the surfers on several occasions. Although the move was generally away from training and patrols to more wave-riding and just hanging out, occasionally the surfers and clubbies joined forces in rescues, and even in the so-called 'Surfie-Rocker Wars'. The first of these bits of biffo took place at Manly Beach in the summer of 1962, much to the delight of the tabloid press.

Australian surfing came to world attention when Phyllis O'Donnel and Midget Farrelly won their divisions of the first World Surfboard Riders Championship held in 1964. The venue was Manly Beach and 60,000 people lined the shore to watch the local heroes beat the world's best. That same year The Beatles visited Australia for the fab four's only tour down under, and Stevie Wright teamed up with some friends at a Villawood migrant hostel to form The Easybeats. It was a different world back then, and Manly's own Robert Askin was the *"less than honourable"* Premier of New South Wales.[21] Surf culture was seen as part

Layne Beachley.
Photo oggy.
Opposite Layne Beachley.
Photo Scott Needham.

Top left *Photo Mandy Zieren.*
Left *Photo Oceaneye.*

Queenscliff. *Photo Oceaneye.*

'Manly—1940s' from shark tower.
Photo Max Dupain.
Courtesy Jill White.

of the rebellious youth culture, but within a few more decades it would become decidedly mainstream.

On 25 September 2010, Manly and Freshwater Beaches were declared the eighth National Surfing Reserve in New South Wales, providing legal protection for the popular surf beaches. The Manly–Freshwater National Surfing Reserve covers the area from Freshwater Beach to a point 500 metres east of Shelly Beach Headland. The dedication of this site as a National Surfing Reserve recognises its importance in the historical and cultural development of surfing in Australia, and offers Manly–Freshwater the same status as Victoria's Bells Beach and New South Wales' seven other National Surfing Reserves at North Narrabeen, Angourie, Lennox, Crescent Head, Cronulla Beaches, Merewether Beaches and Killalea.

For many years the 385 hectares (950 acres) that make up North Head was the realm of the Catholic Church, a sewage treatment works, the military and Sydney's Quarantine Station, but in 1979 it was made part of Sydney Harbour National Park, and in 2007 it was declared a nature reserve. Over ninety species of birds and over one hundred and forty native plants can be found here, and endangered animals are starting to be reintroduced.[22] Cabbage Tree Bay was declared an aquatic reserve in 2002, but the North Head outfall still discharges about 336 million litres of sewage into the ocean daily from its deepwater pipe about 3.7 kilometres from shoreline.

Manly Lagoon was once a critical aquatic nursery and filtering system. It was home to *"a large body of plant, marine and bird species."*[23] Like many of the lagoons, wetlands and mangrove systems along the northern beaches, Manly Lagoon was reclaimed with rubbish and landfill, and has been dramatically reduced to one-tenth of its original size. Toxins leached from the rubbish have destroyed the marine ecosystem and the lagoon is something of an environmental basket-case. Work is currently being carried out to improve the prospects for the lagoon.

Manly shark tower, c.1960.
Photo David Moore.

Left Veteran sweep Harold 'Rastus'
Evans doing a demonstration.
Courtesy North Steyne SLSC.
Opposite David Jackman riding
Queenscliff Bombie.
Photo Ron Perrott.

THE QUEENSCLIFF BOMBIE

Bombora is said to be an Aboriginal word for a wave that breaks outside the normal surf line. Stories recounting how Dave Jackman famously rode the Queenscliff Bombora on 7 June 1961 often credit him for the beginning of big wave surfing in Australia. He certainly was the first person to crack the Bombie on a Malibu board, but Jackman himself credits Claude West, and others, with first riding the break, stating: *"I paddled my board out while Claude says he made his approach from a surf boat."*[1]

There are reports from around 1949 or 1950 of locals 'Lad' Thompson, Bob Evans (founder of *Surfing World* magazine and surf movie fame), Noel Ferry and George Simmer riding it on the 16- to 20-foot hollow plywood boards of the time. Manly surf club legend Roger 'Duck' Keiran claimed to

have ridden a 15-foot Bombie wave on his 14-foot hollow board on the day peace was declared in 1945. Sometime in 1938 or 1939, a 28-year-old ski paddler Bill Hawkins is said to have ridden the 'North Steyne' bombora. There are probably many more unrecorded accounts as well. Snowy McAlister (1904–1988) was always a regular when the swell was up.

Surf boats were also known to take on the challenge of the bombora. Harold 'Rastus' Evans from North Steyne Surf Club, considered to be the greatest sweep (coxswain) of his time, tackled the Bombie with his crew in the club's new boat *Bluebottle* (apparently named because everyone in the club had been severely 'stung' to pay for it). The attempt to ride the massive swell out to sea was described by *Parade* magazine:

The boat was travelling at such a speed when it hit the swell that it continued under water. Complete with crew it was driven on fully submerged for more than 100 yards before the wave spent itself.

The club's committee was not amused by Evans' daredevil bravado, and he came close to being suspended.[2]

In 1960, Freshwater board-maker Joe Larkin constructed an 11-foot balsa gun for local boy Dave Jackman. Joe dressed rough Ecuadorian balsa logs, glued and clamped the balsa into a blank on a rockered jig he had made, and then crafted the square shape into a long pintail gun. The board was conceived for Jackman to ride the Queenscliff Bombora on the biggest possible day,

and that day came on 6 June 1961, when the 21-year-old paddled out by himself. The board that Joe had designed and built performed perfectly and, with no rescue back-up plan in place, Jackman rode three waves successfully. The feat made the front page of the national newspaper, and Jackman had proved that it was possible to ride big waves similar to those being ridden in Hawaii.[3]

MUSICAL FOOTNOTE:
A group of young guys from Randwick on the other side of Sydney Harbour formed a band called The Atlantics in 1961, the year Dave Jackman first tackled the Queenscliff Bombie. Their tune 'Bombora', released in 1963, went on to be an international hit and was covered by many other bands, including The Ventures.[4]

freshwater
and curl curl

"The three great elemental sounds in nature are the sound of rain, the sound of wind in a primeval wood, and the sound of outer ocean on a beach. I have heard them all, and of the three elemental voices, that of ocean is the most awesome, beautiful and varied."

HENRY BESTON, *THE OUTERMOST HOUSE*, 1928

the battle for a name

The name Freshwater is thought to have originated from the freshwater creek that used to flow onto the northern end of the beach. Another opinion is that it was named after Freshwater on the Isle of Wight in England. In the early 1900s, the area used to be a camping area known for drinking and partying. In an attempt to change its image, it was renamed 'Harbord' after the Honourable Judith Harbord, sister-in-law of Lord Carrington, Governor of New South Wales 1885–1890. The name change created much controversy and debate, but the Postmaster-General finally accepted the views of those who wanted a residential image, and Freshwater officially became Harbord in 1923.[1] The locals did not forget their fight, however, and a bid to change the name back to Freshwater led to a vote where 774 voted in favour and 161 voted against. The suburb

of Harbord was officially renamed Freshwater on 12 January 2008.

Some may feel aggrieved that I have combined Freshwater and Curl Curl in the same section, but the name 'Curl Curl' appears to be the original Aboriginal name for the larger area of Manly Vale, Freshwater and Queenscliff, and was probably derived from the Aboriginal words *curial curial*, meaning 'river of life'. It may also have been a corruption of the words *gura gura* or *goorah goorah* meaning 'long and twisting'—appropriate for the lagoon that is in the Manly area. The name Curl Curl Lagoon was originally applied to Manly Lagoon, which empties into the ocean at Queenscliff. North Curl Curl Beach was once dominated by a large sand dune running behind it, but the sand was removed during World War II to aid in defence against shore attacks. Curl Curl Lagoon was substantially larger, and there is now little evidence of the black swans and ducks that were once here in profusion. The freshwater creek that gave Freshwater its name is now a concrete drain, but there have been attempts to protect what remains of the area's natural beauty, including a program to reclaim some of the dunes.

The first land grant in the area, 50 acres behind Freshwater Beach to Thomas Bruin, was confirmed in 1818. In 1827, James Jenkins took up land in the Curl Curl area and built a five-room stone cottage near the beach.[2] Freshwater became an escape from the growing crowds at Manly Beach. In the late 1800s, Freddie Williams had clambered over the headland to get to the uncrowded waves at that beautiful little beach. When Freshwater became popular, Freddie moved over the next headland to Curl Curl, which was

looked upon then as the ultimate extension of the northern surfer's world, a lonely, lagoon-bordered big beach where crashed some of the most treacherous surf to be found in the entire stretch of metropolitan coastline.[3]

Curl Curl. *Photo Alex Marks.*

Previous spread Exploding wave.
Photo Ian Bird.

Randell's Store, Camp City, Freshwater, c.1910.
Courtesy Warringah Library.

Above Rock pool, South Curl Curl, c.1926.
Courtesy Warringah Library.

Kids would follow him, watch him and then pluck up the courage to ask him to teach them how to 'shoot'. Freddie was generous with his knowledge and became a mentor to many aspiring watermen.

Sometime around 1908 a group of local fishermen decided to chisel a tunnel through the headland to allow easier access to the good fishing grounds that lay between Queenscliff and Freshwater. Over the years the elements have enlarged upon their work, but it remains in use for fishermen and adventuring children to this day. In 1912, a Chinese market garden in Bennett Street was purchased by the Holloway family to create a nursery, and C.W. Holloway was praised for his tree planting. Swampy land around Manly Lagoon was reclaimed in the early twentieth century to create Nolan and Passmore Reserves.

By the early 1900s, Freshwater had become a working class retreat, and timber huts with names such as 'Shark Bait' and 'The Ritz' were erected for those who wanted to stay for the weekend. Many of these campers came from the Balmain area. The huts were rented to men only, but women were allowed to visit 'Camp City' on Sundays. According to club histories it was December 1908 when George Young and John B. Steel called together a meeting to form the Freshwater Life Saving and Surf Club. The club was officially opened on Boxing Day 1910, and the maroon and white colours of the club were adopted by the Manly Warringah Rugby League team when it entered the Sydney competition in 1947. The Freshwater club never adopted the name Harbord despite pressure from government officials. Curl Curl Beach has two volunteer surf life saving clubs, South Curl Curl SLSC established in 1918 and North Curl Curl SLSC established in 1922. Warringah Council employs professional lifeguards to patrol the beaches during the summer months.

In December 1914, the great Hawaiian waterman, Duke Paoa Kahanamoku, stayed at Freshwater's 'Boomerang Camp' (so named because the campers would always return). Swimming, surfing and

Freshwater Creek 1919. *Fred and Syd Walters (right) on
the single plank footbridge across the northeastern
end of Freshwater Creek near Gore Street. 'Beach
House' is visible on the high ground.
Courtesy Warringah Library.*

Opposite The 'Wowsers' camp, one of the many early camps established adjacent to Freshwater Beach. *Courtesy Warringah Library.*

Freshwater Surf Life Saving Club members, c.1910. Courtesy *Warringah Library.*

at Freshwater. Jany 1915

Duke Kahanamoku

canoeing were his passion, and when top Australian swimmers had visited the Hawaiian Islands four years earlier, Kahanamoku studied them closely. He used what he had learned from them to perfect his technique, and the rate at which his skills improved astonished everyone. Duke later developed a friendship with Cecil Healy after the Australian's display of great sportsmanship at the 1912 Stockholm Olympics. Duke had been disqualified for missing the semi-finals, but Healy insisted that it would not be a contest without the presence of the world record holder. Following this intervention Kahanamoku was allowed to swim in the final and win his Olympic Gold sprint swimming medal. Duke had travelled to Stockholm by boat with Jim Thorpe, the champion Native American athlete, and

some had suggested that their late arrival had been planned by unnamed conspirators keen on preventing these dark-skinned athletes from winning medals. Instead, both Kahanamoku and Thorpe were called up to the Royal Victory Stand to be awarded medals and wreaths directly from King Gustav of Sweden.

Apparently, Duke had understood that surfing was not allowed in Australia, and so had not brought a board with him. Urged on by his friends, he selected some local timber to fashion a solid wood board modelled on those used in his native Hawaii. The *Daily Telegraph* described Duke's sugar pine surfboard as *"8 ft in length, 3 ft in width, 100 lb in weight and narrowed at one end."* During a demonstration at Freshwater Beach on Christmas Eve 1914,

Above left Isobel Letham.
Courtesy Warringah Library.

Above right The Duke surfing. Isabel Letham sitting in the foreground.
Courtesy Warringah Library.

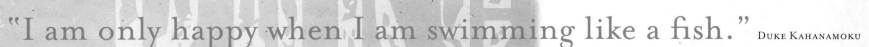

"I am only happy when I am swimming like a fish." DUKE KAHANAMOKU

Duke demonstrated how to surf Hawaiian-style by taking his board out behind the break and riding the unbroken waves, a feat that *"local surfers had not yet learnt to do."*[4]

The event proved was so popular that a second demonstration was given on a Sunday in January 1915. Duke topped the performance by taking a young local girl, Isabel Letham, on the board with him to surf the waves. At just 16, Isabel's life was changed forever. Two years later, Isabel

went to Hollywood to break into the early movie industry as a stunt swimmer but eventually went on to become a swimming teacher at the University of California.[5]

Isobel eventually returned to live at Freshwater until she passed away during the autumn of 1995. Claims that Isobel was Australia's first woman surfer have been challenged by the family of Doris 'Doll' Stubbins, who have a 1911 press clipping of Doll's ride on a surfboard with boyfriend Jack Reynolds at North Steyne. It is obvious that right from the start there were Australian girls who were not going to be content to watch the boys have all the fun in the surf.

The surfboard fashioned by Duke at the Boomerang Camp at Freshwater Beach is said to have originally been given to Tommy Walker's brothers, who later gave it to goofy footer Claude West *"out of respect for Claude's surf stroke."*[6] West later went on to

Above left Duke, 1914.
Courtesy Bishop Museum.

Above right Duke Kahanamoku, 1914.
Courtesy Bishop Museum, Hawaii.

become the very first Australian Board Riding Champion. He eventually donated this historic board to the Freshwater Surf Life Saving Club where it has been proudly displayed since 1952. Duke Kahanamoku has been honoured for his contribution to Australian surfing with a statue erected on the headland at Freshwater. Perhaps one day the original Saltwater People will be acknowledged for their contribution to changing the New Australians from water-fearing immigrants to great waterpeople.

The solid wood boards of the early 1900s were replaced by the long hollow paddleboard, invented by Tom Blake in Hawaii in the early 1930s and made possible by innovations in materials during the First World War. Maroubra surfer Frank Adler announced the arrival of the hollow board to Australia in1934, when he *"easily outpaddled other surfers who were using solid boards."*[7] Around the same time, Dr 'Saxon' Crackenthorp of Manly developed the Australian surf ski, and the design morphed from the original 3-metre shape to the 5-metre 'toothpicks' that were officially adopted as rescue boards by the SLSA in 1937. This type of board construction would be copied under surf clubs and in back yards around Sydney for the next two decades.

The introduction of the lighter Malibu board in the late 1950s and early '60s would change the business forever. With the move to balsa and then fibreglass materials, surfboard production began to boom and shifted from 'hobby' to 'commercial'. Brookvale, named after the vale (or little valley) with its brooks or streams that ran along the track that is now Pittwater Road, would partially 'evolve' into an industrial estate, and the fledgling surfboard manufacturing industry was drawn to this seaside suburb with its cheaper rents. It would soon become the early home of Australian surfboard manufacturing (see page 129).

Guringai descendant Bob Waterer (b.1924) grew up in Brookvale, and remembers it in the early days as

a very rural suburb, with Chinese market gardens, poultry and dairy farms and a pig farm on the hill where Freshwater High School now stands. A large dairy farm was on the present site of Manly High School and covered the area bounded by Abbott and Harbord Roads and Makim Street and back to the top of the Makim Street hill.[8]

Large swathes of Brookvale and parts of neighbouring Freshwater have since been designated light industrial or commercial, and have been transformed over the years with a level of architectural ugliness and lack of sensitivity to the natural beauty of the area that verges on irresponsible. The Harbord Diggers Club has been described by one respected architect as *"a monument to poor taste and a reflection of our culture."*[9] New owners the Mounties group proposed to rebuild the club with a $111.5 million complex on the headland including luxury units.[10] This plan, and another to build a $60 million retail and residential development in the heart of Freshwater, has been met with unprecedented opposition from residents fearing the loss of the 'village' fabric.

The Mounties Group was refused for a second time in May 2011.[11] The planned retail and residential development outlined above was axed by the Land and Environment Court in the same month. Liberal State Member for Manly and newly appointed NSW Treasurer Mike Baird sees the dismissal of these large developments by the Land and Environment Court as a clear *"message to developers to work with the community, not against them."*[12] Warringah Mayor Michael Regan believes that the *"Freshwater community now has a great opportunity to guide the future of the suburb with its site specific development control plan."*[13] One thing is certain, growing population pressure means that the fight will continue.

Opposite Spinner, Midget Farrelly,
Curl Curl, 1963. *Photo Ron Perrott.*

curl curl

Top South Curl Curl 1927. Bill Robinson
   teaching rescue methods. *Courtesy CCSLSC.*
Centre The 'South Curly' girls, 1948. Helen Wood,
   Gladys Brown, Val Smith, Eileen Still,
   Judy Cuneo and Shirly Morrow.
   Courtesy CCSLSC.
Bottom Young South Curl Curl Surf Club members
   on the beach, 1915. *Courtesy Warringah Library.*

Above Standard Life Saving reel.
   Illustration courtesy of ASLA.
Right *Photo Oceaneye.*

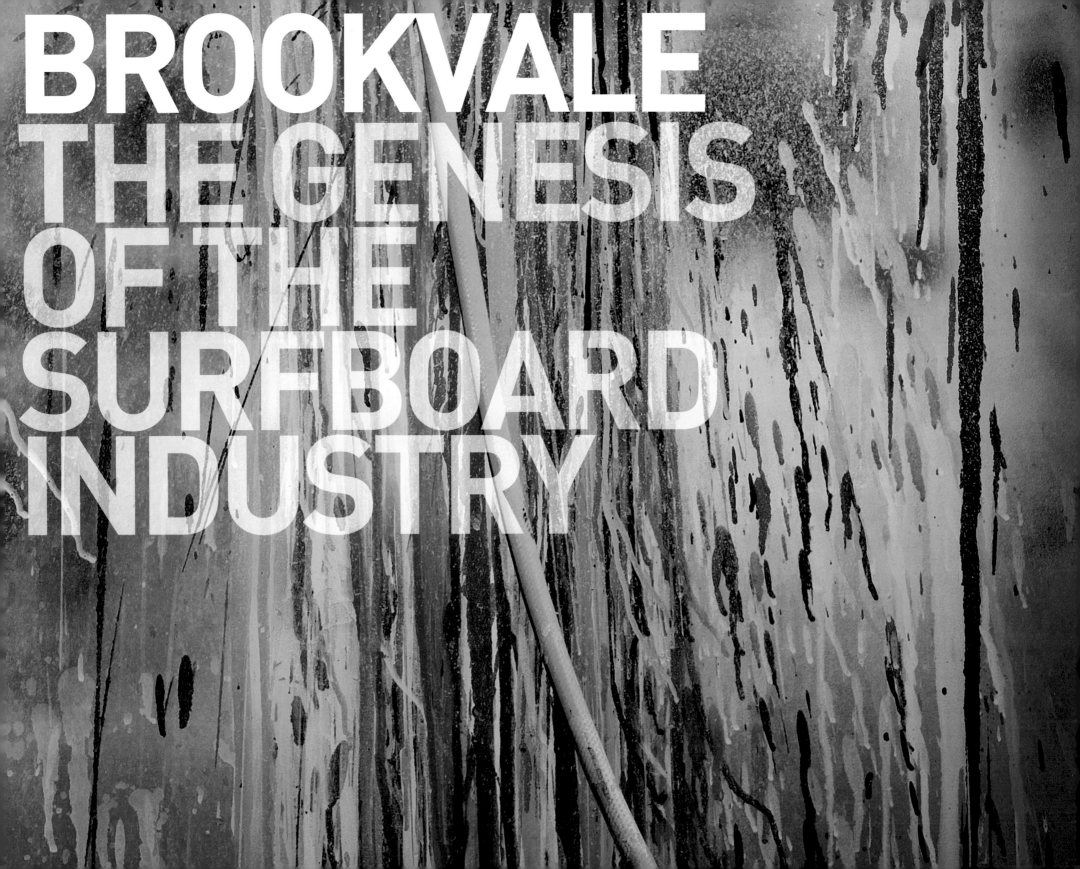

BROOKVALE
THE GENESIS OF THE SURFBOARD INDUSTRY

The Australian surfboard-making industry evolved from the surf life saving movement, and North Steyne surf club member Les Hind is said to have been the country's first surfboard producer.[1] The early days of surfboard construction were very much a back-yard business. Solid wood boards and strutted timber frames with a plywood skin and shellac finish were mainly do-it-yourself jobs built in home garages or at surf clubs. Frank Adler founded the Australian Surf Board Association in 1945 with the *"intention of putting some distance between surfing and life-guarding"*,[2] but it was a demonstration of new skills on smaller balsa wood boards by a team of Californian lifeguards in 1956 that led to some dramatic changes.

Demand for these lighter boards grew rapidly, and by the late fifties several Sydney board builders had begun full-time manufacturing. In 1959, Barry Bennett moved his business from Bronte to the new industrial area of Brookvale, just inland from Freshwater. Within a year, a hub began to develop when Manly Beach surfer Denny Keogh founded Keyo Surfboards and also opened a factory in Brookvale. Drawn by the cheap rents and the proximity to great surf beaches, south-side board builders Bill Wallace, Scott Dillon and Gordon Woods joined them around that same time. With the shift to balsa and then fibreglass materials, manufacturers launched their own labels and Australian board making became a professional craft. At first members of the industry would emulate their big brothers in California and Hawaii, but eventually they stamped surfboard design with their own innovations. Australians were in the vanguard of the revolution to shortboards, and many back-yard artisans would turn into multinational manufacturers.

The second wave of Brookvale board brands were usually owned or supported by top surfers. Midget Farrelly, Nat Young and Nipper Williams established their own businesses, while Ted Spencer and Gary Birdsall shaped signature models for Shane and Kenn Surfboards.

Left *Photo Scott Needham.*
Right *Scott Dillon (left) and Babalooey. Photo Jack Eden.*

BROOKVALE THE GENESIS OF THE SURFBOARD INDUSTRY

THE CRAFTSMEN

Joe Larkin (b.1933)

Freshwater's Joe Larkin began making surfboards in 1949, starting with a 16-foot racing board. After the touring American surf life saving team displayed their skills in Sydney in 1956, Joe began making his own version of the Malibu, nicknamed 'the Okanohue', using a wooden frame and marine plywood, as balsa was initially unavailable in Australia. In the late fifties, Joe and Denny Keogh began making balsa boards in Bill Clymer's garage in Manly. Joe designed and built an 11-foot balsa pintail gun for local lad Dave Jackman to tackle big waves at the Queenscliff Bombora in 1961 (see page 114).

Larkin worked with Bob Evans on his early films and later moved to Queensland, where he started his own label. His surfboard factory became Kirra's unofficial HQ during the 1960s and 1970s, a place where many influential surfers such as Bob McTavish, Peter Drouyn, Peter Townshend, Michael Peterson and Terry Fitzgerald either worked or got boards. In recent years Joe has been coaxed back into making boards, specialising in longboards from original templates as well as making new designs. Bill Clymer moved to balsa boards but then shifted focus to surfboats. His son, Matt Clymer, carries on this work.

Barry Bennett (b.1931)

Barry Bennett, founder of Bennett Surfboards, bought a block of land in Brookvale for his new factory in the late 1950s and became a pioneer of the burgeoning Australian surfboard industry. In 1962, he founded Dion Chemicals and began manufacturing polyurethane foam surfboard blanks. Bennett and Adelaide entrepreneur John Arnold formed Golden Breed, Australia's first international surfwear company, in 1970. Barry Bennett was inducted into the International Surfboard Builders Hall of Fame in 2009. Despite having earned considerable wealth, at the time of printing Barry could still be found working in the factory among the foam dust and resin.

Denny Keogh (b.1937)

Manly boy Denny Keogh was taught to surf by Claude West. Denny started working as a wool classer in winter and a lifeguard at North Steyne during the summer. After attempting to build a few balsa boards in the club's casualty room, he shifted production to his garage in 1957 before founding Keyo Surfboards in Brookvale three years later. Keogh's boards were at the cutting edge of surfboard design from 1963 to 1970, both on the local scene and internationally. Talented board riders such as Midget Farrelly, Nat Young, Kevin Platt and Bob McTavish all surfed and shaped for Keyo at different stages in their careers.

Possibly the pivotal point in the company's early history was the development of the 'shortboard', which occurred in the Brookvale factory between 1966 and 1968. The McTavish 'vee' bottom 'Plastic Machine' was an example of designs being pushed and trialled by shapers such as Neil Purchase and Kevin Platt under Denny. The designs of the boards were kept so secret that the Keyo crew would wait for the right conditions for surf at Box Head so they could trial the boards away from the gaze of competitors.

Left Scott Dillon, Narrabeen 1963. *Photo Bob Weeks.*
Centre Sydney surfboard industry representatives donate surfboards to Australian servicemen in South Vietnam, July 1966. *Photograph courtesy Denis McDonagh. From left to right: Mr Platt, Platts Boardshorts, first local surfwear manufacturer; Denny Keogh, Keyo Surfboards; Colonel P. Trancred, Australian Army; Scott Dillon, Scott Dillon Surfboards; Bob Brewester, Manly Stor-a-Bord and Bower Boy Surf Wax; Gordon Woods, Gordon Woods Surfboards; Denis McDonagh, McDonagh Surfboards Bill Wallace, Wallace Surfboards; Barry Bennett, Barry Bennett Surfboards. Australian War Memorial.*
Far left *Photo Scott Needham.*
Below Scott Dillon (left) and Babalooey. *Photo Jack Eden.*

In 1972 Keogh became the licensee for Hobie Cat catamarans, but Keyo Surfboards continued to be made under licence. Denny's son-in-law John Gill is currently in charge of production.

Gordon Woods (b.1925)

After seeing the performances of American lifeguards in 1956 at Avalon on their 9-foot balsa surfboards, pioneering Bondi surfboard manufacturer Gordon Woods went out and bought one of their boards. That same year he established Gordon Woods Surfboards, and a few years later relocated to Brookvale. In 1960 he began producing his own polyurethane foam. One of the Brookvale Six—manufacturers with national sales and reputations in the ten years from 1962 to 1972—the company boasted a quality stable of shapers and riders, including Midget Farrelly and Nat Young. Woods left the board making business in 1974 and went on to build yachts.

Bill Wallace (b.1926)

Bill Wallace shaped his first hollow wooden paddleboard (a design known as 'the toothpick') under his grandmother's house in Bronte, Sydney, in 1942 when he was just sixteen. In the 1950s he pioneered the introduction of the Okanui and Malibu surfboard to Australia. At the end of the fifties he moved from Bronte to Brookvale, with Gordon Woods at one end of town, Barry Bennett at the other, and the Wallace factory in the middle. He now lives in Noosaville where he still handcrafts wooden replica masterpieces. Bill Wallace was inducted into the International Surfboard Builders Hall of Fame in California in 2010.

Scott Dillon (b.1928)

Boxer, free diver, speedway driver and big wave rider, Bondi lad Scott Dillon became known as a designer and builder of surfboards, opening his first surfboard-making factory in Brookvale in 1956. Many leading surfers began their careers by shaping and finishing surfboards here, including brothers Bob, Peter and Jimmy Pike, Mick Dooley, Bob McTavish, Warrick Smith, Ron 'Little Kiss' Wade, Robert Kennerson and, especially, Gordon Merchant, founder of international surf clothing company Billabong. Future world champion Robert 'Nat' Young rode Dillon's surfboards for several years from 1963.

Scott Dillon conquered big waves at the Queenscliff Bombora 1963, and Bare Island in 1963–64, the same years he travelled to Hawaii with Bob Pike and Mick Dooley. He was photographed regularly riding big swells at Fairy Bower and North Narrabeen in the era from 1963 to 1969. Dillon later moved to Coffs Harbour on the mid North Coast of New South Wales and in 1999 he opened the Legends Surf Museum. Dillon was inducted into the Surfing Hall of Fame in 2004 as one of the true original legends of the Australian surfing industry.

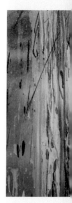

Greg McDonagh

McDonagh built first his own hollow marine ply board at his Freshwater house, now the site of the Harbord Diggers Club. Forced into the industry because there was no one local to make the newer Malibu-type boards, McDonagh was one of the first to work on strengthening the early joined balsa plank boards, covering them with a layer of fibreglass cloth. He actually pioneered the use of Polyfoam in Australia and was the first to mould

BROOKVALE THE GENESIS OF THE SURFBOARD INDUSTRY

Above *Photo Scott Needham.*
Right and below *Simon Anderson 1980.*
Photo Hugh McLeod.
Opposite *Photo Steve Baccon.*

foam blanks for use in board building. Greg was soon joined by his brother Denis, the force behind the Surf Dive 'n' Ski shops.

John 'Nipper' Williams

Nipper Williams of Queenscliff became one of the country's leading board makers in the sixties when the Malibu board became popular. The Malibu made brief appearances as early as 1954, when Australian Hollywood actor Peter Lawford

> "The euphoria from riding a wave has its source in the brief unity between the rider and God given energy." Tom Blake, *Voice of the Wave*, 1969

brought back a board on a return trip from the US. Lawford and Nipper Williams surfed their Malibus at Manly in 1955.

Midget Farrelly (b.1944)

At age 17, Midget Farrelly was working alongside Joe Larkin, Bob Pike and Barry Bennett. Other talented shapers, glassers, sanders, finishers and businessmen also played a part in Midget's early education in the surfboard industry, including Dave Jackman, Mickey McMahon, Denny Keogh and Gordon Woods. Farrelly Surfboards was founded in 1965 at Palm Beach, and the following year he released his lightweight Farrelly Stringerless model. His significant contribution to late 1960s surfboard design would be overshadowed by the work of Bob McTavish and others, who are generally credited with inventing the shortboard and subsequent 'vertical' revolution. In

1972 Farrelly founded the Sydney-based Surfblanks manufacturing company, making it into a successful business.

Shane Stedman (b.1943)

Stedman was the founder of Shane Surfboards and the nation's top-selling board maker in the early 1970s. His talented shapers included Terry Fitzgerald, Butch Cooney, Frank Latta, Ted Spencer and Simon Anderson. Stedman is said to be the 'inventor' of Ugg boots.

Terry Fitzgerald (b.1950)

Terry Fitzgerald made his reputation as an original and flamboyant surfer at his home break, Narrabeen, during the 1960s. In 1969 he moved to Queensland and, after learning some of the surfboard craft while working in Joe Larkin's Kirra surfboard factory, Fitzgerald moved back to Sydney and in 1970 started Hot Buttered in the industrial suburb of Brookvale. That same season he went to Hawaii where he met Dick Brewer and began a great design collaboration with shapers such as Reno Abellira, Sam Hawk and Owl Chapman. This resulted in modern mainstays like the spiral 'V' (a basic double concave) and wings.

Fitzgerald's surfing style and surfboard shaping were based on maximising speed, and Fitzgerald *"played a key role in finally pushing high performance way clear of the sport's longboarding roots and into the realm of the power carve."*[3] Surfers and shapers who passed through his factory over the years include Simon Anderson, Col Smith, Derek Hynd, Steve Wilson, Greg Day, Greg Webber and many more. Along with their unique designs, Fitzgerald's boards were also known for the beautiful airbrush spray work of Martin Worthington.

Simon Anderson (b.1954)

"A large, deceptively casual power surfer, Simon Anderson achieved high renown in both competition and sheer performance through the early days of pro surfing. Like many pros of the day, he also learned the craft of board shaping and design, thinking it might be useful as a career backup."[4] In 1972, he began to shape with Shane Stedman and Fitzgerald in their Brookvale factories before starting his own factory, Energy.

After several big contest wins in 1977, Anderson began to be left behind after Mark Richards' twin-fin had come to dominate the tour, but this design lacked the drive to take him vertically up the face to the top of the wave for his trademark powerful re-entry/cut back. In 1980 he came up with the three-fin 'Thruster', a concept that would quickly make an impact on practically every surfer on the planet. Surfboard design had changed forever, and *Surfer*

magazine listed him as the most influential surfer of the twentieth century.

Geoff McCoy (b.1948)

Born in Gosford, McCoy shaped for Bennett and Keyo before founding McCoy Surfboards in Brookvale, 1970. Damien Hardman, Mark Warren, Cheyne Horan and Pam Burridge all belonged to surfboard designer Geoff McCoy's high profile team. After McCoy moved his operations to Avoca, the McCoy/Horan partnership popularised the tail-heavy Lazer Zap designs. This 'no-nose' design profoundly influenced the style of two time world champion Damien Hardman, helping create a *"back-foot-focused vertical turner whose backside approach was a highlight."*[5] McCoy's designs were also part of the development of the 'Thruster'.

dee why
and long reef

"Dee Why Lagoon—a beautiful sheet of water, upon the bosom of which are frequently seen flocks of wild fowl of many varieties including the black swan floating gracefully among his more diminutive companions."

Town and Country Journal, 2 January 1886

There are many versions of how Dee Why got its name. One opinion is that it is a corruption of an Aboriginal word *diwi*, *dee-wee* or *diwai*, which was the name or noise of a water bird from the area. The earliest European reference to it is in the field book of surveyor James Meehan: "*Wednesday, 27th Sept, 1815 Dy Beach—Marked a Honey Suckle Tree near the Beach.*"[1] Meehan often named locations he surveyed using names from local Aboriginal languages, but it is not noted if this was the case in this reference. It may have been a shortened version of another word, but we can only speculate. After more than a century of being officially known as 'Deewhy', the name was split in two during the 1950s.[2]

Another, stranger, theory offered by Australian pioneer aviator, Lawrence Hargrave (1850–1915) is that Meehan mistakenly read the initials 'DV' carved into the sandstone on the hill above the lagoon as 'DY'. Hargrave believed that 'DV' was the initials of 'de Vega', the Spanish Admiral in command of an expeditionary fleet that set out in 1595 to establish a colony in the Solomon Islands. After leaving the Marquesas Islands group northeast of Tahiti, de Vega's vessel, the *Santa Yzabel* became separated in a fog and was never seen again. Hargrave claimed that the Spanish galleon made it to Port Jackson, and that de Vega made camp at Dee Why Lagoon.[3]

Dee Why Heights or Highlands, known as Narraweena since 1951, on the plateau behind Dee Why apparently means 'quiet place in the hills', but it is also a corruption of the word *nurawina* or *nuraweenah*. Its literal meaning is *nura* (country, place or land) and *wee* (to rest, stay, sit or live), and adding *-na* or *-nah* as a suffix (to see or to watch), so translates as 'place to rest and see'. The area's solitude changed dramatically after World War II when land was subdivided for Housing Commission homes. The name 'Dee Why West' was changed to Cromer in 1969.

Sand dunes once towered over the long beach that stretches from Dee Why point to Long Reef, but were diminished by road-building during the Depression and World War II. Behind the beach's remaining dunes is Dee Why Lagoon, whose entrance marks the divide between Dee Why Beach and Long Reef Beach. Once home to ageless melaleucas, the lagoon was rich in birdlife, fish, shellfish and prawns. From Stony Range Reserve down to the lagoon was once marshland, but much of the freshwater marsh area was filled in with household and industrial waste from the 1950s to 1970s to make way for flats and parkland. The high conservation value of the lagoon and its surrounding area has since been recognised and in 1973 it was proclaimed a wildlife refuge. The Dee Why Lagoon Wildlife Refuge covers an area of 77 hectares, including the 30 acres taken up by the lagoon. It is still an extremely significant area for local and migratory birds, and is listed on migratory bird agreements with China and Japan. A group of dedicated local residents have worked hard for

Previous page Long Reef. *Photo Ian Bird.*
Left Dee Why Point. *Photo Ron Perrott.*
Above Miller's Cup. *Courtesy DWSLSC.*

the last thirty years to preserve the lagoon for future generations, and have been rewarded with sightings of breeding pairs of the once profuse black swan.

The origin of the name of neighbouring Long Reef is obvious, but few would know that the headland with its freshwater spring was an important gathering place for Indigenous women. The rich forests behind the headland were destroyed to make way for a dairy farm that then became a golf course. Griffith Park was established in 1912 and the Long Reef Aquatic Reserve declared in 1980. Approximately 60 hectares aquatic reserve extends from Collaroy rock baths south to Long Reef SLSC, and from mean high water out 100 metres from mean low water. Popular surf breaks on Long Reef include Butterbox and the Bommie, and the area was also a haven for sailboarding at its peak of popularity.

The first land in the area to be listed by the *New South Wales Government Gazette* was 700 acres granted to William Cossar in the early nineteenth century. By the mid-nineteenth century most of the land in what is now Dee Why had been acquired by James Jenkins and his family. In 1900 this land was bequeathed to the Salvation Army by Jenkins' *"eccentric"* daughter Elizabeth to establish an industrial farm, as well as hostels for boys, girls and women. Access to the beach was limited by a wire-netting barrier running along the length of the Salvation Army land, and sunbathing was banned. This changed in 1913 when the Salvation Army decided to progressively sell off most of its holdings on the northern beaches, starting with The Oaks Estate Auction, which gave its name to one of Dee Why's main streets, Oaks Avenue. By 1920, most of Dee Why had been subdivided. Today, Dee Why is regarded as the most multicultural suburb in Sydney, sitting in the middle of the largely conservative, white-bread Anglo-Celtic suburbs that make up the northern beaches.

Dee Why Surf Life Saving Club was founded in 1913. Following an amazing rescue on 22 February 1914 and a subsequent injection

Top left Dee Why clubhouse and shark tower c.1917.
 Courtesy DWSLSC
Top right and centre *Courtesy DWSLSC.*
Left The Dee Why rescue, 22 February 1914. From left to right:
 J.J.K. Taylor, R. Overton, H. Starkey, H. Duckworth (two
 rescued boys in the middle). *Courtesy of the DWSLSC.*

Wheel of Youth, 1929.
Photographed in Dee Why,
Long Reef is in the background.
Photo Harold Cazneaux.
National Library of Australia,
Canberra.

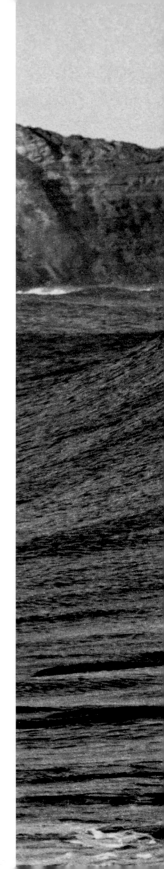

of funds by the council, the original clubhouse opened that same year. Several beltmen had nearly drowned in attempts to rescue a group of youths who had been carried out to sea, and in desperation the life savers turned to a small skiff that was owned by the Salvation Army's Boys Home. A cobbled-together crew of four managed to get past the breakers and collect two of the boys. On the return trip to the beach the skiff was capsized by the waves, but there was plenty of help available and both lads were resuscitated. A rescue like this had never previously been witnessed from any Australian beach. The Warringah Council set aside the then princely sum of £1,250 to distribute to the five life saving clubs then existing within the shire boundaries.

Club members have made thousands of rescues since then, and the club was also involved in many early community projects such as the sea pool and sea wall. During the Depression, the clubhouse was made available for those ex-diggers on the road and battling to make a living. Charles Swancott tells the story of how the cargo ship *Malabar* was wrecked near Sydney Heads and tinned butter, bags of flour and kegs of beer were washed down to Dee Why. The diggers quickly buried one keg in the sand when police were seen coming towards them. A windstorm that night obliterated the markings and the keg was lost until World War II when soldiers bulldozing the dunes as a defence measure uncovered it. According to legend the soldiers were found *"almost insensibly drunk"* and had to be taken to hospital.[4] The Dee Why Ladies Amateur Swimming Club was established in 1922 and has a long history of distinguished competitors.

The Long Reef Surf Life Saving Club was founded in 1950 and a clubhouse was built at the northern half of the 1.8-kilometre stretch of beach. As a number of founding members attended or had attended the Shore School in North Sydney, the school colours navy blue and white were adopted as the club colours. The beach faces towards the southeast and picks up any east to southeast swell, making it a popular surf beach. The beach to the north of the

Above Terry Richardson, Dee Why Point c.1975.
Photo by Hugh McLeod.
Right Bob Pike. *Photo Bob Weeks.*

Long Reef Surf Club is given some protection by the outer reefs (bomboras). In winter, Long Reef is exposed to prevailing winds and is very popular with windsurfers and kite surfers. Long Reef Surf Club proudly boasts 'No Lives Lost' during patrol hours, but recently raised the ire of various community groups who are opposed to the scale of a proposed clubroom upgrade. The original $4.5 million development included plans for accommodation and a private restaurant on the environmentally sensitive site. Many residents fear the commercialisation of the beach by any group—including life saving clubs—and in June 2011, after a torrent of protest, the club informed the council that it no longer wanted to proceed with the development.

In 1958 a group of Californian surfers visited Sydney and was introduced to Dee Why by the late Bob Evans, founder of *Surfing World* magazine. The group included the legendary Phil Edwards, photographer Bob Cooper, and Rennie Yater, one of the most influential surf designers and innovators of the time. Great friendships were quickly established with local surfers, and Dee Why was fast becoming the centre of surfing in Sydney. In 1961 the Dee Why Surfing Fraternity, Australia's oldest surfboard riders' club, was established, with Midget Farrelly as the first President. The first A Grade competition team included Farrelly, Peter Cornish, Bob McTavish, John Dessaix, Kevin Platt, Dave McDonald and Phil Rose.

Peter 'PC' Crawford, one of Dee Why's favourite sons, was an innovative kneeboarder and surf photographer working for both Australian surfing publications and the big US surfing magazines. Even though kneeboarding is a bit of a dying art these days, early practitioners such as PC and George Greenough were at the cutting edge of board and fin design at the start of the shortboard revolution. At his home break, Dee Why Point's barrelling wave, PC was known for his powerful bottom turns, riding deep in the tube, popping 360s and landing barrel rolls. In his day, Crawford was also a master of water photography with the Nikonos water camera

released in 1963. Like many of the play-hard Dee Why crew, PC's life was fast and furious, and he died suddenly in Bali in 1999 from an apparent spider bite. In 2001 he was posthumously inducted into the Australian Surfing Hall of Fame.

Dee Why Point's reputation as a hostile surf spot was underscored by a quip made by Layne Beachley after surfing some big and dangerous waves at Ours, near Botany Bay, in 2009. This white-knuckle ride is notorious, breaking only metres from a rock face and considered to be one of Sydney's heaviest breaks. It is the domain of the aggressive Maroubra-based pack, the Bra Boys, and the territory is fiercely guarded. When asked by one observer what it was like mixing it with the infamous Bra Boys, Beachley joked, *"I've seen scarier people at Dee Why Point."*

Above *Photo Justin Crawford.*
Opposite *Photo Oceaneye.*

Top left Wahini in Dee Why Club boardshorts.
  Photo Ron Perrott.
Left Photo Justin Crawford.

Photo Oceaneye.

collaroy,
narrabeen
and turimetta

Above North Narrabeen Surf Club, 1963.
Photo Bob Weeks.
Previous page Issac Buckley, Narrabeen.
Photo Alex Marks.

Sam Grey, South Narrabeen SLSC member with
a long board used for inter-club racing, 1948.
Surfboard built by Max Whitehead and Adam Fidler.
Courtesy *Warringah Library.*

"Not far off the Pacific boomed. But fifty yards inland started these bits of swamp, and endless promiscuity of 'cottages'."   D.H. LAWRENCE, *KANGAROO*, 1922

Collaroy, originally part of Narrabeen, took its name from the paddle steamer SS *Collaroy* that was beached there in January 1882. It remained there until September 1884 when it was refloated. *Collaroy* is an Aboriginal word meaning 'fresh water reed' or 'long reeds', and the name was given to a sheep station near Merriwa owned by the Clive family and eventually to the SS *Collaroy*. Collaroy Basin was an important fishing place for the Saltwater People. With its deep water enclosed by reefs on two sides, and relatively protected, it was an ideal place to school fish. Dennis Foley states that this was where a few skilled individuals were able to enlist the help of dolphins when fishing.[1]

The origins of the name Narrabeen are uncertain, but there are quite a few theories. In 1802, Lieutenant Grant, in command of HMS *Lady Nelson*, reportedly recaptured two escaped convicts near the mouth of 'Narrabine' creek, but it is not known where he got the name. In his 1815 survey James Meehan mentions *narrabang*, meant to be a corruption of the Aboriginal word *ngarra* (twisted or knotted) and *bong* (separated water), supposedly named after the winding lake entrance to the sea. An article in the *Town and Country Journal* in 1886 recounted the story of how a young Aboriginal girl known as Narrabang tried to prevent the murder of a family of settlers by a band of bushrangers, and that Narrabeen was named in her honour. There seems to be little in the way of proof to verify this story.[2] In other interpretations it is given varied meanings including

On 20 January, 1882, the Newcastle–Sydney coastal steamer ran aground on a lonely beach that would take its name.
Courtesy Manly Gallery.

'place of many swans', 'mouth of the lagoon', or the name of a native plant growing near the lake entrance.

Elanora, the name given to the plateau overlooking Narrabeen, is said to be derived from an Aboriginal word *ella* (the clay used for body painting) and *nura* (country or land). The area of Red Hill was predominantly the Ellanura area. The translation 'by the sea' or 'home by the sea' sometimes given is apparently from distant language groups.

The pristine Narrabeen Lakes were central to the Saltwater People's world, and a *"large semi-permanent campsite once existed on the lakeside of the Mactier Street area."*[3] Traditional life was closely related to fishing and the harvesting of shellfish. Permanent fish traps and fish pens were maintained in many estuaries, with the traps *"used seasonally, for harvesting the migrating or sedentary fish stocks; the cages were used for fattening long-term food supply."*[4] Saltwater People lived in the Narrabeen area right up to the 1960s, and the New South Wales Academy of Sport was built on one of the last camps. The scenic valley behind the lagoon was once a traditional trade route following Deep Creek to Oxford Falls and beyond. Wakehurst Parkway now follows that track, and occasionally when driving through that corridor of bush car windows will suddenly fog up as though a spirit area had been entered.

Above Girls from British Tobacco on the Narrabeen to Newport motor service. *Courtesy Warringah Library.*

Canoes used by Aborigines (New South Wales). The birds moving across the surface of the water are black swans. *Engraving from a drawing by Charles-Alexander Lesueur and published in the Atlas of the Voyage de deconouvertes aux terres australes (1811). Rex Nan Kivell Collection. National Library of Australia, Canberra. nla-an7573675*

The first land grants in the Collaroy–Narrabeen area were made to John Ramsay, John Lees, Philip Schaffer and James Wheeler. Alex Macdonald was granted 80 acres at the beach in 1815, and west of this land J.T. Collins had 93.5 acres by 1857. The Basin and Long Reef were granted to William Cossar in 1819. James Jenkins, a former convict turned stonemason, builder and cedar cutter, acquired large land holdings around Narrabeen in the 1820s, and at one time owned the entire beachfront from the southern end of Dee Why Beach through to Mona Vale Hospital. His eldest daughter, Elizabeth Jenkins, bequeathed some 1,740 acres in portions stretching from Dee Why to

Warriewood to the Salvation Army upon her death in 1900. Following this largesse many of the State's poor, including Aboriginal children from inland New South Wales, were able to visit Salvation Army youth camps that had been set up on the land of the Saltwater People.

During the nineteenth century, travellers from Manly to Newport had to ford the lagoon until the first bridge opened in 1880. From 1903 to 1907, horses were used to pull trams along Pittwater Road until steam services were introduced. With the extension of the tram to Narrabeen in 1913 providing easier transport, the whole area around the lake became popular for holidays and camping. The rapid rise in car-ownership and the opening of the Wakehurst Parkway in 1946 reduced the time needed for road travel to central Sydney and helped fuel Narrabeen's post-war building boom.

The Narrabeen area has undergone substantial change since European settlement, with attempts to reshape the shores, dunes and hills surrounding Narrabeen Lake. As with the Queenscliff, Curl Curl, Dee Why and several other lagoons, extensive ti-tree swamps were filled in with rubbish, destroying breeding habitat for fish, prawns and many other species. At one time prawns were abundant in the Narrabeen Lakes, but now have to be plundered from other more pristine places. High-rise developments now infest the sandy peninsula where trees were once profuse. Collaroy boasts some of those rare Sydney direct-beachfront properties that are now in the process of disappearing as rising sea levels and erosion take their toll (see the end of this section).

Long Reef defines the southern boundary of this long bay. It offers a wide selection of reef and beach breaks that work in a variety of swell and wind conditions. Reef breaks on the north side of Long Reef include White Rock and Little Makaha. These breaks are reasonably inaccessible and can be frustratingly inconsistent. Between Long Reef and Collaroy can be found several other reef breaks of a similar nature.

1940 flood outside Bryson's store.
Courtesy Pittwater Library.

Narrabeen. *Photo Alex Marks.*

Christo Hall, South Narrabeen.
Photo Justin Crawford.

Collaroy is known by surfers as Powder Puff Point because of its gentle waves. In contrast, Narrabeen Lagoon empties into the ocean at the far northern end of the beach, providing a steady flow of sand for the famous North Narrabeen banks. This classic break has been a hot-bed for talented surfers including Simon Anderson, Terry Fitzgerald, Damien Hardman, Colin Smith, Grant Oliver and numerous others. Narrabeen Beach is exposed to most available swell and its consistent waves have created respect as well as some heavy localism. In recent years one particularly aggressive surfer was banned from the beach for his acts of violence. Ironically, when hearing the court's decision he broke down and complained of the unfairness of it all, seemingly immune to the notion that he had been doing this to others for years.

A Narrabeen Beach surf club was functioning at North Narrabeen in 1908, followed by Collaroy in 1911 and South Narrabeen in 1923. Many watermen were drawn to the waves rolling in at the famous Alley, and Narrabeen SLSC was officially established in 1964 when it was realised that the beaches were not being adequately covered. The North Narrabeen Boardriders Club was also formed in 1964 to allow its members more acceptance and control of the beach. Stretch Cooper recalls working as a lifeguard at North Narrabeen in the 1980s:

I found this an extremely difficult period as even though I was a keen surfer Lifeguards were perceived as 'clubbies'. Many older and heavier locals like Richard Damph used to tell me where to put the flags on the beach in relation the best surf on any given day. Generally this worked well … as long as I complied. Noncompliance was not an option![5]

Just north of Narrabeen Head is a small cove named Turimetta Beach. At the northern end is Turimetta Head, home of one of

Sydney's most recent sewage outfalls. The name 'Turimetta' is believed to be derived from a local Aboriginal clan or family name, because, in this area, the suffix *-etta* was part of a family name. The Turimetta foreshore was isolated from predators by the inland swamp and marshes, and the area once supported large shearwater and fairy penguin rookeries. These barren dunes were sacred 'women's country' watched over by Saltwater women who protected this place.[6] Turimetta Point provides some excellent waves, but the beach is unpatrolled so it is recommended to surf with others.

Above *Photo Dave Fairbairn.*

Left Narrabeen. *Photo Oceaneye.*   **Above** J.P. Slupnik. *Photo Alex Marks.*

warriewood,
mona vale and
bongin bongin bay

"The waves dash and break with spiteful fury upon the rocks of the cliff; but, rolling majestically in a succession of transparent breakers, they burst with a loud and hollow roar upon the far sounding beaches." WILLIAM GOVETT, 1829

The exact meaning of the name Warriewood is not clear, but it is thought to be a mixture of the English word 'wood' and an Aboriginal word *warra* (a type of swamp tree in the area) or *warrie* (wild or untamed) to describe the wild swampy wooded area. Another interpretation is that Warriewood translates as 'much swampy water'. The Warriewood Valley was indeed swampy land, with two creeks, Narrabeen and Mullett, flowing through the area. In 1829, James Jenkins was granted 350 acres in the Warriewood area, which he named Cabbage Tree Hill Farm. Part of the suburb was also once known as Sheep Station Hill.[1]

Mona Vale was originally known as Bongin Bongin until it was renamed in 1858 after the first farm in the area, 'Mona', which means 'high born'. There is a Mona Vale in Scotland, and this may have inspired settler Robert Campbell in the choice of name for his property. The name Bongin Bongin Bay still remains for the small bay to the north of Mona Vale Pool. The original land grant of 700 acres to Campbell in the Mona Vale area had passed into other hands, and in the middle of the nineteenth century had been rented to David Foley. Foley's success had provoked *"the envy and jealousy of unscrupulous neighbours"*, and after series of thefts and skirmishes Foley was shot dead. No one was ever found guilty of the crime. At length the land was rented again in 1863 to a James Therry, and the

outrages continued. With the help of his neighbours, including John Jenkins, Therry received the support of the police and the culprits were arrested and sentenced,[2] but following several other incidents the Therrys sold up and the bad luck plagued subsequent tenants.

After inheriting considerable wealth, George Brock bought the estate in 1894 and began building *"a grandiose, Riviera type resort on the beach which eventually became known as Brock's Folly."* He then proceeded to drain and fill unclaimed swamp to build a lake, racecourse and polo ground. With a change of government, the earlier promise to extend the tramline to Newport and past his estate soon evaporated, and Brock *"lost every penny he possessed."*[3] In later years it was variously used as the La Corniche Resort, the Mona Vale Hydro and as an Officers' Training School during World War II before finally being demolished to make way for home units.

Mona Vale and Pittwater Roads had their beginnings as Aboriginal pathways. By the end of the nineteenth century horse-drawn coaches were regularly making the leisurely journey from Manly to Newport, stopping at the Narrabeen Inn and the Rock Lily Inn in Mona Vale. The Rock Lily, named after the wild lilies that grew in the foothills, was constructed by a burly Frenchman named Leon Houreaux in 1866. The Gallic touch was appreciated and the inn flourished for twenty years under Houreaux and Madame Boutin,

Previous page *Photo Oceaneye.*   Right *Photo Jedd Cooney.*

his *"jolly manageress"*, who was well known for her *"earthy humour."*[4] Located near the corner of Mona Vale and Pittwater Roads it remains a Mona Vale fixture.

Warriewood Beach, Mona Vale Beach and Bongin Bongin Bay all lie between Turimetta Head to the south and Bungan Head to the north. Warriewood is a relatively narrow beach facing east-northeast, attracting a good amount of swell. Turimetta Head affords the beach some protection from southerly waves and winds. It is most popular during moderate southeast swell when the southern point offers a fullish right that finally closes out on the bar. Mona Vale Beach faces south-southeast and is also open to the swell, producing some good waves on the reef and beach. Bongin Bongin Bay is better known to surfers as the Basin. This small, sheltered cove provides a right breaking wave across the rocks on the northern side of the pool during big seas.

The first mention of a surf club in Mona Vale was in 1907, and by 1910 the Surf Bathers Association was happy to claim that this small club was *"doing good work."* The Mona Vale Surf Life Saving Club as it is known today was re-formed in 1922, and Fred Lane was voted the first president. Lane was the first Australian swimmer to win an Olympic gold medal (1900), and went on to hold seven world records before retiring at age twenty-two. In 1934 the Warringah Council constructed a brick clubhouse at the northern end of the beach near the rock pool shared with the Basin. The Warriewood SLSC was established in 1949 and is located on the southern slopes, providing members with a superb view up the beach.

Since the 1980s, one of the major risks to the northern beaches has been from pollutants discharged from the North Head and Warriewood sewage outfalls. Out to sea, outfalls continue to be a hazard to marine life, increasing mercury levels in fish stocks, as well as endangering bathers with bacterial infections.[5] In 1990 the North Head outfall tunnel was extended and improved, effectively reducing

Left Hayden Cox. *Photo Alex Marks.*
Top *Photo Bruce Usher.*
Bottom Old Warriewood 'Turn of the Century'.

threats to beach users, but the long-term impact has not been fully investigated. Warriewood outfall continues to discharge 16 million litres of effluent into the sea every day at the cliff face, and discolouration of the water here is still apparent on a regular basis. In 2007 the Surfrider Foundation, as part of its annual conference held at Narrabeen, organised for more than seventy surfers to paddle out to the beautiful Turimetta Head, the site of the largest remaining cliff-face sewage ocean outfall in Sydney.

The Warriewood wetlands were important sites to the Guringai due to the abundance of resources—both food and materials. They were also a permanent source of fresh water, and therefore had a spiritual significance to Aborigines. Scar trees can still be found in the area surrounding the wetland. In the late 1970s, the then Wran Government agreed to let developers build the Warriewood shopping centre on part of the site on the condition that Warringah Council would purchase the remainder of the site for retention as a natural area. After much negotiation, and action by concerned residents and conservationists, the wetlands came into public ownership when Pittwater Council brought the remaining land in 1996. The Warriewood Wetland, at 26 hectares, is the largest remaining remnant sandplain wetland in northern Sydney. Located near the base of the escarpment adjacent to Irrawong Reserve, you can also find here the most significant stand of swamp mahogany (*Eucalyptus robusta*) in the Sydney region. These trees usually flower in winter and attract a wide variety of birds.

It is one of those quirks of nature that we now benefit from the fact that the swampy and flood-prone low-lying coastal areas were previously considered useless as building grounds. Large tracts of prime beachfront land were left largely untouched, and many of these areas are now parklands and golf courses. Even these developments had a major impact on the environment. When the golf course in Mona Vale needed extending, the 20-acre Black Swamp

behind the beach was drained and filled. During the drought of 1983, the peaty soil under the fill dried out. Enormous cracks appeared, some as large as a metre wide and four metres deep. The peat caught fire and continued to burn underground for more than a year. The only way of stopping it was to dig the swamp out again, right back to the water level, and refill it.[6]

The Mona Vale Basin was once the food bowl for the area, with field crops, and in the 1930s a proliferation of glasshouses built by migrants from the former Yugoslavia. Eventually some 3,500 glasshouses dotted the area and spilled into neighbouring Mona Vale. Production boomed in the 1940s and '50s, but the market declined

Photos oggy.

in the '60s and the area was subdivided. Light industry began to infiltrate the district despite the fact that it was zoned rural until 1991.[7] In the noughties, the State Labor Government legislated to open the area up to housing to take population pressure off the western suburbs. Much of this land was converted into new homes and town houses, but a decision to allow a multi-unit development in the Warriewood Valley was reversed following a change of government in 2011. It is hoped that the local community will now have a real say in planning proposals that will affect their neighbourhood.

One of those light industries to infiltrate the Mona Vale Basin is the surf industry. The Mona Vale industrial estate has become a satellite hub to Brookvale for surfboard manufacture. Channel Islands, Ozzie Wright and Ron Wade make their boards here, and the Insight brand set up by Greg Webber in the 1980s is recognised globally. Former world surfing champion Damien Hardman began surfing at age 10 at sleepy Warriewood Beach before moving with his family to Narrabeen in 1984. As a teen, Hardman joined surfboard designer Geoff McCoy's high-profile team alongside seasoned pro Mark Warren and rising stars such as Cheyne Horan and Pam Burridge.[8]

Mona Vale was once a quiet spot. In the 1950s, surfers Peter Hughes and Ian Wallace had built a little shack on the beach at The Basin. On the way to the beach in the morning they would collect a couple of bottles of milk left out at someone's house by the milkman, and if the surf was flat they would dive for a fresh feed of crayfish and abalone. On the site where their shack once stood are now luxury homes. One nearby belonging to property developer and former Manly Sea Eagles co-owner Max Delmege was said to be on the market in 2011 for around $7 million.

Mona Vale line-up.
Photo Alex Marks.

Photo oggy.

bungan
beach

Bungan Beach is located on the southeastern extremity of the Barrenjoey Peninsula. The name is thought to be a corruption of Bongin Bongin, the Indigenous name for the swamp grounds in the area. A. Metson gives another version of how Bungan Head was named in a romantic tale called *Bushranger's Hill* (1908) concerning two escaped convicts who lived on the peninsula. The story goes that while trying to protect the convicts from capture, eight Aborigines were shot by soldiers between Bushrangers Hill and the headland, and that from that time onwards *"the blacks called that headland 'Bung-an Bung-an' their expression for a musket and the sound of the report and its echo from the hill."* This story is not backed up by the historical record and is thought to be a piece of fiction.

The name 'Bungan' was first recorded in a survey in 1814 as Bongin Bongin, referring to an area which encompassed present-day Mona Vale and Bungan Beach granted to Robert Campbell, Jr. Bushrangers Hill marks the northern end of the beach and rises to a height of 103 metres at the summit. Despite the claim in some local histories that there is no known connection with bushrangers,

Bushrangers Hill provides a natural lookout point said to have been used by bushrangers to observe the approach of troopers. In 1861, John Farrell, Jr, told journalist Charles de Boos that a bushranger by the name of Casey frequented Casey's Hill, now known as Bushrangers Hill, and that he had been shot by 'Black Bowen'.[1] Bowen Bungaree was employed to track escaped convicts and bushrangers in the Pittwater area near the mouth of the Hawkesbury River. An account by Maybanke Anderson tells of his role in the capture of two assigned servants of James Jenkins who had escaped and taken refuge in a cave near Bushrangers Hill.[2] After an adventurous life (see page 63), Bowen was murdered in 1853, with his friend Farrell claiming that he had been ambushed, shot and killed by bushrangers while sitting at a campfire near Bushrangers Hill, Newport.

In the 1890s Alfred Yewen built a cottage, 'Bungania', at the north end of the beach on the headland. Before the 1920s few people lived at Bungan. In 1908 Napier Thomson built the 'Eyrie' and in 1914 Betty Morrison, née Pollock, lived on the slopes above the beach. Artists' agent Adolph W. Albers started building 'Bungan Castle' at the top of Bungan Headland in 1919, which became known for its *"riotous parties."* Transport was by horse and cart or on foot, and time was spent walking, fishing, boating, or bathing.[3] The Mona Vale Company land was subdivided and sold in a number of sections, with most of the lots surrounding Bungan Beach sold between 1907 and 1914. Gradually the area has become residential, but Bungan Beach remains one of the most undeveloped of Pittwater's ocean beaches, with a wild and unspoiled character enhanced by limited access.

During World War II, a tank trap was dug, and stretched from Bungan Beach to Pittwater spanned by a single timber bridge which was bolted together in such a way that *"if you knocked one bolt out, the whole bridge would fall into the trap."*

"The waves dash and break with spiteful fury upon the rocks of the cliff; but, rolling majestically in a succession of transparent breakers, they burst with a loud and hollow roar upon the far sounding beaches." WILLIAM GOVETT, 1829

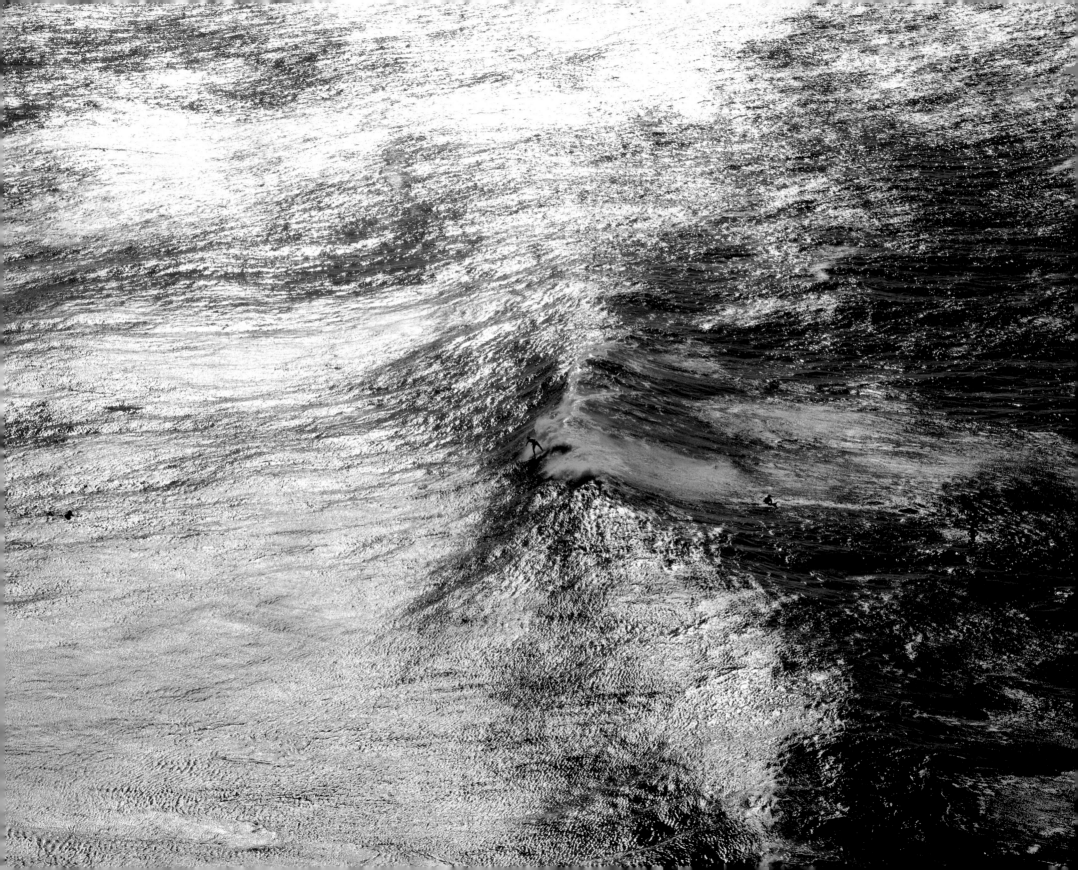

South Bungan.
Photo Bruce Usher.

Above Ian Usher, Bungan Beach, 1975.
Photo Bruce Usher.

This bridge, mined with explosives for good measure, allowed cars to drive north along Barrenjoey Road. The trap was lined on the southern side with large poles that presented a high vertical face to any intruders, and at the end of the trap there were large concrete blocks shaped like pyramids which extended part of the way up to Winji Jimmi.[4]

The dramatic coastal scenery of Bungan, particularly the rugged beauty of the cliff areas, is a great attraction for sightseers, bushwalkers, surfers, beach-goers and local residents. The rock platforms at each end of the beach support significant ecosystems and are Intertidal Protected Areas where all collecting is prohibited. A natural bushland reserve named after early resident Betty Morrison has been established next to the dunes and beach. Local residents of Bungan have been actively involved in managing and conserving the beach and reserve. A bush regeneration program has been underway for many years led by local volunteers, the Friends of Bungan.

The reserves support a range of coastal bushland types, including areas of coastal scrub, cliff-face open heath and coastal closed heath communities. These vegetation communities are regionally significant as they do not occur in either Ku-ringai Chase or Garigal National Parks and have only a limited distribution within the Pittwater Council area. There are also small pockets of littoral rainforest. These reserves also provide a range of habitat resources for native fauna. The variety of reptiles and small birds found here (such as the yellow-faced whip snake and eastern whipbird) indicates the importance of the reserves for providing habitat to species that are scarce or missing from residential areas. Significant animals that have been sighted in the reserves include the long-nosed bandicoot

(*Perameles nasuta*), peregrine falcon (*Falco perigrinus*) powerful owl (*Ninox strenua*),[5] osprey, pied oyster catcher and little penguin.

Bungan Beach itself runs in a southeast direction and is open to most available swells, with the northern corner offering good protection from the northeasterly winds. The wave quality varies from ordinary to excellent depending on the conditions, and is sometimes overlooked by surfers. Volunteers of the Bungan Beach Surf Life Saving Club patrol the beach during the swimming season. A temporary clubhouse was erected when the club was established in 1953, and would remain until 1970 when a new clubhouse was approved by Warringah Council and the old clubhouse demolished. It did not last long. On the night of 28 May 1974, huge surf generated by winds reaching 200 kilometres per hour washed through the club and swept away the southeast corner of the building. Rebuilding was not completed until 1977. Women were admitted to the club in the 1980s and an association was formed with Barker College.

Olive Cotton (1911–2003), a pioneer of Australian modernist photography, was drawn to the solitude of Bungan Beach and took the photograph *She-oaks* in 1928, aged seventeen. Bungan Beach remains a quiet haven only really known about by the locals, but visitors occasionally manage to discover its secluded charms. The renowned Irish rock institution, U2 front man Bono, secretly slipped into Sydney and spent two weeks at the beach with his family in 2006 relatively undetected.

Hayden Beck, Rock Pools tube.
Photo Alex Marks.

newport
beach

FARELL'S BEACH FROM MT LOFTUS,

Previous page Farrell's farm from
    Mt Loftus. *Courtesy Pittwater Library.*
Top left Newport storm.
    Photo Nathan Smith.
Above *Photo Steve Killelea.*
Right *Photo Nathan Smith.*

Newport marks the beginning of 'the peninsula', the narrow finger of land running from Newport to Palm Beach that separates Pittwater and the Pacific Ocean. In 1788, Governor Phillip named the lake behind the peninsula after William Pitt the Younger (1759–1806), statesman and British Prime Minister. Pittwater remains a slightly unfortunate misnomer for this beautiful place, described by Phillip himself as *"the finest piece of water which I ever saw."* Maybanke Anderson believed that Phillip was attempting to please Pitt as he *"had no doubt found him interested in this new scheme for emptying the prisons, by using inmates to found a colony."*[1]

Newport took its name from the 'new port' established on the Pittwater side for steamers carrying cargo and passengers between Sydney and the Hawkesbury area. Due to the lack of good roads to the area, shipping had become the main delivery system for all the produce, mail, local shell lime, firewood, etcetera, and Pittwater was officially designated a port from 1843 until the end of 1900. A small town grew up around the wharf, and in 1880 a weatherboard residence was built near the new pier that would later become the Newport Hotel. Newport Beach, on the Pacific Ocean side of the peninsula, was originally known as Ocean Beach, or Farrell's Beach, named after the first John Farrell who had successfully bid for 30 acres, including a dairy and house along the beach, in 1822. Three generations of the Farrell clan built up their holdings in the area until they held about 1,000 acres between the beach and Pittwater.

It was John Farrell, Jr, who told early traveller Charles de Boos the story of how Bowen showed him how to fish at night on the rock platform at the southern end of Newport Beach. Family members would congregate at low tide when black fish and others seeking refuge from predators could be found in small pools linked to the ocean by small channels running through the reef. Twisting dry stringy bark together to make a torch, they would then

Bottom The Thompson Family on the beach with surfboat, 1928. *Courtesy Newport SLSC.*

Top The southern end of Newport Beach and the opening of Farrell's lagoon, c.1918.

First Women's Life Saving Team

NEWPORT LIFE SAVING CLUB
1910

Left 1910 postcard of women's team with reel.
Photographer unknown. Courtesy Newport SLSC.
Below The world's first girls life saving team.
Courtesy Newport SLSC.

"This picture is historic and represents the first girls' life saving team formed in the world. They succeeded in reaching the buoy at their first public surf carnival at Dee Why in 1910. The men's team failed. Water was rough and heavy with kelp which tangled lines."

POST CARD

214 039.

This picture is historic & represents the first girls life saving team formed in the world. They succeeded in reaching the buoy at their first public surf carnival at Dee Why in 1910. The mens team failed. Water was rough & heavy with kelp which tangled lines.

light it and take that in one hand, and a good
lump of waddy in the other, ... surround the pool,
placing in first instance a sharp hand to guard
the outlet. As soon as the fishes see the light,
they begin to jump up and dart around in all
directions. Then the fun begins.[2]

After the fish were stunned with the waddy, they would be *"flicked
onto the rocks to be gathered up by the children."*[3]

The Saltwater People also fished in the lagoon where Newport
Oval now lies, and settlers were known to fish for eels and hunt
quail in this area. The lagoon near the Newport SLSC, once referred
to as Farrell's Lagoon, was filled in and is now a concrete drain.[4]

Newport is a decidedly Anglo name for the area, but there are
many Aboriginal words to be found in local street names: Bardo—
the word for 'saltwater'; Karloo—meaning 'water'; Kalinya—'good';
Mitala—'green point'; Nullaburra—possibly a combination of *nulla*
meaning 'wood' and *burra* meaning 'big stone'; Wiruna—possibly
meaning 'setting of the sun'.

Arthur Phillip explored the northern beaches by land and sea
as early as 1788, but it would be another fifteen years before land
grants were made in the area. Early Newport was neatly divided
along class lines, with the area south of the present site of the surf
club and extending to Mona Vale part of a 700-acre grant to Robert
Campbell, Jr, a merchant, entrepreneur and pastoralist. To the
north, smaller allotments were granted to either ex-convicts or
'currency lads' (born in the colony of convict parents), including
Robert Melville, Richard Porter, Robert Henderson, James McNally,
Martin Burke and John Farrell. The Farrell family would go on to
own much of the land around Newport for the following 130 years.[5]

By the end of the nineteenth century, horse-drawn coaches
were regularly making the leisurely journey from Manly to

Roy Cane, Standard bearer, late 1930s.
Photo Robin Cale .

Newport, and a motor bus service was begun in 1906. The Spit Bridge was opened in 1924, but there was little traffic during the war years as petrol rationing was in force. Mid-twentieth century Newport was a rustic place, with several dairies still active in the area and only 175 people recorded in the 1931 census. Despite this isolation, there was a fear of Japanese invasion during World War II and all the beaches to the south were barricaded with barbed wire and steel posts. As Newport had no barbed wire, servicemen could come to swim and surf, but as protection *"Mr Vincent's house at the southern end of Myola Road was requisitioned by the army and fortified with a gun trained on the beach."*[6] Guy Jennings relates:

> In the Avenue there was at least one fox hole and all the families living north of the tank trap had to be ready for evacuation at a moment's notice.[7]

Newport was a gathering place for many creative people, including photographers Max Dupain, Olive Cotton and Damien Parer. Dupain met his future wife Olive Cotton in Newport, and some of his earliest work was created here. The cliff-top cottage that Max Dupain's father built in Calvert Parade provided a holiday sanctuary for him and many of his friends throughout his life.[8] Steps down the cliff face gave direct access to the beach, and Newport Rock Pool lay directly below. A rock pool had been built at Newport as far back as the early 1900s, but had been rapidly rendered useless by the pounding surf. The rock pool shown in the Dupain photo was built at the southern end of the beach in 1925, and has so far proved better able to withstand the sea. Max Dupain's *Sunbaker 1937*, his iconic image of Australian beach culture, was not taken at Newport; it was actually taken while Dupain was holidaying on the south coast of New South Wales.

The Newport SLSC was first formed in 1909 with a clubhouse

'Ray Payne with wooden ski, late 1940s'.
Photo Robin Cale.

"… the large waves of the vast Ocean meeting with so sudden a resistance make a most terrible surf breaking mountains high …" JAMES COOK, 1770

in Neptune Street, as the beach was still owned by the Farrell family. In 1911 the Council took control of the beach and a clubhouse was built there in 1915. The current clubhouse was built in 1933. Newport is also home to the famed Newport Plus Boardriders Club and back-to-back World Title winner Tom Carroll. There were early confrontations between the board riders and life savers, notably with the surfboat running over surfers at the Newport Peak, but the two clubs eventually enjoyed mutual respect. It is worth noting that at a particularly difficult time for the Newport SLSC club following the big storm of 1974, Newport Plus saved the club by having its members also join the surf life saving club.

The Peak, situated at the northern end of the car park, is the most consistent surf break on the beach. At the southern end of the beach, near the pool, can be found a right-hander called Newport Reef. The long, low island reef jutting out beneath the southern headland is one of the landmarks of the peninsula. This reef catches swell from all directions, but the rideable waves are on the northern side, with powerful rights at a spot known as Crosswaves (also known as the Path, the Pass and the Island). The swell wraps around the exposed outer reef and intersects with itself on the shallow water covering the inside reef, where Bowen and his family once fished on the low tide. The effect of the swell being parted and then reuniting in a crash of waves is both unique and entertaining.

The Path (Little Reef) diamonds. 2007
Photo Tom Carroll.

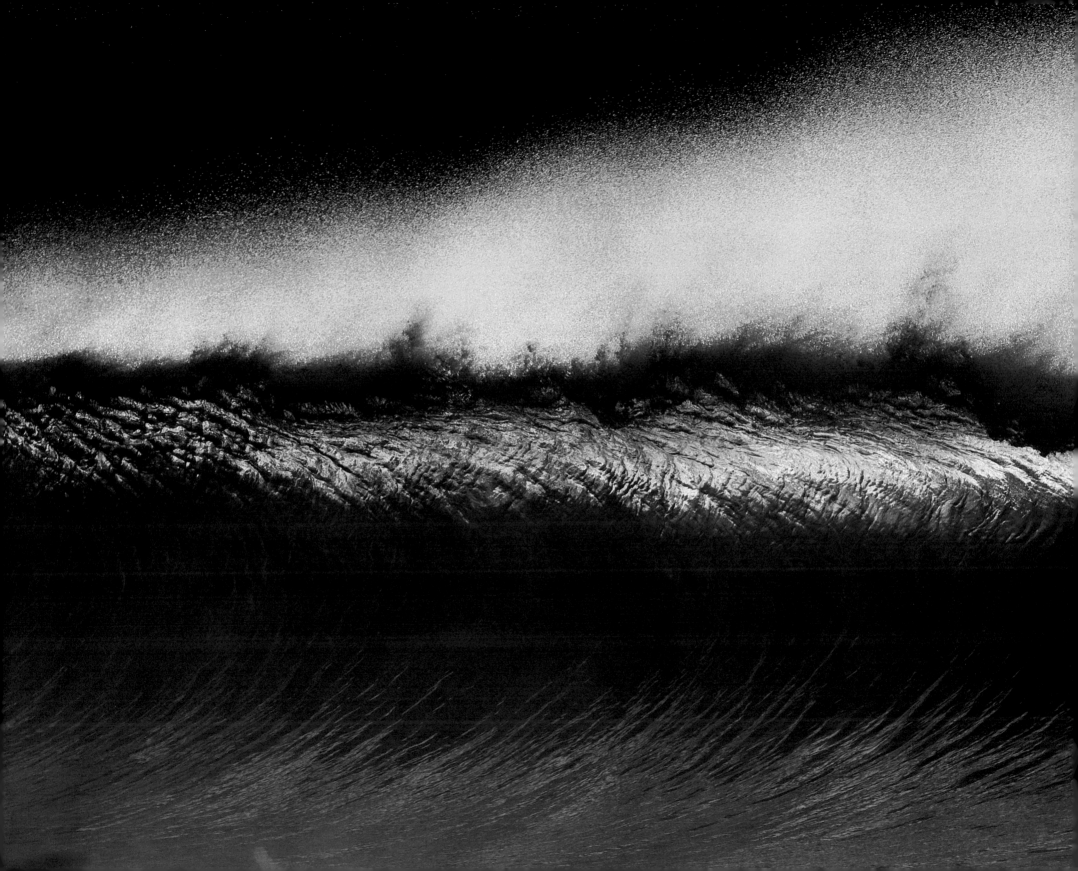

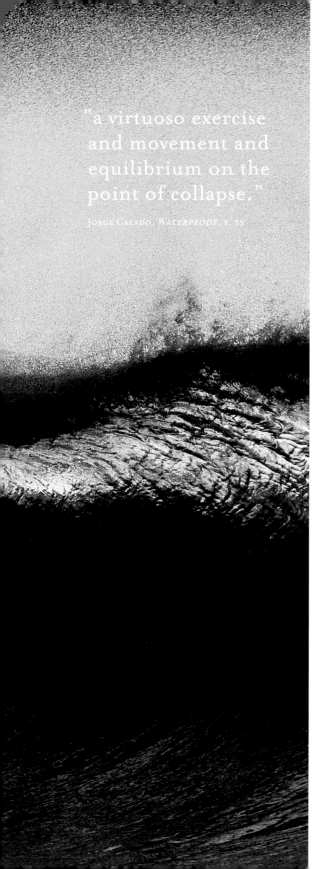

"a virtuoso exercise and movement and equilibrium on the point of collapse."

JORGE CALADO, *WATERPROOF*, P. 55

Left *Photo Nathan Smith.*

Above At Newport—1952
Photo Max Dupain.
Courtesy National Gallery Australia.
Accn No: NGA 79.61 NGA IRN: 115709

UNFETTERED TEENAGE BOYS

A QUICK FLASHBACK BY NICK CARROLL

Ever since a Manly councillor complained to the local newspaper after being struck by a solid wooden surfboard at Freshwater in 1908, surfboard riders and the general Aussie beach culture have enjoyed a relationship touched by some wariness. Like ... what the HELL are they DOING out there, hour after hour, sitting on their boards, facing away from land, speaking their own language, menacing strangers, waiting for the perfect wave? What are they thinking? Don't they know there's more to life? Or something?

That wariness has often touched the special relationship between surfers and surf clubs. Sometimes it's flared into turf wars or calcified into prejudice. Almost always it's left a gap between the cultures that seems awkward, hard to cross.

At Newport Beach, we were lucky. We never engaged in the ugly surfer-clubbie wars that tainted Palm Beach and Collaroy in the mid-1960s. When I began surfing the beach for real, on a fibreglass surfboard in the summer of 1972, I surfed where every other kid surfed—in the rips and rocks near the Peak, well to the north of the surf club. Other than in the non-

patrolled winter months, when good sandbars often formed in front of the clubhouse, the beach's natural geography kept surfers and clubbies out of each other's hair.

The mood was so relaxed that when Alastair Walker, eldest of the terrible Walker brothers and captain of the surf club, sent out a general call to arms for new members, many of us surfer larrikins immediately leapt at the chance. There were a couple of excellent reasons for our enthusiasm. First: Alastair told us, we would be vital new blood in the club, and thus would have the run of its facilities, whatever the hell they were. (We didn't know! God, it was a big building at the beach! What else did we need to know about it?) Second: according to him, Newport SLSC was planning on being a pioneer of the new IRB technology, and we could get our hands on a power craft built specifically for surf zones. (Yeah.) And third: the club owned a motor vehicle—a ridiculously clapped-out bus, wobbly, ragged and held together by grease and good luck, but big enough to fit a pack of us along with our boards. We were

15 years old for christ's sake. We dived in head first.

None of us could believe the hilarious Bronze process. The whole reel, line and belt thing actually happened! We did our exam on a freezing sou-west day, one of those freak cold snaps of early summer, in a heavy six foot swell chock full of freshly harvested seaweed. It probably shoulda frightened us, but it was too funny to be scary ... and besides, we'd already seen more frightening things close-up, the way you do as a young hardcore surfer. Weird things. A big tiger shark swimming off the northern point late one autumn afternoon. Diving ten-foot waves off the southern tip at six in the morning with no legropes. Crazy shit that you'll see sometimes glittering in a longtime surfer's eye.

I think our craziness must have quietly warmed the heart of Bert King, because he and the other patriarchs of the club let us get away with a great deal. (Jeez, maybe he didn't know! Sorry Bert.) That bus took us to surf carnivals in distant locations, like Bancoora in Victoria, where we won the Malibu Board Display titles. It also took us on surf trips to places

from North Narrabeen to Crescent Head. At some stage the engine fell clean out; fortunately we had apprentice mechanics among us. The IRB exceeded our wildest dreams. Alastair was very serious about it, to the point where he re-designed its floor to allow it more flexibility in wave impacts, and built an anti-cavitation device around the propeller, all of which allowed us to drive it even faster and more recklessly around the lineup. We even invented tow-in surfing, without realising it, thanks to an uncrowded day and a nice length of rope.

Being a surfer and a part of the surf club didn't seem odd to us at the time, not even when we began to compete as surfers at national junior level—partly because some of the hottest juniors we met, from places like Burleigh Heads in Queensland, were also surf club members. The membership was a benefit to us as we scratched our way to surf contests with barely enough money for baked beans—back then you could stay in most surf club bunkhouses for two bucks a night. At Bells Beach, we crashed at the Torquay clubhouse which was under the curatorship of old time surfer Owen Pilon; Owen had been there when the American lifeguard team had shown up for the Olympic surf carnival in 1956, and stunned the surfing world with their lightweight Malibu boards.

We didn't understand any of this history, nor did we really feel connected to it, and it was only many years later that I came to realise the costs of the split between surfboard riding culture and the surf clubs generally—that both had lost out somehow. But in any case, by 1980 we were drifting away from the surf club, surfing manically in Newport Plus contests, spending half the Aussie summer in Hawaii and the other half playing surf-stars at home. Hell, given the encroaching glamour of international pro surfing, wearing sluggoes and a cap on a Sunday afternoon just didn't fit any more.

Rejoining the club in recent years has been really wonderful, although a bit odd at times. On my part, among other things, it's been a quite deliberate effort to get past that old wariness and try to bring some of the good stuff you learn from surfing across into the surf life saving arena; in another way, it's been an attempt to show the surfers, who can be a pretty lonely and anti-social bunch, that maybe the club has something for them too. The more of my older mates who're showing up with their kids at Nippers these days and seeing the benefits of a flowering beach community, the more I have hope that both cultures will grow a bit closer and thrive as a result.

Courtesy Newport SLSC. From *Newport Surf Life Saving Club, 1909–2009: The First Century.*

Left Newport pipe. *Photo Bruce Usher.*

bilgola
beach

'swirling water'

Bilgola is said to be a corruption of the Aboriginal word *belgoula* or *belgoola*, meaning 'good water'. Other translations are said to be 'swirling water' and 'spinning water'. The word 'Belgoula' was noted in Surveyor James Meehan's records of 1814. Robert Henderson received a grant of 100 acres (0.40 square kilometres) in 1822 which he named 'Belgoola'. The current spelling derives from 'Bilgola House', built by William Bede Dalley, the son of former convicts, in the 1870s when he acquired land from the Therry estate. The Rev. J.J. Therry had been granted 1,200 acres at Pittwater by Governor Bourke back in 1833, and the estate stretched from Bilgola to Whale Beach.

In the early days of Pittwater, Bilgola Beach became known as Dalley's Beach, named after the flamboyant lawyer and politician who built his holiday house there. The Hon. William Bede Dalley, former Attorney General and Acting Premier, was a jovial and

Previous page Bilgola to Avalon. *Courtesy Manly Gallery.*
Left Bilgola. *Photo oggy.*

generous man, so it is ironic that Bilgola was once also referred to as 'Mad Mick's Hollow' and 'Cranky Alice Beach'. Apparently this name was used by locals after two old people who once lived there and *"were in the habit of pouring out their wrath on the children who passed by."*[1] In 1912, Dalley's 'Bilgola House' was purchased by World War I aviator W. Oswald Watt, who had been awarded the Legion of Honour and Croix de Guerre by France for his bravery. Watt drowned at Bilgola in 1921, and the land was subdivided the following year when the celebrated hotelier and writer Hannah Maclurcan purchased and rebuilt the house.

Many of the northern beaches, especially those with

escarpments running behind, boast a natural look with plentiful trees, but the amount of foliage begins to increase dramatically as you leave Newport and head north. Bilgola Beach is backed by a deep gully with a remnant of subtropical rainforest thick with cabbage tree palms. The main road north reduces to two lanes after Newport and winds around the escarpment creating a bottleneck affectionately known to locals as 'the Bilgola Bends'. Due to visionary planning and sympathetic councils, much of the coastline along the peninsula retains a natural look and Bilgola Beach is one of the most beautiful beaches in Sydney.

A relatively small beach at approximately 500 metres long,

Above Bilgola Beach, 1914.
Courtesy Warringah Library.

Post-Edwardian Bilgola, 1916. Miss Strickland, Miss Cadman and Margaret Allen, Bilgola Beach, 1916.
  Margaret was the daughter of the photographer, Arthur Wigram Allen.
  From Allen Family Album/Mitchell Library, State Library of NSW.
  *Call number: PX*D 604*

Bilgola is popular with sunbathers. Although it faces southeast it is offered some protection by Newport Head and rocks to the south, and to the north the beach is protected by 60-metre-high Bilgola Head. The surf at Bilgola consequently consists mostly of small shorebreak waves of inconsistent quality for surfing. Bilgola SLSC was formed in the summer of 1949 with construction of the clubhouse beginning in 1950. The clubhouse has undergone many renovations over the years, with a major addition and rebuild completed in 2003. The first Bilgola surfboat was an old double-ended craft affectionately known as 'Irene', so named because every time the crew caught a wave it was 'good night Irene'. Since those days the club has enjoyed considerable success in both men's and women's divisions.

Bilgola Headland, like most headlands north of Long Reef Point, is covered with a fine, dark soil created from the shale bedrock. The shale creates deeper, more fertile soil that is better able to hold water than the sandstone headlands, and the better soil conditions make life easier for the heathland plants. On shale one is likely to find more vigorous groups of plants of the same kind, such as casuarinas, ti-trees, paperbarks and bottlebrushes. Only a narrow strip of coastal heathland remains on the cliff tops of Bilgola South Head (Newport Head), cut off almost completely from other bushland by major roadworks. Looking west into the Bilgola Valley, there is a change in the vegetation with cabbage tree palms (*Livistona australis*) following the valley floor, marking the path of a river which has long since disappeared. These palms occur in isolated pockets in moist, sheltered sites all along Sydney's coast, but this stand is regarded as one of the largest, and finest, examples.[2]

Isabel Letham and friend, Bilgola Beach, c.1917.
Courtesy Warringah Library.

Photo Matt Hunt.

avalon
beach

"On one side lay the Ocean,
and on one Lay a great water ..."

ALFRED LORD TENNYSON, *MORTE D'ARTHUR*, 1869

First spread Tube and tanker. *Photo oggy.*
Second spread Tom Carroll, North Avalon. *Photo Mandy Zieren.*
Left Swimmers in the mist. *Photo oggy.*
Above *Photo Mandy Zieren.*

Avalon rock pool, 1918.
Courtesy Warringah Library.

It would come as no surprise that there is no Indigenous origin to the name Avalon. After a few ultimately unsuccessful attempts by earlier landowners to subdivide the area under the names Josephton and Brighton, Arthur Jabez Small bestowed the name Avalon in 1921 acknowledging the Arthurian legend of Avalon. This was the place where King Arthur retired to enjoy *"perpetual youth and bliss"*,[1] and local historian Geoff Searl believes that this may have been the intention of the modern-day Arthur. The Avalon in Celtic mythology was a fabled island, and this new manifestation, with its sheltered valley nestled between the Pacific Ocean, enjoys something of an island feel. There are some who believe that a 20-metre feature in the cliff-face near Indian Head is an ancient symbol or rune symbolising fertility and fertile ideas.

Bangally Head was named after the bastard southern mahogany trees (*Eucalyptus botryoides*) which grow in the area and provides an impressive backdrop to Avalon Beach. But the headland was not always known by this name. Surveyor William Govett wrote in 1829:

> The headland named the 'Hole in the Wall', has been so called, from its having in its projecting wall of rock a huge and lofty archway, close to the water, which appears so perfect in its formation, as to excite great curiosity and admiration. Not far from this, in a steep declivity of the coast-range, are the entrances of one or two subterraneous caverns, wherein one man informed me that he had entered more than eighty yards.[2]

Bangally Head has changed shape over the years and the 70-foot high natural rock archway, also known as St Michael's Arch, collapsed in 1867. From a distance this *"Gothic arch"* was said to look *"exactly like the altar window of some huge ruined cathedral erected by the*

Top left Avalon Service station with the first tenant Bert Ward and his daughter. Erected by A.J. Small in 1934 on the site of the current Shell garage. *Courtesy Geoff Searle, ABHS.*

Bottom left The first general store, built by A.J. Small in 1922, on the site of the present Woolworths building. *Courtesy Geoff Searle, ABHS.*

Top right Lot's Wife (The Stone Lady) 1944 with Gwen Geoff, patron of the Avalon Beach Historical Society. *Courtesy Geoff Searle, ABHS.*

Bottom right Avalon beach looking north, c.1920s. *Courtesy Geoff Searle, ABHS.*

sea-side."[3] Only drawings of the arch survive, but the two caverns, St Michael's Cave and another at sea level, are still there.

Martin Burke, 1798 Irish patriot and convict, was a pioneer of Pittwater, and received a grant of 50 acres on the peninsula in 1814. In 1833 Governor Bourke gave a 1,200 acre grant at Pittwater to Irish-born Catholic priest the Rev. J.J. Therry (1790–1864). This land eventually stretched from Surf Road in Whale Beach to Atunga Road, Newport, and included Taylor's Point, Clareville and most of Careel Bay. Following the discovery of coal at Coalcliff (near present-day Wollongong) in 1797, Father Therry (pronounced Terry) was advised that there might be a coal seam on the peninsula. In 1861 he began an exploration shaft on the current site of the Avalon Golf Course, but after spending a considerable amount of time and money his attempts proved unsuccessful. This was a fortunate result for the Avalon, which may have otherwise been reduced to a quarry like areas around Newcastle and Wollongong.

Father Therry died some twelve months before his beloved St Mary's was destroyed by fire, but the sale of his land at Pittwater helped finance the splendid new St Mary's Cathedral. Arthur Jabez Small purchased a parcel from this estate in 1915, about the same time that another parcel was sold to Dr Chisholm Ross. In 1923 Dr Ross onward sold his property to H. Ruskin Rowe.[4] At that time Avalon had ten houses, and most were only wood or fibro holiday houses, topped with tin or fibro roofs. A.J. Small and H. Ruskin Rowe moved in similar circles when it came to town planning, and both men were influenced by the architect John Sulman (1849–1932) who advocated the importance of the natural land form in the planning of a town. Sulman was the also the connection with Walter Burleigh Griffin whose Chicago-born Prairie School 'organic architecture' followed a similar philosophy. They, along with local architect Alexander Stewart Jolly, would all help shape the early development of Avalon (see page 268).

Photo Mandy Zieren.

Photo Nathan Smith.

Above Chris Beecham, North Avalon, c.1964.
Photo John Pennings.

Right Avalon 1991.
Photo attributed to Murray Close.
Courtesy Beach Without Sand.

For many years LA was considered unrideable with
its 'sucky' take-off exposing bare rock. In the 1960s
a new kind of body-surfer began to emerge who
sought out the hollow reef breaks.

LA. *Photo Hugh McLeod.*

Above LA bodysurfers. May, 1964.
From left to right: John Holden, Adrian Parsons,
Dennis Markson, John Dunn & Paul Coller.
Photo John Pennings.

By the 1940s the area attracted a vibrant bohemian community drawn to its natural beauty and holiday atmosphere. Avalon artists included Arthur Murch (winner of the 1949 Archibald Prize), Sali Herman, Bonar Dunlop and visiting friends such as Hal Missingham and William Dobell. When Morris West arrived on the peninsula in 1953 he wrote:

> The sun and the sand and the surf were free. The food at the wayside stalls was cheap, the bush full of firewood, the coastal waystations—Mona Vale, Newport, Avalon—were still villages.[5]

Founded in 1925 at the request of A.J. Small, the Avalon Beach Surf Life Saving Club is a relatively new club by Sydney's standards, but it has been home to some remarkable innovations. The 1956 Avalon Beach International Surf Carnival was the first place Malibu board riding was seen in Australia, when visiting American lifeguards, including Greg 'Da Bull' Noll, put on a display that would begin a tidal wave of interest in surfing. In the late 1960s local member Warren Mitchell OAM introduced the use of the IRB, or inflatable rescue boat, for surf rescues, revolutionising life saving methods in Australia and around the world. Members of the club are credited with introducing surfboard riding to Britain and started the Avalon stomp during the sixties.

When the *Baywatch Down Under* series tried to turn Avalon Beach from a peaceful reserve into a long-term film-set, the community rose up and overthrew government assurances to the producers that it was a done deal. Many locals work in the film industry and low-key productions such as the *Home and Away* had been accepted by the community for years, but the thought of the beach being taken over on the scale indicated by the pilot series was a step too far. Ironically, the producers had poured fuel on the fire when at a fiery public meeting held at Barrenjoey High School they condescendingly suggested that *Baywatch* would teach the locals about surf rescue. The controversy shone a light on the club's need for funding, and plans to upgrade the clubhouse to include a commercial development are currently being assessed.

Avalon's famous curved surfing beach offers protection from the dominant northeasterly winds in summer. The beach is popular with swimmers, offering tidal platforms and rock pools. Avalon has the lowest tidal rock pool on the northern beaches, so on a high tide and a big swell you have to time your launch off the rocks carefully when going for a surf. Good waves break at each end of the beach. It is also the home of the North Avalon Surfriders Association, or NASA, the Avalon rivals of Newport Plus. In 1963 Toowoomba-born Bob McTavish made an old car wreck at North Avalon his home for a while, and famously came to international attention when he and David Chidgy stowed away to Hawaii on board the *Orsava* while saying goodbye to some Avalon surfers. North Avalon is consistently rated in surfer polls as one of the best surfing spots in Australia with picture-perfect waves peeling along the point. The line-up has featured a veritable who's who of surfing over the decades. The recently relaid Avalon skate park is well used by skateboarders, BMX cyclists, and even a few inline bladers able to ignore the derision of the local skateboarders.

On the southern headland, Little Avalon, or LA as it is known to the locals, offers a short but memorable wave that breaks over a shallow rock ledge. For many years it was considered unrideable with its 'sucky' take-off exposing bare rock. In the 1960s a new kind of body-surfer began to emerge who sought out the hollow reef breaks, and in late 1964 LA was pioneered by body surfers such as Tony Hubbard and Andre Byron. They were later joined by Don McCredie, Michael Fay and others. When surfboards got shorter the wave became more accessible, and board riders started to claim the

wave along with kneeboarders and body boarders. On a big day LA will challenge the best of surfers. Ten times World Champion and one-time Avalon resident, Kelly Slater, snapped three boards in a memorable session in 1999 and claimed it as one of his most fun surfs ever. Over the decades tube hunters who dominated this spot include Roger Buckingham, Ronni Berzelli, Peter 'Marsupial' Horton, Michael Northcoat, Ben and Toby Player, and Paul 'Sea Bass' Standon.

Since its beginning, the good burghers of Avalon, especially town planner and developer A.J. Small and architect Harry Ruskin Rowe, campaigned against greedy development and urban ugliness which threatened their vision of housing blended with the environment. As well as allowing for environmental housing, substantial reserves of bushland were protected. Angophora Reserve was opened in 1938 to preserve a healthy stand of *Angophora* (or Sydney red gum) and to act as a refuge for koalas. The koalas have long disappeared from Avalon, however, unable to survive in an increasingly urban environment shrinking their feeding habitat and from attacks by domestic dogs.

The Avalon community has also been active in conserving the fragile beach ecosystem. The Avalon dunes cover about 4.5 hectares and are a rare example of high dunes (to 22 metres) in the Sydney urban area. By the mid-1960s, sand mining and sand removal was impacting on the dunes to such an extent that local activists staged protests to stop the mining. Shaw Brothers had a lease to mine an area behind the dunes, and were taking away tons of sand on their lease area as well as the sand that would then fall onto their property. Members of the Avalon Preservation Trust began to take picnic blankets and baskets down to the dunes each morning and set up in front of the dozers, successfully foiling efforts to take away sand. Warringah Council eventually bowed to pressure and finally cancelled the lease. The flat grassed area to the north known

Kelly Slater LA. *Photos Nathan Smith.*

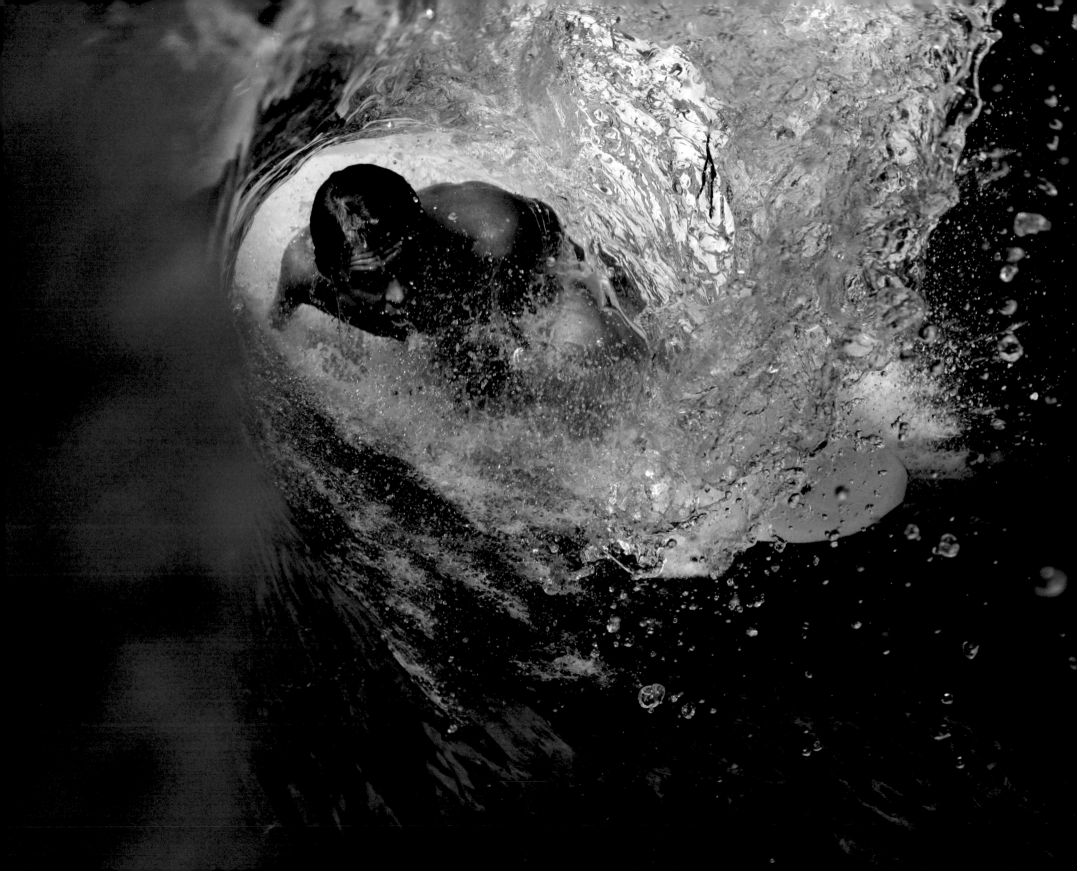

as Des Creagh Reserve, named in honour of a local environmental campaigner, is now all that remains of the once impressive northern spur of the dunes.

Camping and unrestricted access (that once included grazing by circus elephants), continued to degrade the vegetation, and in an effort to stabilise the dunes some reshaping, fencing and revegetation, including the introduction of bitou bush (*Chrysanthemoides monilifera*), was done by the New South Wales Soil Conservation Service in the early 1970s. Warringah Council initiated bitou clearing in 1989, and concern over seedling regrowth triggered the formation of Friends of Avalon Dunes in 1990. The group has been working monthly on the dunes ever since. Through development and application of best practice, successful grants and partnerships with State Government, Coastcare and Pittwater Council (after the 1992 split from Warringah), the dunes now provide vastly improved sustainability in this coastal ecosystem.[6]

Careel Bay, on the Pittwater side of the peninsula, is an extremely important area from an environmental point of view, providing habitat for marine life and bird species. This sheltered bay is home to extensive marine sea grass flats and a large stand of mangroves on its southeastern shores. Careel Bay Creek once ran parallel to the northern spur of the Avalon dunes allowing a flush mechanism for the Careel Bay mangroves after heavy rains. The creek was dammed around 1840 and much of the mangroves were filled in during the 1970s to provide sports grounds. In the 1970s the Careel Bay Pittwater Protection Association was set up to preserve and protect Careel Bay for current and future generations. This unique area is currently under threat from overdevelopment, namely the construction of a large and exclusive marina. The area has long been a popular playground with locals and visitors, and the public wharf adjoining the boatshed in the bay has serviced the boating fraternity since the early 1900s.

Left *LA. Photo Mandy Zieren.*

Above *Photo Oceaneye.*

Left *Photo Oceaneye.*

Above Harley, LA. *Photo Toby Player.*

Big Day At North Avalon

By Kirk Willcox

A deep depression had edged into the Tasman Sea, pushing up the swell from a clean four in the morning to six foot around the middle of the day. Perfect six foot, with some real open barrels. Considering that the centre of the low hadn't even moved out into the ocean, it was obvious that this was going to be serious business.

By the next morning it was there. Giant, peaking waves were pounding the beach with huge clumps of spray being lifted off their backs as they lumbered towards the shore. Ten to twelve foot solid, with some 15-foot sets pushing through from the east. And it was still offshore. A lot of surfers who attempted to ride it didn't even get past the shorebreak. Some who made it out questioned why they were there when they were confronted by solid 12-foot sets.

About 10 that morning, Stuart 'Stretch' Cooper waited more than 30 minutes for a gap in the lines before attempting to jump off the notorious North Avalon rock platform. Huge waves were washing across the platform under the steep cliff face. Stretch, an experienced big wave man with plenty of Hawaiian hours under his belt, including Sunset, Pipe and clean-up sets at Waimea, hadn't seen the beach that big for years. And Stretch knows Avalon well, having spent five years on the beach as a lifeguard. Plus he was well-equipped with a 9'6" purpose built for a swell like this.

Waiting with three other surfers, Stretch saw his chance, raced to the edge of the platform alone and jumped in. About 100 metres out, he was confronted by a set first hand and thought to himself, *"This is way bigger than it looked from the beach."* A few other guys also got out, including Colin Bernasconi and Marsupial. The take-off was in line with the outside headland and the waves were peeling off for about 400 metres down towards the surf club at the south end of the beach. *"They were perfect conditions, but the worrying part was that the offshore wind was so strong that you had to take off blind with your eyes full of spray,"* Cooper said. But he got a few, in full survival stance racing them down the line, before quickly scratching out again in case a set came through.

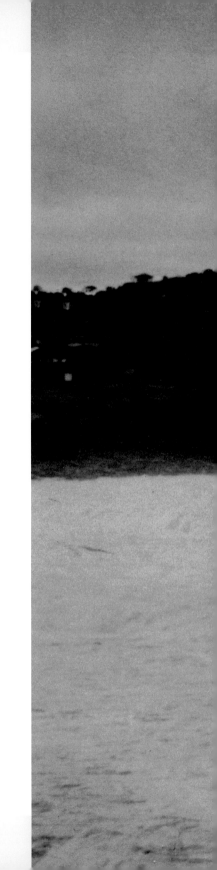

Right Avalon 1991. Photo attributed to Ian White or Murray Close. *Courtesy Beach Without Sand.*

"Good yarns always come out of a big swell."

The other guys also caught a few and either went in or couldn't get out again. Stretch ended up out there alone, picking off a couple more waves. After one big one he paddled back to what he thought was the take-off area. He was sitting there for ten minutes when he heard people in the car park whistling and he turned around to see them jumping up and down and waving towels. *"I thought it must have been a set so I paddled out another 50 or so metres,"* Stretch said. *"I paddled over a ten-foot wave and when I got to the top I saw this wave stand up like a block of home units."*

It was solid 14–15 foot easy and as soon as he saw it Stretch knew it was going to close out the whole beach. Surfing in Hawaii he had once been caught inside 20-foot Waimea and had had the same feeling—*"This wave is bigger than I can handle."* Thinking logically Stretch knew he was in a bad situation. *"I got the 9'6" in planing mode out of the water trying to get over the set, but realised that the whole wave was going to close out five feet in front of me."*

Stretch went with panache. He stood up on his board, and did the whole Hawaiian-style bale, diving as deep as he could, trying to reach the end of his 12-foot leg rope. He had got a fair way when he heard the wave impact, and can just remember *"going through the whole spin cycle."* Stretch went with it for a while but was running out of air pretty quickly. *"I tried to head to the surface but got held down for ages. When I came up I was probably one-third the way up the next face."* He still had his leg rope, but he then realised it was tied to only half a board, and Stretch felt like he was a mile out to sea.

Stretch took the leg rope off and started swimming for the beach, fully conscious that he didn't want to be caught by another close-out set. It took him about 20 to 25 minutes to get in and he landed right in front of the surf club at the southern end. His board had been snapped clean through and was heavily creased in another four places.

Stretch's big wave philosophy is simple. From the beach he will look at the biggest wave possible to ride and pictures himself wiping out on it. *"If I think I can handle that wipe-out, I'll go out and surf it."*

Story courtesy *Tracks* magazine, 1991.

Right Matt 'Tiny' Thomson, South Avalon, 2001. *Photo Hugh McLeod.*

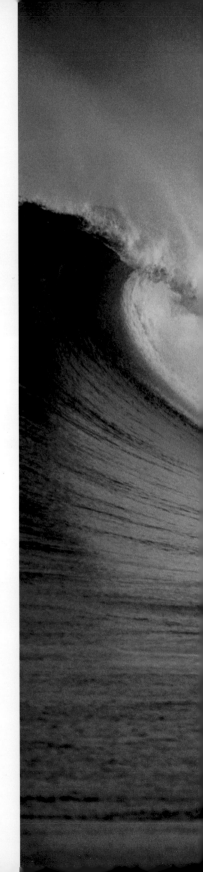

whale
beach

WHALE BEACH

Previous page Jason Salisbury, The Wedge.
Photo by Alex Marks.

Above Early Whale Beach. c.1930.
The National Library of Australia, Canberra.
EB Studios. nla.pic_vn3418797

Whale Beach faces east to the ocean, with Palm Beach to the north and Avalon to the south. The origin of the name Whale Beach is unclear, but is understood to be associated either with the shape of its prominent headland, or a beaching of a whale in the late nineteenth century. Dolphin Bay at the southern end of Whale Beach is named after the dolphins which frequent the area. A low ridge runs adjacent to the beach and a short distance to the west of this ridge lies the shoreline of Careel Bay, Pittwater.

Shipbuilding and boatbuilding were carried out in Pittwater soon after first settlement, at Clareville and Stokes Point. The name Careel Bay is recorded in the Grant Registry of 1816, and is thought to be named after an Aboriginal man long forgotten. Captain F.W. Sidney, however, surveyed the area between 1868 and 1872 and *"noted the bay on his chart as Evening Bay, with the southern entrance noted as Stripe Bay."*[1] Stokes Point takes its name from a shipbuilder said to be a convict transported for a crime he claimed he did not commit, who worked and lived there. Local histories tell us that despite the fact that he worked with the rough tools of his trade Stokes was somewhat of a dandy, and every Sunday he wore *"a tight bottle-green coat with large buttons, a remarkable tall hat, and a stock which might have belonged to Beau Brummel."* These clothes, purchased in London when they were the latest style, remained his Sunday best well into his declining years.[2]

Whale Beach was part of a 400-acre grant to James Napper in 1816, and the land remained virtually untouched during the nineteenth century. In 1900 it was offered for sale by the Barrenjoey Land Company in large blocks suitable for pasture, but none of the land sold. In 1912, the land was offered again in smaller blocks with more success, marking the beginning of development at Whale Beach. In 1913 Whale Beach Kiosk was built and supplied the needs of visitors, and by 1918 Whale Beach Road had been laid down. Jack Webster was employed by the Palm Beach Land Company in 1927 to build roads throughout the area. The company also built Webster a cottage at Whale Beach where he lived for over forty years. Gradually several holiday homes were built, but the beach didn't become a residential suburb until the 1950s when transport became easier and motorcars more common.[3]

Architect Alexander Stewart Jolly built his truly remarkable 'Loggan Rock' house on the headland at the south end of Whale Beach in 1932. The house was owned by the Commonwealth Film Censor, Colonel Lionel Hurley, and it became well known not only for its design but also for its parties. Model Patricia Minchin, known as 'Atlantic Ethel' after her posters for the oil company, recalled lively parties held there with her film and radio friends at the end of the war. The Antarctic photographer and adventurer Frank Hurley would rent or borrow the cabin from his relative to host these events fondly remembered for their *"wonderful cocktail concoctions"* and *"summers of happiness"*.[4] The legend of Loggan Rock would

Careel Bay. *Photo oggy.*

"There is more bounty, more possibility for us in a vista that moves, rolls, surges. Twists, rears up and changes from minute to minute." TIM WINTON, LAND'S EDGE, 1993

Left The Wedge. *Photo Louise Whelan.*

Above *photo oggy*

carry forward into later decades with the Dunlops and other artistes in the 1950s.

Jolly and other 'organic' architects made the area unique in its protection of the natural setting, a principle later enforced by council regulation regarding clearing trees. Unfortunately, the desire for bigger housing has meant many concrete and glass edifices have been built close to the beach and dominating the headlands without any regard to the natural setting. Wealthy owners and developers consider paying the relatively small fine to the land and environment court for clearing bush illegally a small percentage of the multimillion-dollar building projects.

Whale Beach is a popular swimming beach, and has excellent rock fishing off both north and south points. In the northern corner of the beach is an excellent surfing wave known as the Wedge. It gets its name from the heavy pitching peak created when a solid northeast swell refracts off the north point, especially on a low tide. On smaller days good surf banks can usually be found along the beach and the southern corner will occasionally provide some excellent barrels. With a medium south to southeast swell, low tide and offshore winds the waves here can jack-up as outgoing wash collides with them. The take-offs can be frightening, as I found out in 1999 when my right eye was removed by one of my surfboard fins after blowing a late take-off.

Following several near fatalities in the surf in 1925–26, locals formed a squad of life savers with a council-supplied reel, line and belt and began irregular patrols. With beach visitors growing in numbers, Whale Beach SLSC was formed in 1937, and the following year an old windmill frame was adapted to house a reel and provide a lookout for sharks. In 1941, a stone boatshed was built, doubling as an air-raid shelter during World War II, but was eventually destroyed in the 1974 storm. In that same year the club held the first Palm Beach to Whale Beach Ocean Marathon Swim and 28 club members

Foundation members with the first Whale Beach club house and shark tower, c.1937–38. *Courtesy WBSLSC.*

From left to right: Hal Baily, Doug Hall,
and Neville Gough, surf race c.1945–46.
Courtesy WBSLSC.

Whale Beach. *Photo oggy.*

swam in atrocious conditions, making it the first of many fundraising surf club ocean swims in Australia. Following the death of club member Bob Lynch, father of surfing champion Barton Lynch, the swim has been held in his honour. In recent years around 2,000 competitors lodge entries for the event now known as 'The Big Swim', considered to be the premier ocean swim in New South Wales.

Club members eventually raised funds to purchase land, and built a large clubhouse with volunteer labour. Along with neighbouring Palm Beach SLSC, Whale Beach is one of only two New South Wales Surf Life Saving Clubs to own its own club premises. The first major rescue by club members was on 26 January 1938, when a disabled motor launch with two men on board was swept by heavy seas toward the south end rocks. Noel Greenfield of Whale Beach and James Barnes of Palm Beach SLSC donned belts and swam through the heavy seas to rescue the men, and received the Meritorious Award from the SLSA. In 1956, cadet member Colin Timms rescued two men in a mass rescue in big seas when five people were swept out to sea in a fierce undertow. Another man drowned from a suspected heart attack, and this remains the only fatality experienced at Whale Beach during patrol hours.

Betty and Hal Baily were among the early characters who chose Whale Beach to settle. Originally a member of North Bondi SLSC, Hal began to visit the Whale Beach clubhouse as an 18-year-old before enlisting for World War II. He was wounded while fighting in Palestine and spent a year convalescing in hospital. In 1943, Hal joined the Whale Beach SLSC and began swimming again to improve his damaged back. He and Betty rented a small beach shack from F.J. 'Pop' Timms, one the founders of the WBSLSC. The shack had few amenities, and while out walking one day Hal and Betty came across a block of land for sale at the southern end of the beach. The owner Mrs Lewis happened to be walking by and stopped to tell Hal that she appreciated his "*great service*" to his country. She then informed

Photo oggy.

Betty worked as an actress, performing in the stage play of *South Pacific*, playing roles in films such as *Mad Max 2*, *They're a Weird Mob* and *Babe*, and even doing a memorable stint on *Red Faces*.

Hal and Betty that she owned the listed block and adjacent blocks, before offering them their pick of any of them for the princely sum of £65. Betty exclaimed that they could not afford it but Mrs Lewis replied, *"I'm sure you will be good for it Betty."*

Betty worked as an actress, performing in the stage play of *South Pacific*, playing roles in films such as *Mad Max 2*, *They're a Weird Mob* and *Babe*, and even doing a memorable stint on *Red Faces*. Hal worked as a photoengraver at the *Sydney Morning Herald* newspaper, and in the early days would ride his motorbike to the city. His surf skills are legendary. At 52, in 1970, he revelled in heavy seas to win the open surf race at the Whale Beach carnival and, as a Life Member of the club, Hal won numerous medals in Masters swimming in Australia and overseas. Hal would swim the length of the beach every day, right up to the year prior to his death in 2009. Betty celebrated her ninetieth birthday with her children, Jill and Kim, in October 2010.

At the beginning of the 1970s, John Witzig and fellow *Surfing World* photographer Albe Falzon teamed up with *Go-Set* editor David Elfick to create *Tracks*, promoted as 'the surfers bible'.

The original office was in Whale Beach and John Witzig recalls that he and Alby *"did the layout of the first issue at a ratty old house that I was living in next door to the shop at Whale Beach."* There were few youth magazines back in that time, and the anti-authoritarian, counterculture surf tabloid would certainly make waves of its own. The *Captain Goodvibes* cartoon series about a surfing 'Pig of Steel' by Tony Edwards would become an icon of Australian surfing culture.

With their box seat to witness the annual migration of whales, many residents of the aptly named Whale Beach take a fierce interest in these mammals. Everyone living here has a story to tell how their spirits were uplifted at some time by the sight of whales and dolphins playing in the ocean. During the late nineties, the owners of Whaleys, the now defunct local café reputed to make the best hamburger in Sydney, was also known for the controversial notice displayed near the door. The handwritten sign said something along the lines that citizens from a certain country known for its government's support of the whaling industry would not be welcome until their countrymen stopped killing whales. Nothing personal … just looking out for some old friends who drop by each year.

Right Betty Baily. *Photo oggy.*

Left *Photo Oceaneye.*

Above Whale Beach. *Photo Sean Davey.*

palm
beach

The beach is named after the *Livistona australis,* cabbage tree palms, still prevalent in areas such as Dark Gully on the Pittwater side and in the southern corner of the beach, which is still officially known as Cabbage Tree Boat Harbour. Palm Beach is for the most part a shore-parallel sand barrier stretching between two bedrock headlands, Observation Point and Barrenjoey Headland. To the north of Barrenjoey lies the mouth of the Hawkesbury River, known as Deerubbun to the Saltwater People. The river was renamed by Governor Phillip in 1788 after Sir Charles Jenkins, a Minister in the Pitt government who had recently been raised to the peerage as Lord Hawkesbury. Pittwater, like Port Jackson, is a drowned river valley created when sea levels rose after the last ice age.

Barrenjoey (it has also been spelt Baranjuee, Barranjoey, Barranyu and Barranjull) was once an isolated hill on a broad peninsula, but with a rise in the sea level some 16,000 to 6,000 years ago it was converted into an island, and eventually a 'tied island'. It is a sacred place to the Guringai. Local historian and former judge Jim Macken believes that one of the rock carvings on the America track at West Head depicts the one-legged Daramulan (emissary to the sky god 'Biami') as an aerial view of the Barrenjoey land formation with nominal human characteristics. Macken also states that another carving further along the Hawkesbury basin depicts the Kuringai equivalent of the Rainbow Serpent of the Aboriginal dreaming, that is in fact an uncannily accurate aerial map of approximately eight miles of the river system.

It may surprise some to hear Barrenjoey being referred to as an island, but it is only since colonisation that the sand dunes have built up with shore drift over the shallow water between Barrenjoey and the mainland. Maybanke Anderson recorded how 'Old Pat' Flynn, an early settler who had a vegetable garden near Palm Beach, would tell tales *"of a day when, during a furious storm, the waves of the ocean had swept across the isthmus."*[1] According to Dennis Foley, *"this was once*

Previous page *Photo oggy.*

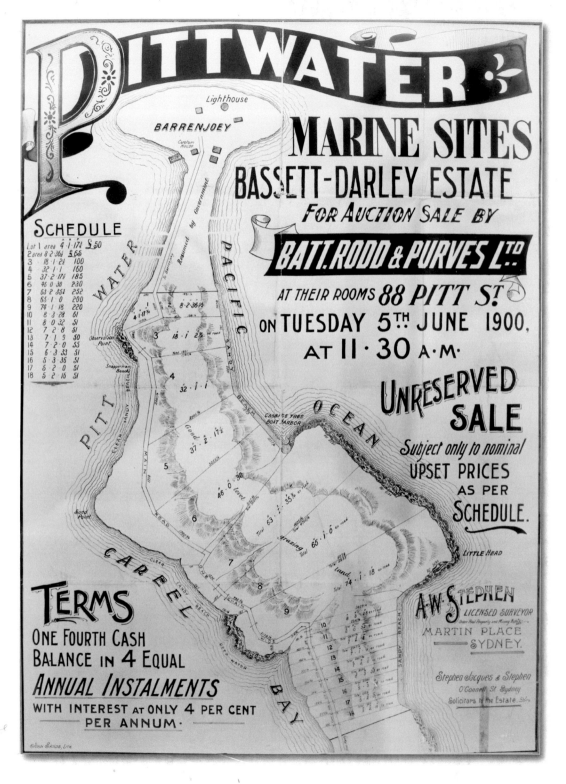

... one of the rock carvings on the America track at West Head depicts the one-legged Daramulan (emissary to the sky god 'Biami') as an aerial view of the Barrenjoey land formation with nominal human characteristics. Macken also states that another carving further along the Hawkesbury basin depicts the Kuringai equivalent of the Rainbow Serpent of the Aboriginal dreaming, that is in fact an uncannily accurate aerial map of approximately eight miles of the river system.

Left *Barrenjoey and Palm Beach as presented in the 1900 real estate subdivision. Courtesy Nicholina Ralston.*

Opposite *Daramulan (emissary to the sky god 'Biami'), as represented in a rock carving at West Head. The carving appears to depict an aerial view of the Barrenjoey land formation with animal characteristics.*

Kiddies Corner, Palm Beach, before road.
Courtesy Nicholina Ralston.

"... I have seen the hungry ocean gain
Advantage on the kingdom of the shore,
And the firm soil win of the watery main,
Increasing store with loss, and loss with store."

WILLIAM SHAKESPEARE, *THE SONNETS*

Kids with seaplanes, Palm Beach. c.1935.
Courtesy Warringah Library.

a place where sick whales beached themselves and our people would gorge themselves for weeks on the carcases." [2]

In fact, North Head and Barrenjoey, the two islands that bookend the section of coastline discussed in this book, were both known to the Saltwater People as whale beaching areas. One theory for this is that shore erosion and subsequent geomagnetic changes in the shore confuses the whales' biomagnetic and echolocation senses. There are early stories of washthroughs on the sand spit at Manly near the present site of The Corso, as happened at Barrenjoey. It is thought that migrating whales may have been lured by calls from whales inside the waters of Sydney Harbour and Pittwater, or sung to by Aborigines, causing the whales to beach themselves.

Governor Phillip explored Broken Bay in March 1788 and, although Pittwater was used for shelter by passing ships, Palm Beach remained a remote and little-frequented area until the second half of the nineteenth century.[3] In 1829 Govett wrote:

Pittwater, a quiet inlet of the sea, protected from
the boisterous waves within by a ridge of mountain
and a narrow sandbar, forms a beautiful and
romantic lake, and is found a convenient shelter
in adverse weather.[4]

There had also been a lagoon in the southern corner of the ocean beach, near the site of the current change sheds, where ducks had been hunted. Before the road to Newport was completed in the early 1920s, Gow's Wharf (near the Palm Beach Ferry Wharf) was Palm Beach's link to the outside world, and visitors would climb over the hill to get to the beach. Gadigal descendant Dennis Foley states that the ridge at the top of Palm Beach where they would have passed is the site of an ancient Guringai burial place.[5]

In 1816, Palm Beach, Barrenjoey and most of Whale Beach

The view looking north-east from Sunrise Hill
    to Lion Island, Barrenjoey Headland, and
    Palm Beach, 1925.
    State Library of New South Wales.

(400 acres) was granted to James Napper. In 1836, Bowen (Toura Bungaree) and his wife Maria, Jonza, Nan and daughters Theda (Jane), Theela Bowen and son Mark, move to Pittwater, near Barrenjoey. Bowen may have decided to lead his clan away from the destruction and poverty of Sydney life back to a semi-traditional existence. He found work as a black tracker, catching fish to trade with settlers and working beside Customs Officer Howard. In 1843: *"As a result of increased smuggling in Broken Bay, a customs station was established on the western foreshore of Barrenjoey Peninsula."*[6] Governor Gipps, who ordered the customs house, once wryly remarked that smuggling was the chief industry of Pittwater.[7] The customs station was located on what came to be known as Station Beach, but was burnt to the ground in 1976.

The first reference to a light from Barrenjoey was from an 1855 government report that mentioned a light sheltered in a weatherboard building in rough weather. This was replaced by two wooden towers in 1866 and eventually by the current lighthouse in 1881 after Barrenjoey Headland was purchased by the government. Built with Hawkesbury sandstone quarried from the top of the headland, other materials were horse-hauled up a trolley track from the jetty below. This stone wharf *"has long since become part of the landscaping and houses around Palm Beach."*[8] When the original red (non-flashing) kerosene light was replaced with an automated white group flash (four every twenty seconds) gas lamp in 1932, the lightkeepers were withdrawn from duty. In 1972 the light became electrified in order to overcome acetylene gas resupply problems. Jervis and Bridget Sparks were the unofficial caretakers of the light station for three decades up until 1999 and were awarded the first-ever Pittwater Medal in recognition of their preservation work.[9]

In the late nineteenth century, a Chinese firm ran a prosperous fish-drying business at Snapperman Beach. The manager, Ah Chuney, was *"much respected by residents and was a general favourite"*

Men with boat full of fish, Cabbage Tree Boat Harbour, Palm Beach, c.1950.
Courtesy Warringah Library.

SECOND ORDER DIOPTRIC
RED LIGHT
FIXED

FOCAL LINE 50 FEET ABOVE
GROUND AND 5/1 FEET ABOVE
HIGH WATER MARK

PLAN. AT. G.

PLAN. AT. H.

Left James Barnet's 1877 drawing
of the lighthouse tower.

Right Barnet's Lighthouse,
Barrenjoey Head, c.1945.
*E.W. Searle Collection. National
Library of Australia, Canberra.*
nla.pic-vn4654085

who was *"exceedingly fair in his dealings."*[10] Fish and abalone were sent to either Sydney and subsequently to China, or to Melbourne where there was a large Chinese population following the gold rush. At that time Melbourne was considered the richest city in the world. Abalone, known to the locals as 'mutton fish', had been a favourite food of the Saltwater People before the Asian emigrants arrived, but it was not appreciated by the English settlers in those early days, although its shells were used for buttons and pearl inlay.

In 1900, the area was divided into eighteen large blocks listed as good grazing land and offered for sale. None sold. In 1912, the land was offered again in smaller residential blocks, promoting the area for its fishing, sailing, golf and rowing. Most houses were built from

local sandstone quarried on the block, creating a distinctive architectural style. Some of these dwellings were guest houses, but many were holiday homes for those who could afford them. Palm Beach Wharf in Pittwater was the terminus reached by boat from Newport or Bayview. The hill overlooking Palm Beach was known to locals as 'Pill Hill' because of the large number of homes owned by Macquarie Street doctors. 'Kalua', an old-style plantation home opposite the beach, was built by Hordern family in the early 1920s. This elegant and historic property still boasts over two acres of gardens in an exclusive part of Palm Beach.

It was probably less an act of xenophobia and more an attempt to keep the hustle and bustle of the city away that the people of the peninsula lobbied against the Manly–Warringah District Railway League's 1933 attempt to introduce a train line to Newport. Despite the lack of public transport, Palm Beach has become more residential since World War II, while retaining a sense of seclusion at the northern point of Pittwater. The Palm Beach residents' committee comprises some very influential people and lobbies hard to protect the natural beauty of the area against over-development. Hordern Park, Wiltshire Parks and McKay Reserve were donated by long-time resident R.J. Hordern, who was also responsible for the planting of the Norfolk Island pines along the beach front.

In recent years, Barrenjoey Headland has been added to Ku-ring-gai Chase National Park, and the entire rocky platform around the headland extending 100 metres seaward from the mean low-water mark is designated an Aquatic Reserve. At the entrance to Broken Bay is Lion Island, 560 metres long, 280 metres wide and rising to 93 metres above sea level at the eastern end. This island, resembling a crouching lion guarding the Hawkesbury, is a nature reserve not open to the public, as it is a breeding ground for fairy penguins and other sea-birds. With the completion of the sale of Currawong to the State Government a new State Park encompassing

Members of the PBSLSC show their flag outside their second clubhouse at Hordern Park 1920s. Second from left is Adrian Curlewis.
Courtesy PBSLSC.

Palm Beach 1930s.
From left to right: John Ralston, unknown,
Alrema Samuels, Herb Tattersall, R. Mant,
possibly Lister Ifould.
Courtesy Nicholina Ralston.

Pittwater's northern and western foreshores is being considered as the best way to protect public land around the foreshores for future generations. Three council-owned sites, including Mackerel Beach Reserve, McKay Reserve and a block of bushland in Newport, will be united with the crown land sites of Currawong, Pittwater Park at Palm Beach and the ferry wharf, Barrenjoey Beach and North Palm Beach to create the State Park.

'Kiddies Corner' at the southern end of the beach offered some protection and it was here that the Palm Beach Surf Life Saving Club *"was founded in November 1921."* Early Vice-Presidents of the club included such luminaries as Dr H.H. Bullmore, Judge Clive Curlewis and A.J. Hordern. The nephew of Clive Curlewis, Adrian Curlewis, was captain of the club from 1923 to 1928 and would go on to become the president of Surf Life Saving Australia for thiry-seven years. The Palm Beach Surf Life Saving Club, Cabbage Tree and Pacific Club (strictly for women) together form one of the more exclusive clubs in New South Wales. The North Palm Beach SLSC is a little more working class, with its origins in the Beacon Store in 1939, followed by a more permanent clubhouse in 1946. Many worthy and aspiring volunteer lifeguards who did not fit the social criteria of the exclusive Palm Beach club found acceptance at North Palm Beach.

The North Palm Beach Surf Life Saving Club gets some valuable support by providing a part-time location for Summer Bay, the fictional town in television soap opera *Home and Away*. The presence of the film crew is low key and unobtrusive, unlike the overblown circus seen during the making of the pilots for the controversial *Baywatch* Australian episodes filmed at Avalon. It is also worth noting that the North Palm Beach club runs an 'Outback Meets the Beach' program. Once a year around Easter a group of Jawoyn Aboriginal kids and traditional owners from the desert country near Katherine Gorge come down and stay at the clubhouse. This is is often the first time that these people have seen the ocean and the trip

Left Cloudy Rhodes. *Photo Mark Onorati.*
Above Nora Ralston c.1930s.
Courtesy Nicholina Ralston.

is eagerly anticipated. In exchange a group of privileged northern beaches kids visit one of the Jawoyn communities in the Northern Territory. Both groups share culture and lifestyle, and challenge stereotypical views. Project coordinator Terry Kirkpatrick has noticed that *"a level of trust has grown."*[11]

In the days before clubs could afford the cost of road transport to get their boats to carnivals at distant beaches, the Palm Beach club made a *"highway of the seas to Newcastle in the 1920s and early 1930s, completing at least half a dozen return trips over the fifty-miles-odd journey."*[12] Many tales of adventure and misadventure are told of these long journeys, beach to beach. A leatherjacket fisherman by the name of Coltman tells the story about one trio when he had been at one of the oars:

> We cleared from the beach in a mist that quickly
> hid the shore, and had hardly got out before a
> nor'-easter blew right up in our faces, bringing
> a lot of water into the boat. Everyone baled but
> it came in so quick we couldn't get rid of it. The
> dead pull against the headwind, too, had us all
> in by midday, and we'd about decided to go ashore
> and camp when a steamer came up astern. For
> four hours we towed behind her ... My, it was cold!
> And how cheering the first sight of Newcastle,
> the boat crew rowing out to meet us, the chap
> in the in the bow waving a bottle of whisky.[13]

An interesting character from the Palm Beach SLSC in the 1930s was Reginald Keightley Russell, a.k.a. 'Blue' Russell. Russell's interests had turned to surfboard design and construction after his wool brokerage business collapsed in 1937. His hollow boards were longer than traditional boards, ranging in size from 11 feet (3.35 metre) to the

Wayne Lynch, Palm Beach 1968.
Photo John Pennings.

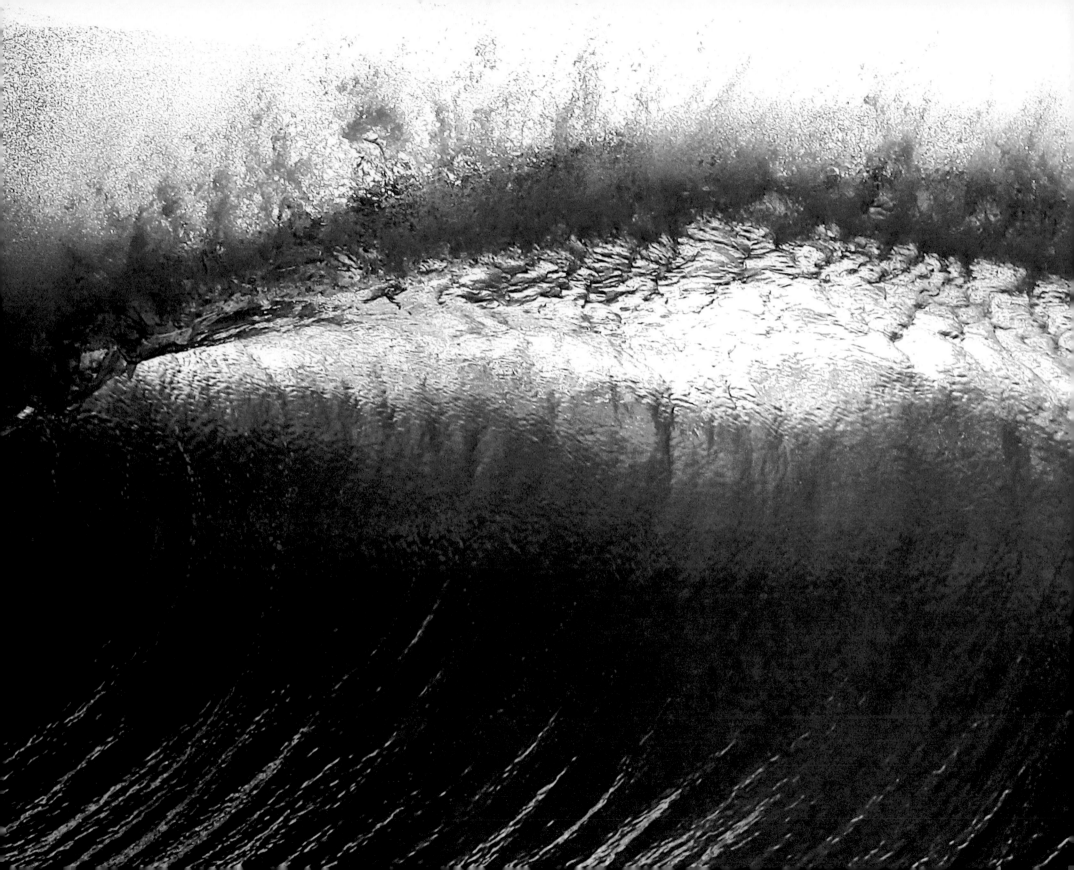

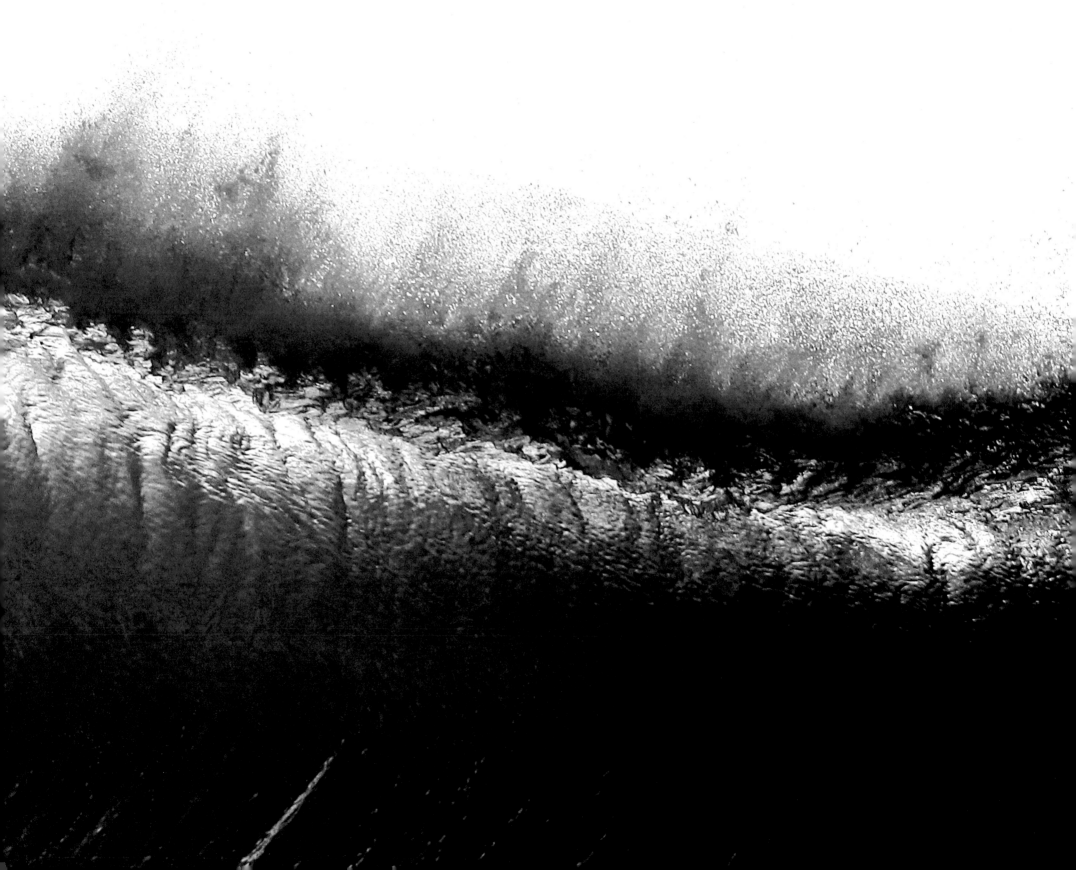

13-foot (3.96-metre) 'Queen Mary'. Hearing of a *"new type of board"* in Australia, the *Honolulu Star Bulletin* sent a challenge to the *Sydney Daily Telegraph* for the Australians to send their best board riders to see if they could beat *"Honolulu surf-board men in their own surf."*[14] Frank Packer, annual Palm Beach summer resident and proprietor of the *Telegraph*, accepted the challenge and insisted that Russell was selected for the team. Russell stayed on in Hawaii after the competition, becoming friends with surfing icon Duke Kahanamoku and later marrying the heiress to the Heinz soup empire. He went on to head the Olympic Record Company in Los Angeles, with the whole recording plant, considered among the most modern in America at that time, built to his own design.[15] One of Blue Russell's boards can be still found at the Manly surf club museum.[16]

Another colourful Palm Beach SLSC character and club stalwart is John 'Johnny' Carter. Carter became the club's permanent lifeguard at the age of 18 at the end of World War II. To supplement his income he conducted swimming lessons in the Palm Beach Pool, and has since taught generations of children how to swim. Carter's most daring rescue occurred in 1958 when two teenage boys were washed off the rocks by large surf. After locating the two boys and stabilising them he decided to wait for a rescue craft. The condition of one of the boys was deteriorating and no help had arrived, so Carter swam the boys towards the beach. It was obvious that the boys would not survive a swim through the dumping shorebreak, so Carter waited for the right wave to launch himself and his two patients onto the rocks. Landing on his back to protect the boys he was badly cut on the rocks, but was assisted by others. Johnny Carter was subsequently nominated for a George medal for one of the most courageous rescues in Palm Beach history. He retired from life saving duties in the late 1960s but can still be found giving the occasional swimming lesson. Carter was awarded an OAM in 2005 and Lifetime Membership of Palm Beach SLSC in 2010.

The increased popularity of the Malibu surfboard in the late fifties resulted in an increase in surfboard-related injuries. In 1959 the Council allowed for a board flag system to be introduced, and boards entering the area could be confiscated by the club's honorary beach inspectors. The introduction of this system angered the non-surfclub board riders and there were acts of civil disobedience. The council and Surf Club responded by increasing the exclusion zone and confiscations, while club members continued to ride boards in the area. Things came to a head in the mid-1960s when the Windansea Surf Club advocated a more hard-line attitude, and on the morning of 6 November 1966 over 150 board riders gathered at the beach and began surfing in the restricted area. The confrontation threated to turn into a serious brawl before the police were called. Eventually meetings between the ASA and the club saw some concessions, but the relationship between 'surfies' and 'clubbies' remained poor for many years.

The Surf Life Saving movement is a volunteer community service that relies on limited government funding and corporate largesse, so it is in its interests to keep detailed accounts of all rescues and assistance given to beachgoers. Less known are the hundreds of unrecorded rescues performed by surfers who patrol the beaches daily looking for waves. In some places surfers and life savers have been in conflict, often portrayed as a clash between the regimented and the free spirited, but there is also a long history of these two tribes assisting each other in rescues. There is growing recognition that they both share a love of the ocean and a more harmonious relationship has been developed. Midget Farrelly is a good example of a waterman who bridged the divide. Midget was the first president (1961) of Australia's oldest surfboard riders' club, the Dee Why Surfing Fraternity, and is now 'sweep' on one of the Palm Beach Surf Life Saving Club's classic Australian surfboats.

Palm Beach can offer a series of options and many excellent

Above Tommy Carroll, Barrenjoey.
Photo Hugh McLeod.

Pittwater surfing.
Photo courtesy Stretch.

waves when the conditions are right. It is also an excellent location for beach fishing and kite-surfing. The north end of the beach provides relatively uncrowded waves, and Barrenjoey will serve up some of the best waves on the northern beaches during a big northeast swell. Alternatively, the south end of the beach sometimes offers the only option during a big easterly storm or southerly buster, with the headland giving some protection from the winds. The sand banks along Palm Beach can be fickle, but when favourable will supply beautiful fun waves year round. The Palm Beach Longboard Club meets on the first Sunday of each month and often runs events in conjunction with the Disabled Surfers Association.

On rare occasions, when monster swells make all the northern beaches unsurfable, an event takes place where surfable waves can be found in Pittwater. In 2009 a one-metre high wave began breaking from approximately 100 metres southwest of Carmels (the seaplane wharf) then running down Pittwater cutting past the shoreline beneath multimillion dollar homes past Gonsalves Wharf. A few sets even passed under the Palm Beach Ferry Wharf, offering a 500-metre ride and ending up on the beach opposite Barrenjoey House. As word got out, everyone wanted to be part of this freak event, and by the afternoon there were about eighty surfers and stand-up paddle riders all sharing the novelty wave.

Since the beginning of the twentieth century Palm Beach has been the playground of the rich and powerful. There were the eccentric ones like Bee Miles in the 1920s who swam with a knife to protect herself against sharks. And then there were the Packers. Three generations of the family spent most summers at their beachfront holiday home, and the stories are plentiful. In 1986 lifeguards at Whale Beach received an urgent radio call for IRB *"rubber duckie"* assistance at Palm Beach where a catamaran with two young teens on board was being swept onto Mushroom Rock at South Palm Beach in strong winds and heavy seas. As Stretch Cooper and Martin Linz

were launching the IRB a huge man appeared running down the beach yelling at them to take him with them as it was his kids in distress. The lifeguards politely refused due to space restrictions and suggested he meet them on the beach at Palmy. They reached the youngsters and took them from the boat as it was being pounded against the rocks.

On returning to the beach, the big man, Kerry Packer, greeted his kids Jamie and Gretel with bear hugs, and then did the same to the lifeguards. Later Kerry asked Stretch why the Palm Beach Lifeguards didn't have an IRB, and he answered that the council didn't have the budget and Palm Beach only had one lifeguard when two are required to run an IRB. The next day Stretch was transferred to Palm Beach to take delivery of a brand new, fully operational IRB donated by Kerry to the then Warringah Shire Council Lifeguards at Palm Beach. This was soon followed by a motorised tractor to get the IRB from the club to the water. As the richest man in Australia at that time, Kerry exerted considerable power. When the thick black cables required for cable television were rolled out by Foxtel along existing power poles, the word allegedly went through from the boss that this was not going to happen in Palm Beach … and it didn't. They went underground in that suburb to avoid the eyesore.

Above *Photo oggy.*

bohemians and blue bloods

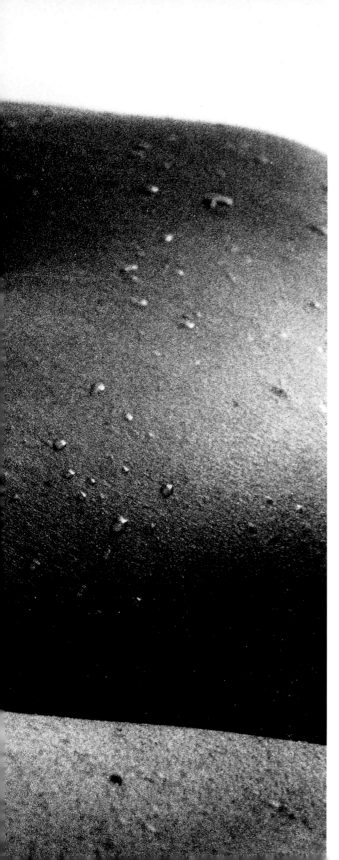

Landscape Nude 1, 1973.
Photo David Moore.
Photographed at Lobster Bay on the north
side of Broken Bay. David had a house there.
Courtesy National Gallery of Australia, Canberra.

"Part of the attraction of the coast is undoubtedly the quality of the light; it has a luminosity which never occurs inland. We have all seen the extraordinary effects of light on the sea, even on grey misty days: the burning midday glare, or the spectacular beauty of a sunset, or a gleaming ray of sunlight illuminating a patch of ocean on a dark, stormy afternoon. Such elements have been the inspiration for countless painters and composers."

Stafford Cliff, *The Way We Live: By the Sea*, 2006

A/P 'Shell Surfer' for Isabel. Bruce. '10

Shell Surfer.
Artist Bruce Goold.
Hand coloured linocut 17 x 13.5cm.
Based on Botticelli's 'The Birth of Venus',
supposedly born from a shell.

The blue-ribbon Liberal conservative politics of the northern beaches often seems to sit at odds with the creative and usually left-leaning artisans and bohemians who have been drawn to the fabled beaches, waterways and bushland of the area. But the beach is a great social leveller, where pretense, heritage and the outward signs of wealth can be peeled off and a form of stripped-down egalitarianism takes place.

For many cultures over the centuries, a strong link has existed between creativity and immersion in the ocean. The ever-changing nature of the ocean, especially at the interface of sea and land, is the space which shapes and inspires the creative spirit. This book acknowledges those surfers, sailors, swimmers, divers, fishermen, photographers, filmmakers, musicians, artists, writers and poets, and all who have been inspired by the ocean to live extraordinary lives.[1]

writers

In *The Iliad*, Homer declared the ocean *"the genesis of all."* Coleridge surrendered to the seduction of the sea, declaring: *"… my whole Being is filled with waves that roll and stumble, like things that have no common master."* Ernest Hemingway wrote about the eroticism of the unknown in *The Old Man and the Sea*, when the old man thinks of the ocean *"as feminine and as something that gave or withheld great favours, and if she did wild or wicked things it was because she could not help them."* Tim Winton constantly draws inspiration from the ocean and his love of surfing, and in his book *Land's Edge* states his belief that *"The ocean is the the supreme metaphor for change."*

"The ocean is the supreme metaphor for change."

Tim Winton, *Land's Edge*, 1993

"It looks a bit sharkey out there".
Photo Tim Hixson.

Many writers have drawn inspiration from the northern beaches, and many have made it their home. Morris West OA (1916–1999) wrote of his life on the northern beaches: *"Some of my best work was written here, the friendships made here have held rock solid through the ages."*[2] West authored *The Shoes of the Fisherman*, *The Ambassador*, *The Devil's Advocate* and *Children of the Sun* from his *"privileged corner"* near Pittwater.

D.H. Lawrence (1885–1930) used Narrabeen as the location for *Kangaroo*, and Frank Hardy (1917–1994), author of *Power Without Glory*, once lived there. Ion Idriess (1889–1979) lived in the Mona Vale area and had great success with his popular novels. Successful author Frank Clune (1893–1971) would often be visited by William Dobell in his northern beaches retreat.

His gallery in Kings Cross would later become the home of noted artist Martin Sharp and was known as 'The Yellow House'. Current northern beaches resident Thomas Keneally AO (b.1935) is a prolific author, perhaps best known for *Schindler's Ark* (1982), *The Chant of Jimmy Blacksmith* (1972), *A Dutiful Daughter* (1971) and *Bring Larks and Heroes* (1967). He has won the Booker Prize and several Miles Franklin Awards.

Bob Ellis (b.1942), author, journalist, playwright (*The Legend of King O'Malley*), screenwriter (*Newsfront*), director (*Nostrodamus Kid*) and political activist has long lived in Palm Beach. Outlining the depth of Australian creative talent living on the northern beaches, Ellis once wrote about his house in Palm Beach that *"on our hilltop lived Weir and Noyce and Elfick."*[3]

Former *Tracks* editor Phil Jarratt (b.1951) wrote *Peninsularity*, a collection of stories about life on the peninsula, while he lived in Avalon. Kate Grenville has never lived on the northern beaches, but *The Secret River*, her 2005 book about the devastating impact of Europeans settlement on Aboriginal land along the Hawkesbury River, is based on her ancestors, the Wisemans.

artists

The non-Indigenous artists who first depicted this region's strange plants and animals and the changing landscapes were Europeans. Among the artists on voyages of exploration were Thomas Banks, Nicolas-Martin Petit, Charles-Alexandre Lesueur and Pavel Mikhailov. The first artists in the fledgling colony were

Above left Mick Glasheen.

Above Mick Glasheen painting.

convicts who delivered the naive works of the Port Jackson painters. These early attempts were followed by the likes of Joseph Lycett and Thomas Watling, who were also convict artists but with skills developed through their crimes of forgery. The early attempts translate the 'exotic' Indigenous peoples, landscapes and unfamiliar wildlife through European sensibilities soon gave way to a more native and unique view.

Well-known artists who came from the northern beaches or lived here include: James Auld (1879–1942), Lawson Balfour (1870–1966); Sydney Long (1871–1955); Arthur Murch (1902–1989), winner of the 1949 Archibald Prize; Wendy Sharpe (b.1960); Robert Lovett; Neville Cayley (1886–1950); Sali Herman OBE (1898–1993), whose awards include the Wynne Prize 1944,

1962, 1965 and 1967, and the Sulman Prize 1946 and 1948; Martin Sharp (b.1942); and Brett Whiteley (1939–1992).

Current resident artists include Michael Glasheen; former Mambo artist Bruce Goold; Gretel Pinniger (a.k.a. Madam Lash); Rachel Newling; Joshua Yeldham; Mark Rhodes; Linda Dry-Parker; Stephen Glassborow; Ben Brown (illustrator); and Peter Rushforth (ceramics).

photographers

Photographers like to document the miracle of existence in all its aspects whether they be wonder, joy or calamity. Since the first cameras arrived from Europe around 1846, many photographers have attempted to capture that peculiar alchemy that happens when the

ocean meets the shore. The significance of humanity is made insignificant when compared to the power of the sea.

Early masters of the craft such as Harold Cazneaux (1878–1953) and Frank Hurley (1885–1962), best known for his work on Antarctic expeditions, lived along these shores. They inspired and mentored the next generation, which included Max Dupain (1911–1992), Olive Cotton (1911–2003) and David Moore (1927–2003). Too many to list have called this coast home, but I will attempt to name a few: Gervaise Purcell (1919–1999), Richard Bailey (1959–2010), Ray Leighton (1917–2002), Roger Scott, Hugh McLeod, Tim Hixson, Sally Mayman, Louise Whelan and Murray Vanderveer.

Above Brett Whiteley. *Photo oggy.*

Above right *Painting of Gretel.*

film & television

The variety of locations on the northern beaches has made them a popular choice for film and television dating back to *The Sunny South,* filmed in 1913. Artransa Studios in Frenchs Forest were opened in 1956, creating diverse productions ranging from *Whiplash* to the 'Louie the Fly' TV commercial and parts of *Summer of the Seventeenth Doll* (1959). The bushland featured in *Ben Hall* and *Skippy the Bush Kangaroo,* while the beaches provided locations for *Home and Away, Baywatch, BMX Bandits, Paperback Hero, Looking for Alibrandi, Holy Smoke, Dark City* and *Superman Returns.*

Well-known actors including Chips Rafferty, Jack Thompson, Bryan Brown, Rachel Ward, Peter Phelps and Toni Collette have lived on the northern beaches. Rachel Ward has recently turned her talents to directing with the feature film *Beautiful Kate* (2009) and the television show *Rake* (2010). Other directors who have made the northern beaches their home include Peter Weir, who won the Academy Award for *Master and Commander* (2003); David Elphick, producer and director; Alby Thoms, avant-garde filmmaker at 'The Yellow House' and director of *Palm Beach* (1980); Yahoo Serious, writer and director of *Young Einstein*; and Bob Ellis, writer and director of several films. Chips Rafferty once described Pittwater as *"Sydney's best kept secret."*

musicians

The northern beaches can also boast some talented singers and musicians, including Dame Joan Sutherland, Winifred Atwell, Tamam Shud, James Morrison,

Above 'Ascension'.
Artist Mark Rhodes.

bohemians and blue bloods   269

Harry Seidler and Sydney Ancher, led a more modernist approach, as evident in the Seidler buildings at Bungan Beach and Avalon, and Ancher's 'Windy Drop Down' in Molong Street, North Curl Curl. Built in 1946 during the post-war boom, 'Windy Drop Down', with its flat roof design, unusual for its time, had its critics, but the house still stands today as part of the architectural history of the northern beaches.

Since its beginning, the good burghers of Avalon, such as town planner and developer A.J. Small and architect Harry Ruskin Rowe, campaigned against the inappropriate development and urban ugliness which threatened their vision of housing blending with the environment. In some cases, private properties have attempted to limit public access to the foreshore. Concerned citizens continue to fight against the huge concrete and glass edifices now swamping the more

organic early dwellings all along the peninsula, but responsibility for this excessive building and the destruction of the environment lies with the individual owners as well as with councils and government planners of urban consolidation.

Harry Ruskin Rowe (1884–1956)
Harry Ruskin Rowe came from a long line of builder-architects and was a founder and president of the Institute of Architects of NSW. He was also the first mayor of Manly, and initiated the planting of the famous beachfront Norfolk Island pines. A.J. Small and Ruskin Rowe moved in the same town-planning circles, and when Small was planning his Avalon subdivision Ruskin Rowe was examining the work of Louis Sullivan and others in America.

Alexander Stewart Jolly (1887–1957)
Few records exist of Alexander Stewart Jolly's Avalon years and some of his major buildings have been demolished, but some truly remarkable works remain, including 'Careel House', 'Loggan Rock' and 'The Gem'

(now 'Hy-Brasil'). It is generally thought that Jolly left the city and arrived in Avalon at the time of the Great Depression towards the end of the 1920s. Here he would team up with Harry Ruskin Rowe.[6]

Walter Burley Griffin (1876–1937) and Marion Mahoney Griffin (1871–1961)
American architect Walter Burley Griffin is best known for his role in designing Canberra, Australia's capital city, and as perhaps the greatest exponent of 'organic architecture'. Greatly influenced by Frank Lloyd Wright's use of site-specific natural materials and by his emphasis on horizontal design, the experienced, successful architect duo of Walter Burleigh Griffin and his wife Marion left Chicago for Canberra in 1914 to continue the mission to build in harmony with the landscape. It would be 1933 before they found their way to Avalon, where they would build 'Burley Griffin Lodge', formerly 'Stella James House'.[7] This lodge stands as one of Burley Griffin's finest surviving examples of a small domestic residence and organic design generally. The preservation of the bushland setting on a sloping site, surrounded by tall stands of eucalypts, reveals the original character of Newport–Avalon district.

Peter Muller (b.1927)
Peter Neil Muller was born and educated in Adelaide, but moved to the northern beaches in the 1950s after returning from a Fulbright travel scholarship at the University of Pennsylvania. Muller developed an alternative to the Modern Movement, the 'organic' conception of architecture using natural materials, valuing craftwork and the regional context in which his buildings were set.[8] Muller built his own house at Whale Beach in 1955, followed by the 'Richardson House' at Palm Beach (1956), a radial design which

featured a fibreglass domed foyer and circular rooms. He visited Bali in 1970 and the experience transformed him. He would later design the Oberoi hotel, then called the Kayu Ayu, in Seminyak, Bali (1974), but his best-known work is perhaps the Amandari Hotel in Bali (1989), which was awarded the title of Best Hotel in the World in 1992 and 1995.[9]

Richard Leplastrier (b.1939)

Living near Pittwater on the northern beaches has had a strong influence on Leplastrier's 'organic architecture'. He makes the distinction that using materials from the site is sustainable building, but he is open to new materials being 'organic' if *"added to and can grow"* the structure. A pivotal moment in his career was his experience working alongside Jørn Oberg Utzon, AC (1918–2008) and other young Australian architects on the Sydney Opera House. Utzon's influence on Leplastrier was similar to that which Louis Sullivan had on the young Frank Lloyd Wright and Walter Burley Griffin, and others in Chicago.[10] Since Leplastrier's early years he has also had a passion for sailing boats, and many of his buildings, which are scattered across Australia's eastern seaboard, have been inspired by the thought of such vessels. In 1999 Leplastrier received Australia's highest architectural accolade, the Royal Australian Institute of Architects Gold Medal. In 2011 he was appointed an Officer of the Order of Australia.

Glenn Murcutt (b.1936)

Pritzker Prize-winning architect Glenn Murcutt was born in London, but grew up in the Morobe District of New Guinea, where he learnt to appreciate simple, primitive architecture. Murcutt's father introduced him to the streamlined modernist architecture of Ludwig Mies van der Rohe and versed him in the philosophies of Henry David Thoreau, who believed that we should live simply and in harmony with nature's laws. He would later be inspired by the architecture of Californians Richard Neutra and Craig Ellwood, and the crisp, uncomplicated work of Scandinavian architect Alvar Aalto. Murcutt's designs quickly took on their own distinctively Australian flavour. He avoids grand structures and showy, extravagant materials. Instead, Murcutt prefers smaller projects that allow him to work alone to design economical buildings that will conserve energy and blend with the environment.[12]

Peter Stutchbury (b.1954)

Peter Stutchbury is regarded as one of the leaders of a new generation of Australian architects, and recognised for his innovative approach to sustainability and design. His projects have been published and acclaimed internationally. Stutchbury has also taught widely, most recently as visiting professor at Tecnológico de Monterrey, Mexico, where he held the Catedra Luis Barragáßn. He is currently a Conjoint Professor at the University of Newcastle, Australia, and one of the distinguished 'masters' with the Architecture Foundation Australia.[8]

FOOTNOTE:
Several builders along the northern beaches should also be given credit for the environmental sensitivity of their creations. Andrew Minter is known both for his creative designs, and also for his ability to integrate recycled materials to help his houses blend with the surrounds.

Polar to this effort, it is interesting that many of the worst examples of concrete monoliths inflicting themselves onto the neighbourhood are holiday houses for those with more money than sensibility. It brings to mind the Sufi saying: *"When a thief sees a saint, all he sees are his pockets."*

"Life is not about maximising everything, it's about giving something back—like light, space, form, serenity, joy. You have to give something back."[13]

Glenn Mercutt, 2002

Right Ken's house. *Photo oggy.*

future planning

the view through the windshield while checking the rear vision mirror

The architecture of the Saltwater People consisted of a simple shelter known as a *gunyah*. Usually made from bark and branches, these shelters were functional and left almost an almost zero footprint. The original fibro holiday shacks along the northern beaches (often called gunyas) were small by necessity, thanks to the post-Depression scarcity of money and building materials. With the post-World War II building boom the houses were kept *"small by intent—less housework meant more leisure, and with the superb beach and climate no one spent much time indoors"*,[1] but the design and choice of building materials were more sympathetic to the natural setting.

As real estate values increased, so too did the demand for enormous, multimillion-dollar, energy-guzzling mansions which dominate the skyline and clutter once pristine headlands. In the preface to his landmark 1952 book *Australia's Home*, Robin Boyd wrote that *"this is the story of a material triumph and an aesthetic calamity."*[2] Council regulations on development and tree preservation on the northern beaches are breached on a daily basis as owners up-scale and developers try and wring as much value as possible out of their block of land. Big is not necessarily better in regard to home building and sustainability. Richard Leplastrier asks: *"How much room do we need to live?"*[3] I am certain that the neighbours are not impressed by those who destroy the integrity of the beaches with their need to dominate the environment by building monuments to both their success and excess.

Another area of concern is the push to commercialise the beaches. Cash-strapped surf life saving clubs such as Avalon, North Palm Beach and Long Reef have plans to enlarge their beachfront clubhouses considerably, allowing room for accommodation and private enterprise such as restaurants. Many Australians see the beach as one place where they can all go for free and are completely opposed to having the integrity of the beaches compromised. This was made clear in Avalon in 1999, when deals were made to make Avalon Beach an ongoing film set with limitations placed on access to the beach and pool. Communities do value the good work of the surf life saving clubs, but definitely draw a line in the sand when the clubs try to impose large-scale developments on beachfront land. Funds need to be made available to clubs from other sources to remove the need to commercialise the foreshore.

With global warming, there will be other concerns facing the northern beaches. Experts predict that rising sea levels will make coastal erosion, tidal inundation and flooding an increasing problem. The northern beaches can claim many of Sydney's absolute waterfront properties, with Collaroy Beach identified as one of

Australia's most at-risk—and most capitalised—coastlines. In August 2010, the State Government released guidelines for coastal management regarding development and coastal erosion. The Coastal Protection and Other Legislation Amendment Bill 2010 allows landowners the right to place sand or sandbags on beaches to reduce the impact of coastal erosion on their homes. It will also have wide-ranging implications for development proposals. It is not just beachfront property owners that will be affected. The guidelines also take lakeside properties and low-lying land surrounding these areas into consideration. Estuaries damaged by man-made intervention will begin to rise up and swamp these developments.

It is estimated that the current (2011) 4.5 million population of Sydney will almost double by 2056, to 7.64 million. The State Government's metropolitan plan released in December 2010 outlines plans for

> "Nature is my manifestation of God. I go to nature every day for inspiration in the day's work. I follow in building the principles which nature has used in its domain."
>
> Frank Lloyd Wright (1867–1959)

770,000 extra homes in Sydney by 2036 to cope with the area's rapidly growing population. For a glimpse into the future, people on the northern beaches only have to look at our neighbours in the eastern beachside suburbs where people-pressure has covered the area in high-density housing. In an attempt to take some of the pressure off the inner city and rapidly growing western suburbs, politicians have decided that land previously set aside as local food bowls will soon be completely covered in housing. As food-growing areas get further away and shipping costs increase, we may well see the development of new architecture, with the roofs of houses becoming gardens for food plants. The monopolisation of supermarkets, future oil shocks and increasing food prices (40 percent rise in 2010) will add to this shift.

The secession of the Pittwater Council from Warringah (an Aboriginal word meaning 'signs of rain') in 1992 to administer what had been the northern part of Warringah Shire was an extraordinary example of people power at work, going against the tide of local council amalgamation by government authorities. Its success has proved that bigger is not always better, and that small can be efficient and sustainable. Its creation reflected the strong community spirit of Pittwater people and their desire to protect the area from over-development and preserve it for future generations.

Unfortunately, the development plans of the council and wishes of residents were overruled in early 2011 by the State Government-appointed Planning Assessment Commission (PAC) who gave the green

"Touch the Earth Lightly"

Aboriginal saying

light to a four-storey, multi-unit development by Meriton at Warriewood. Pittwater Mayor Harvey Rose stated that this decision set *"a precedent for gross overdevelopment in Warriewood."* These decisions were reversed following the change of State Government in March 2011. The axing of the contentious Part 3A of the *Environmental Planning and Assessment Act 1979* and the Affordable Rental Housing policy also put a stop to this backdoor means of developing multi-storey flats in areas of Elanora and Newport where they were otherwise prohibited.

Recent wins here and with the Currawong estate are good signs, but there are still challenges ahead. The recent land release at Warriewood and the next one at Ingleside will add an extra 20,000 people to the local population, increasing by one third the number of people relying on the Warriewood sewage treatment plant. Pittwater MP Rob Stokes believes that *"there should be no further land releases in the area until a proper solution is found"* to this and other infrastructure problems.

the surfing tribe

Ocean commemoration for Andy Irons.
Photo oggy.

"More than anything, I just want to be remembered as someone who passionately loved surfing." Andy Irons, *Surfing* Magazine 2005

Surfing has its genesis in a frightening display of cosmic alchemy. As the sun's rays enter the earth's atmosphere they cause a reaction of breathtaking proportion. Enormous pressure systems are created, generating wind and fierce storms that churn the surface of the sea. Waves mass and merge, eventually forming a pulse of powerful groundswells radiating out across vast oceans. As these swells near landfall they begin to slow, and finally, when the water is shallow enough, individual waves will rise up and their crests pitch forward. It is here that "*the silent swell becomes surf.*"[1]

A new swell announces its arrival with the thunder of surf crashing onto a reef or the final graceful symmetry of sets of waves peeling along a sandy beach or curve in the shoreline. This 'surf zone' is the intersection of ocean and shore where surfers play on a variety of craft, or just with their bodies, in a joyful, sometimes perilous, dance with nature. It is here where the moon plays its role in the formation of the wave with the tides lowering and raising water levels over reefs and sandbars. The wind exerts its force once more to further shape the wave in its final act by fanning it with an offshore breeze or whipping it into whitecaps.

Surfriders innately understand that "*ocean waves are not moving humps of water but invisible pulses of power pulsing* through *water.*"[2] Early quantum physicist Louis de Broglie (1892–1987) theorised that all matter has wavelength, and thus "*all nature is a great wave phenomenon.*" This in part explains the feeling of interconnectedness and vague mysticism shared by surfers. Dale Jones-Evans writes that surfing

"Like as the waves make toward the pebbled shore, So do our minutes hasten to their end." William Shakespeare, *The Sonnets*

represents a powerful notion of freedom, provides an enviable sense of belonging and sits in the psyche as an indigenous spatial condition … Aboriginal people interest them, people whose traditions are most close to the phenomena of the natural world.[3]

Waves can frighten or thrill us, but good surf only happens when it is ready. Going for a surf is not like booking a tennis court or going for a bike ride. Week after week may pass without swell, and when it does come you have to be ready to abandon all else, rescheduling abruptly for an unknown time set by nature. An African friend of mine who had not previously visited the coast much found herself standing on a headland among a group of surfers. She looked from person to person as they quietly gazed out to sea, their faces deep etched with lines from too much sun and set in concentration. Finally she turned to one of the party and asked in her rich African accent: "*What is everyone looking at?*" Men, women and children who ride the waves take part in this ritual, often daily, analyzing the conditions, waiting for the swell, the wind and the tides to cooperate in creating the perfect wave.

A surfer's gaze reflects a life spent observing minute movements across the ocean's surface. Acute and focused, it is orientated out to sea, drawn to the horizon like an iron needle to magnetic north. In the water the gaze intensifies as it scans distant humps of moving water adjusting to the contours of the seabed and land mass formations. The gaze when directed to the land is used as a marker, critically locating the body in space in response to the demands of what lies out to sea.[4]

Surfers ride as individuals, but they share mysteries that bond them into a tribe, complete with invisible kinship and territorial values. Even the death of a respected member of this tribe is ritualised in a unique manner with friends and admirers, sometimes in their hundreds, paddling out to form a circle beyond the waves. By way of honouring the deceased they will join hands, say a few words, perhaps chant and scatter ashes or flowers. This usually takes place at the surfer's favourite beach, but occasionally, such as when Andy Irons died at a young age in 2010, these ceremonies break out around the globe. Irons may well have been a flawed hero, but the surfing community respected his surfing ability and his bravery in taking on terrifying waves.

world champions

The essence of surfing has been defined as 'grace under pressure'. High-performance surfing demands precision, power, speed and style. Dale Jones-Evans describes surfing as *"a creative act practiced at high speed on an unpredictable field."*[1] Contest surfing is regarded as anathema by purists, who regard the real challenge as between man and nature, but whatever your opinion it cannot be denied that Sydney's northern beaches have produced, or given home to, more than its fair share of surfing champions.

Phyllis O'Donnell (b.1937)

It might come as a surprise to some that Australia's first world surfing champion was a woman. Phyllis O'Donnell took out the women's division of the 1964 championships in Manly shortly before Midget Farrelly won the men's division. In winning the title, Phyllis beat the American favourite Linda Benson. Phyllis recalls, *"I used to do a lot of spinners and that was probably what won me the title."*[2] Phyllis grew up in Drummoyne, in Sydney's inner west, but began surfing at Freshwater. She counts Manly surf pioneer Snowy McAlister as a friend and mentor. In 1996, Phyllis was inducted into the Australian Surfing Hall of Fame, only the second woman, after Isabel Letham, to win the honour.

Bernard 'Midget' Farrelly (b.1944)

Nicknamed 'Midget' for his slight build, Farrelly was just 12 years old when he saw California's Greg Noll and others surfing Sydney waves on their Malibu-style boards during a lifeguard-sponsored visit in 1956. This was to be a pivotal moment for the quick, light-footed kid, and by 1961 Midget was the Australian surfing champion. The following year Farrelly travelled to Hawaii and became the first Australian to win a major surfing title, the Makaha International championship. Farrelly's status as a local surf hero was cemented when he won the inaugural World Surfing Championship in 1964, taking the men's crown ahead of such surfers Joey Cabell and Mike Doyle.

Farrelly remained a successful competitor throughout the '60s, and went on to establish a career as a board and blank maker. He also contributed many articles to surfing magazines and published two books—*A Surfing Life* and *How to Surf*—in collaboration with journalist Craig McGregor. Midget remains a great waterman who manages to bridge the divide between surfers and the surf life saving movement. He can occasionally be seen riding a Blake-style 16-foot hollow board, or being 'sweep' on a classic Australian surfboat in the waves near his Palm Beach home.[3] Farrelly was inducted into the Australian Surfing Hall of Fame in 1986.

Nat Young (b.1948)

Robert Young grew up in Collaroy, and the slight 10-year-old surfing on his big balsa-and-redwood log was nicknamed 'the Gnat' by the local clubbies. After a growth spurt that saw him grow into a lanky six-foot-three, the 'G' was dropped from his nickname, creating *"Nat's Nat, and that's that."* As he grew in size his surfing style would become bruisingly powerful.

In the 1966 World Surfing Championships held in San Diego, an 18-year-old Nat Young blew the field apart and helped cement a 'new era' of power surfing. Nat only dabbled in competitive surfing but retained a competitive attitude in his surfing and skiing. In 1974 Nat donated his Surfabout prize money to the Australian Labor Party, and later ran for State parliament on the northern peninsula. Campaigning on the issue of beach pollution, his spirited bid was only narrowly defeated. Nat has also produced a historical surfing film, and books including *The History of Surfing*. Young was inducted into the Australian Surfing Hall of Fame in 1986.

Tom Carroll (b.1961)

Tom Carroll's dominance in Australian surfing began with winning the 1977 Pro Junior in Sydney. After a few setbacks early in his career, Newport's 'pocket rocket' won the 1982 World Cup and followed up in the next season with the first of two back-to-back world titles.

Portrait of Tom Carroll.
Photo Bruce Usher.

As Newcastle's Mark Richards stepped aside, heir apparent Tom Carroll filled the void, becoming the first goofyfoot to earn a professional world title and remaining in the top five in 1982 for the rest of the decade. His precision and power, and ability to perform in small waves and big surf, earned Tom the 1984 Surfer Poll, proving he was a surfers' surfer and the people's choice. Tom was inducted into the Australian Surfing Hall of Fame in 1990.

In 1985 Tom inspired many when he decided to boycott the South African leg of the tour because of his opposition to apartheid. This personal stance contributed to the loss of his title to Tom Curren, but also earned him the respect of the Australian Prime Minister, Bob Hawke. At Tom's 1993 retirement dinner a misty-eyed Hawke declared: *"There is no Australian sporting hero or legend, at whose name I have a greater surge of affection than [that of] Tom Carroll."*[4] Tom earned the most lucrative sponsorship deal of the 1980s when he and manager Peter Colbert negotiated surfing's first million-dollar contract with longtime backer Quiksilver.

Stuart Entwistle (1949–2002)

Stuart Entwistle moved to Manly with his family at age 6, trying kneeboarding and riding shortboards before moving to new-era longboarding. He defeated Australian icon Nat Young at his home break in Manly to win the 1987 World Longboard Champions. Stuart died of skin cancer aged fifty-two.

Tommy and Barton.
   Photo Scott Needham.

Barton Lynch (b.1963)

Barton started out as a scrawny kid from Mosman with big dreams of surfing greatness. First recognised as an unconventional talent for his wild and flexible back-hand surfing, he quickly mastered the contest format. After years of fluctuating fortunes, in 1988 Barton came from behind to snatch the world crown in the last contest of the year, the Billabong Pro at Pipeline, Hawaii. He achieved nine straight years in the top ten, and thirteen years in the top sixteen. Barton sums up his ability to combine natural talent and tenacity with an analytical, technical approach with the statement that *"pure ability will only take you so far, then your head has to take you the rest of the way."*[5]

The 'thinking man's surfer' Barton has been a strong advocate for the rights of professional surfers, and served ten years on the ASP board. Always capable of expressing a view outside the narrow confines of surf world orthodoxy, Barton is regarded as one of the sport's wittiest and most articulate figures. He is Patron of the Disabled Surfers Association (DSA) and organised the surfers' protest against French nuclear testing in the South Pacific. Barton was inducted into the Australian Surfing Hall of Fame in 1998, and into the Australian Sporting Hall of Fame in 2000.

Damien Hardman (b.1966)

Damien Hardman emerged from the talent hotbed of North Narrabeen during the 1970s with his vertical, top-to-bottom surfing, and developed a reputation as a tactician and fierce competitor during the 1980s. By the age of 19 he had won a world junior crown, and in the 1987 Coke Classic used all his 'Iceman' control to beat tour favourites Tom Carroll, Mark Occhilupo and Tom Curren. Hardman picked up a second world title in 1991. Hardman's style was a back-foot-focused vertical turner approach with an impressive back-side attack. He was inducted into the Australian Surfing Hall of Fame in 1999.

Pam Burridge (b.1965)

Originally from the Manly area, Pam Burridge began her professional surfing career at age fifteen. A strong field of female surfers such as Lynne Boyer and Margo Oberg filled the top spots when Burridge started her career, and after many years as the perennial bridesmaid she would become World Champion in 1990 with an emphatic win at Sunset Beach. Burridge quit the tour in 1998, and now spends her time raising her family, running surf schools and enjoying the waves near her home on the south coast of New South Wales. Burridge was inducted into the Australian Surfing Hall of Fame in 1997.

Layne Beachley.
Photo Scott Needham.

Layne Beachley (b.1972)

Layne Beachley was adopted as a baby by Neil and Valerie Beachley, who gave her a home in Manly. At the age of 16 Beachley began her career as a professional surfer, and by 20 she was ranked sixth in the world. Beachley became the Women's ASP World Champion in 1998, and won the title again in 1999, 2000, 2001, 2002, 2003 and 2006. Beachley is the first woman in the history of the sport to gain seven World Championships, six of them consecutive. Her competitiveness and courage would also drive her in her quest to ride the biggest waves ever caught by a woman.

Media savvy and entertaining, Beachley is popular with the media for her insight and quick wit. For several years she was the sole female board member of the ASP, pro surfing's governing body, where her commitment to the betterment of women's surfing has also been felt.[6] Among her many awards Beachley was inducted into the US and Australian Surfing Hall of Fame in 2006, and announced her retirement from full-time professional surfing at the conclusion of the 2008 ASP Women's World Tour.

Chelsea Georgenson Hedges (b.1983)

Chelsea Georgenson (now Hedges) morphed from being a *"gifted grom who caught the eye of four-time world champion Lisa Andersen while she was scratching into shorebeaks at Avalon to becoming a surfing superstar."* In 2005 she won the world title after beating Brazil's Jacqueline Silva in the final at the season-ending event in Hawaii. 'Chels' displays an easygoing grace and carefree attitude in life, but there's nothing laid back about the focus, drive and talent she exudes in the lineup and competition.[7] Georgenson was recognised as Surfer of the Year in the 2005 Australian Surfing Hall of Fame awards.

Ben Player (b.1978)

Avalon-based bodyboarder Ben Player was world champion in 2005, 2007 and 2013. In the 2006 Pipeline final he placed second and has finished number two overall on the world bodyboarding tour several times. Player and his brother Toby honed their skills riding Little Avalon. Player now also helps run *Movement*, the specialist bodyboard magazine.

"You must live in the present, launch yourself on every wave, find your eternity in each moment."

Henry David Thoreau (1817–1862)

honorary residents

Kelly Slater (b.1972)

Having claimed his eleventh world surfing championship in 2011, the boy from Cocoa Beach, Florida, has broken every single record in professional surfing history. Forests of text and photographs have been printed recording his remarkable career. Perhaps less known is that Slater lived in Avalon for a while during the 1990s and entertained guests such as Pamela Anderson, Eddie Vedder and Chris Isaac in his apartment overlooking the beach. His surfing at L.A. is featured in many early surf movies, like *110/240*, *Momentum* and *Kelly in Colour*.

Lisa Anderson (b.1969)

Like her friend Kelly Slater, Florida-born four-time world champion Lisa Anderson spent large amounts of time in Avalon during her years as a professional surfer. Her presence proved inspirational for up-and-coming surfers like Avalon's Chelsea Georgenson, who later went on to a world title of her own. Anderson began her reign as the new surfing queen when she won her first World Championship Tour title in 1994. During her four years of domination on the circuit, Anderson earned respect and changed many things in the world of surfing and women's sports in general.

Martin Potter (b.1965)

South African-born surfer Martin Potter, known as 'Pottz', was drawn to the northern beaches during the 1990s. A performance pacesetter of the 1980s and 1990s, he won the ASP World Title in 1989. He linked futuristic aerial manoeuvres with an impressive repertoire of powerful carving arcs. Once labelled the *"world's most exciting free surfer"*, Pottz *"genuinely loved the northern beaches lifestyle and the numerous high energy and testing surf spots as well."*[8]

Wendy Botha (b.1965)

Wendy Botha was born in East London, South Africa, and began surfing at the age of thirteen. She won four consecutive South African National Championship titles, from 1981 to 1984, and after turning pro went on to claim four world championships, in 1987, 1989, 1991 and 1992. Botha became an Australian citizen in 1989, making Newport her home, to keep surfing without sanctions. Botha retired in 1993 and moved to New Zealand.[9]

Above Martin Potter, Whale Beach.
Photo Sean Davey.

surfers' surfers

Bob Pike.
Photo Jack Eden.

For every surfer who has forged respect and recognition in the field of contest, there are many other extraordinary surfers from the northern beaches who are respected by their peers, either for their athleticism, their natural ability or just through the sheer force or fun of their characters. Many have sacrificed other parts of their lives to make themselves available to the whims and vagaries of the ocean. Some have benefited from the commercialisation of the sport while others see that development as anathema to its inherent purity. This latter group can be recognised through the lack of logos on their surfwear and boards.

Whether they ride shortboards, longboards or bodyboards, or just slip out to shoot a few body waves, the northern beaches are rich in surfing heroes and legends. Not every surfer of interest can be listed here, but these few profiles and short roll call acknowledge some known, and some lesser known, contributors to the sport.

Roll call: A.W. Relph, W.G. Gotcher, Bill Walker, Frank Bell, Mick Dooley, Pearl Turton, Dorothy de Rooy, Tanya Binning, Will Evans, 'Tank' Henry, Neil Purchase, Mick McMahon, Robert Coneerly, Butch Cooney, John Dessaix, Peter Cornish, Kevin Platt, Dave McDonald, Bob Boot, Robbie Lane, Danielle Dubois, Lynne Holmes, Jonty Evans, Sheree de Costa, Nick Carroll, Rob Bain, Larry Blair, Greg Reilly, Col Brooker, Ian Bolland, Richard Harvey, Richard Cram, Richard Bailey, Tiny Thompson, Cloudy Rhodes and Laura Enever.

Freddie Williams (c.1875–1940)

Freddie Williams learnt to 'surf-shoot' by watching Tommy Tanna at Manly in the 1880s. Although a shy man, Williams soon progressed to being the most admired bodysurfer in Sydney. His *"quick sparing motion, perfected in the endless hours of practice"* was an austere *"streamlined motion of over with one arm, side stroke with the other, a single trudgen kick."*[1] After years of riding the waves he retreated to *"the isolation of a little green-painted humpy at the base of Dobroyd Point"*,[2] where he died just before the outbreak of World War II.

Isabel Letham (1899–1995)

Isabel Letham was in the right place at the right time when Duke Kahanamoku called for someone to help demonstrate tandem surfing at his historic exhibition of surfing at Freshwater Beach in 1915. Plucked from obscurity at age 16, it was to be the beginning of Letham's long involvement with the ocean up until her death in 1995. Isabel was inducted into the Australian Surfing Hall of Fame in 1993.

Background Butch Cooney,
Newcastle Championship, 1965.
Photo Jack Eden.

Charles Justin 'Snowy' McAlister (1904–1988)

At age 11, Snowy McAlister witnessed Duke Kahanamoku's demonstration of surfing in 1915, and, as with Isabel Letham, it would prove to be a defining moment in his life. Snowy used to ride in what were then called Board Display contests, and was the winner of the surfboard division of the Australian surf life saving championships from 1925 to 1928. He sealed his first national title in Newcastle by performing a headstand all the way to the beach. He stopped competing during the war years, but made a comeback at the 1956 Olympic Carnival in Torquay, Victoria. He was still on his surf ski catching waves at Manly's Fairy Bower well into his seventies. McAlister was inducted into the Australian Surfing Hall of Fame in 1985.

Above Isabel Letham.
Courtesy Warringah Library.

Robert Hughes (Bob) Pike (1940–1999)

Bob Pike grew up one street back from the Manly Surf Club and began riding waves in 1955. The following year Pike witnessed the Californian lifeguards Greg Noll and Tom Zahn when they came to Australia to demonstrate the first lightweight Malibu-style boards, and the 16-year-old managed to acquire Zahn's surfboard. In 1961 he travelled to the North Shore of Oahu, Hawaii, and rode with the legends—Hawaii's Jose Angel and Buzzy Trent, and California's Pat Curren, Rick Grigg and Greg Noll—pioneering big wave riding. Surfing the monster waves of Sunset Beach and Waimea Bay back in the early 1960s was a lonely, white-knuckled experience with frequent long swims and little in the way of rescue support.

Pike thrived in these wild conditions, riding immense waves on a surfboard made by Curren and dubbed 'the ultimate gun'. He stayed on in Oahu and in 1962 joined the Americans on a trip to Peru, where he won the waveriding division of the Peruvian International Surf Championships—the first international surfing win by an Australian. Back in Australia by early 1965, Pike avoided the emerging surf industry by working as a fireman, surfing North Narrabeen in his spare time. He remained fit and strong well into his fifties, but was later injured in an accident. Bob Pike died by his own hand in 1999.[3]

Bobby Mills (?-1992)

Manly identity Bobby Mills was *"an absolute loose cannon."* *"No matter how big the surf was, he'd paddle out … and he had to catch the biggest wave of the day, whether it was closing out or not. He just had to take it."* Bobby took his own life at North Head in 1992.[4]

Col Smith (b.1948)

Born in Sydney, Col Smith was a leader of the Narrabeen power school of surfing in the 1970s and became Australian Champion in 1977, but was perhaps too advanced for the contest judges of his time. He is widely credited with pioneering vertical back-hand surfing, and respected surfers such as Simon Anderson and Damien Hardman cite Smith as a strong influence.

Col Smith, North Narrabeen.
Photo Hugh McLeod.

Terry Fitzgerald (b.1950)

Terry Fitzgerald emerged from the Narrabeen push in the 1960s and was there at the start of surfing's true pro era in the 1970s. Footage from the pivotal surf movie *Morning of the Earth* shows him on his first trip to Hawaii surfing Rocky Point and Sunset with incredible speed and flair. Fitzgerald's competitive surfing hit a peak in 1975, and if there had been a World Tour that year he may have been professional surfing's first world champion. Nicknamed 'The Sultan of Speed', Fitzgerald's involvement in surfing went far beyond competition. He was a founding member of Australia's original pro surfing organisation, the Australian Professional Surfers Association, and became one of the first big-name surfers to explore Indonesia. Fitzgerald was inducted into the Australian Surfing Hall of Fame in 1995.

David 'Baddy' Treloar (b.1951)

Known as 'Baddy' since he was a grommet, big, bad and brawny Treloar grew up in Manly and did well in the Australian National Titles in the late sixties, usually finishing second behind Lorne super-surfer Wayne Lynch. Treloar moved to Angourie in 1971 and featured in Albe Falzon's seminal surf film *Morning of the Earth*. He remains one of the best surfers at Angourie, living a simple but full life fishing and surfing.

Grant 'Dappa' Oliver (1952–1994)

Born in Sydney, Dappa was one of the leaders of Narrabeen push in the late 1960s and early 1970s. He was at the forefront of the shortboard revolution and pioneered new moves inside the pitching lip of the wave.

Mark Warren (b.1952)

Born in Gundagai in country New South Wales, Mark Warren moved to Sydney and became Australian schoolboy champion in 1972. He went on to win the 1976 Smirnoff Pro at Sunset and the Duke Kahanamoku Trophy in 1980. Along with Ian Cairns and Peter Townshend, he was a founding member of the Bronzed Aussies—the world's first sponsored surf team. Dubbed 'Mr Teflon' for his clean image and smoothness, Mark was inducted into the Australian Surfing Hall of Fame in 2008. He is also active in the media, and published the *Atlas of Australian Surfing* in 1988, for which he won the Surf Culture Award.

Simon Anderson (b.1954)

Simon Anderson is considered to be one of the most influential surfers in the world who never won a world title. Born in Manly and growing up in a house overlooking Collaroy Beach, the beach where Nat Young had learned to ride, Anderson became part of the North Narrabeen power surfing push of the 1970s. He went on to win several pro events, but it was his 1980 three-finned 'Thruster' concept that revolutionised surfboard design to such an extent that within a year 95 percent of all surfboards were Thrusters. (See 'Brookvale—the genesis of the surfboard industry', page 129.)

Inspired by Col Smith's vertical North Narrabeen surfing, Anderson was a surprise winner of the Australian Junior title at Bells Beach in 1972. During a three-week burst in 1977 he won the Bells Easter event and Sydney's Coke Surfabout back to back, putting him into the top ten and world title contention. In 1980,

after developing the Thruster, Anderson won the Bells-Coke double again and, to prove this was no fluke, later that same year won the most prestigious event in professional surfing: the Offshore Pipeline Masters in Hawaii. Simon was inducted into the Australian Surfing Hall of Fame in 1989.

Bruce Raymond (b.1954)

Bruce Raymond grew up on the beaches from Bondi to Bronte, but surfed on the northern beaches as much as possible. Since those early days he has travelled the globe, first as a professional surfer in the 1970s and later as an executive for Quiksilver. He also did some stunt surfing for the Hollywood blockbuster *Big Wednesday* and starred in Harry Hodge's film *Band on the Run*. Even after sampling the beaches of Europe, California, Hawaii and Victoria, Bruce never forgot the beauty of our northern beaches, and the Raymond mob came home to the peninsula.

Simon Anderson.
Photo Steve Baccon.

Shane Herring sequence.
Photos Justin Crawford.

Derek Hynd (b.1957)

Hynd's family moved to Newport in 1966 and Hynd soon began surfing. Joining the world pro tour in 1979, by the following year he was rated twelfth in the world before being blinded in his right eye during competition. Hynd proved his tenacity by finishing the 1981 season with a highly respected 7th place world ranking. Derek Hynd is not just a stylish surfer, he is also a very articulate and intellectual writer with an Economics/History degree. As the former head of marketing at Rip Curl, Hynd implemented 'The Search', allowing him to travel the world with Tom Curren and other pro surfers. When not in Jeffreys Bay, Chile or some other far-flung destination, Hynd can be seen anywhere on the northern beaches when the waves are good, surfing his distinctive no-fins style of board riding.

Shane Herring

"When the young, freckly, Dee Why natural footer defeated the all-conquering Kelly Slater in the final of the Coke Classic at Narrabeen in 1992, a veritable media stampede proclaimed him our great, red-haired hope to take on the American wonderchild."[5] Herro was quickly dubbed by the surf media as *"our newest star."* Somehow, in the subsequent years his career prospects were harpooned by equally well-publicised overindulgence and personal turmoil. Herro shirks none of the blame for his own undoing. *"I'm from Dee Why and we're pretty much mongrels down there,"* he says, while warning kids to *"Watch your drinking and watch your intake of substances and stuff because it can wear you down and you'll end up losing what you've got, and you won't even know you've lost it until you get older."*[6]

northside
surf media

THE
SURFING
WORLD
MONTHLY

PRICE
3/6

THE AUSTRALIAN SURFING MAGAZINE

SEPTEMBER
1962
Vol. 1. No. 1.

surfing magazines

The first known publication oriented towards surfers, *The Surf*, was produced by Manly's surf club in Australia in 1917. In all, twenty issues of *The Surf* were published, every Saturday from 1 December 1917 until 13 April 1918. This paper ran a cover beachgirl, and weekly columns such as 'Surf Shooters and Sirens' covered all aspects of beach life including board riding around Manly. Its masthead objective boldly read: "*The Development and Protection of our Beaches.*"

In 1961, Lee Cross published *The Australian Surfer*, but it only lasted two issues. Bob Evans released *Australia's Surfing World* early the following year and the magazine is still in production today. Jack Eden's *Surfabout Australasian Surfer* (based on Sydney's south side) also came out in August 1962 and was soon followed by a tsunami of fledgling surfing magazines such as *Surf Scene*, *Surf International* and *Tracks*. It must be remembered that before the 1960s there was very little in the way of youth magazines, and surf magazines became immensely popular.

Bob Evans (1928–1976)

Manly surfer turned surf-photographer, promoter, magazine editor and publisher, filmmaker and contest director, Bob Evans was a mentor to many in the fledgling Australian surf media. He also helped the surfing careers of many surfers, especially Midget Farrelly, Nat Young and Peter Drouyn, who would make substantial contributions to the surf media through articles and books.

The Australian surf media grew on the back of Bob Evans, dubbed 'Mr Surf' by the local press. In 1961, he organised the first Australian push to Hawaii, taking Dave Jackman and Bob Pike. The following year he released his first full-length movie, *Surf Trek to Hawaii*, and went on to produce twelve full-length surf movies. In 1962, Evans also launched *Australia's Surfing World*, which has since become one of the world's most enduring surf magazines. In 1963, Evans formed the Australian Surfriders Foundation and initiated the Australian National Titles and, perhaps his major triumph, the first World Surfing Championships, hosted in Manly the following year. He was inducted into the Australian Surfing Hall of Fame in 1987.

John Witzig (b.1944)

Photographer and journalist John Witzig had his first piece of surf journalism published in 1963 for *Surfing World*, and later worked full time for the magazine. In 1966, he produced the pivotal 'New Era' issue that documented for the first time the rapid changes in performance and equipment taking place in surfing and being led by the Australians. Following Nat Young's win at the World Championships in San Diego in 1967, he wrote 'We're Tops Now' for the American publication *Surfer*, an article later described by Nick Carroll as "*splendidly inflammatory.*" Witzig went on to edit *Surf International*, considered by Drew Kampion in his history of surf culture, *Stoked*, to be "*one of the most artistic and innovative publications to ever come out in the field.*"[1]

Witzig co-founded *Tracks* in 1970 with Albe Falzon and David Elfick. Interviewed in Cyrus Sutton's film *Under the Sun*, Steve Pezman, editor of *The Surfer's Journal*, described *Tracks* as "*an Australian take on a surfing magazine that was completely fresh, journalistically sophisticated and maybe the hippest youth culture magazine being published in the world at that time.*"[2] Another view, also expressed by Drew Kampion in *Stoked*, was that *Tracks* "*broke barriers into new territory—the brutally frank world of tabloid 'surf journalism'*",[3] and some criticised it for being reckless in the way it appeared to promote drug use. Frank Pithers, Tony Edwards, Phil Jarratt, Richard Bailey, Kirk Willcox and Nick Carroll represent just some of the other talent that emerged from this magazine in its early years. Witzig founded the short-lived *Sea Notes* in 1977, and has published several books on Australian photography, including his own 1960s and '70s surf photography in 2008.

Left   First *Surfing World* magazine cover, 1962.
    Courtesy Surfing World.
Right   *The Surf*, 1917.
    Courtesy Mitchell Library, State Library of NSW.
Background   *Photo oggy.*

Phil Jarratt (b.1951)

Phil Jarratt was an editor during the golden years of *Tracks* magazine in its early days based at Whale Beach, and is one of the world's best-known surf writers. Jarratt is the former editor of the *Australian Surfer's Journal*, and contributing editor to the *Surfer's Journal, Surfer, Surfing* and *Pacific Longboarder*. He is also the author of several surfing bestsellers, including *Kelly Slater: For the Love* (2008), *The Mountain and the Wave: the Quiksilver Story* (2006), *Mr Sunset* (1997) and *Salts and Suits* (2010). Scriptwriting credits include *Bustin' Down The Door* and *Going Vertical*. His work was recognised with the 2007 Australian Surfing Hall of Fame Media Award. Jarratt now lives with his family in Noosa Heads.

Hugh McLeod (b.1951)

Hugh McLeod had been contributing to *Surfing World* magazine as a graphic designer since the early 1970s. By necessity, he evolved into photographer (a.k.a. 'Aitionn'), writer and co-editor in 1974, and joined forces with Bruce Channon to buy the title in 1978. Over the next three decades this talented Mona Vale-based duo combined their skills as designers and photographers to turn Australian *Surfing World* into one of the world's most creative and successful surfing magazines. Channon and McLeod sold *Surfing World* in 1997, and the magazine is currently partially owned by Coastalwatch (based in Avalon). McLeod continues his writing and photography, and his iconic portraits have been published worldwide, notably for *Pacific Longboarding* and *Surfing World*.

Bruce Channon.
Photo Hugh McLeod.

Bruce Channon (b.1950)

Bruce Channon was already a top surfer, industry craftsman and cinematographer before he joined Hugh McLeod at *Surfing World*. Channon learnt to shoot film from the Sheppard Brothers and Bruce Usher when they were making their film, *A Winter's Tale*, and worked on other surf films including *Drouyn* with Bob Evans. Channon's photographic legacy from his magazine work will no doubt point to his unique short telephoto water shots. He is currently the editor of *Australian Longboarding* magazine and runs the website surfinfo.com.au. Channon and McLeod were recognised with the Surf Culture Award in the 1985 and 1998 Australian Surfing Hall of Fame awards.

Peter Crawford (1952–1999)

Like many others, Dee Why surfer Peter Crawford began his career in the surf media at *Surfing World* magazine. He became a masthead photographer for *Surfer* from 1977 to 1994 and co-founded *Waves* magazine in 1980 while remaining a regular contributor to virtually all Australian surf magazines. His work was recognised posthumously with the Media Award in the 2001 Australian Surfing Hall of Fame.

Nick Carroll (b.1959)

Nick Carroll, the elder of Newport's famous Carroll brothers, had his first article on surfing published in *People* magazine in 1975—an interview with 'Mr Pipeline' Gerry Lopez. After a stint as a professional surfer, Nick got a job at *Tracks* in 1981 and would eventually become editor of both *Tracks* and *Surfing*. He later became the editor of *Deep*, and has authored several books including *Fear-Less-Ness: The Story of Lisa Anderson, Visions of Amazing Waves, Complete Guide to Surfing* and *An Endless Wave*. Nick also wrote for the TV documentary series *Bombora*.

surf photographers

In the 1940s and 1950s, the era before surf magazines, several commercial photographers began to photograph the surf scene on the northern beaches. Ray Leighton in Manly, and Robin Cale and Max Dupain in Newport, were the standouts. With the increased popularity of the sport and the arrival of surf magazines in the following decade, some photographers began to specialise in surf imagery.

In the 1960s it was difficult to make a living from surf photography, but northside photographers such as John Pennings, John Witzig and Bruce Usher recorded some memorable surfing imagery from that era. The first wave of professional surf photographers started to appear in the 1970s and 1980s, and included Albe Falzon, Frank Pithers, Hugh McLeod, Bruce Channon, Peter Crawford, Laurie McGinness, Guy Findlay and Phil McAusland. In the modern age there are new outlets for surf imagery with online magazines and blogs. Local photographers such as Nathan Smith, Alex Marks, Mark Onorati, Justin Crawford, Jules Phillips, Ian Bird, and Mandy Zieren represent some of the current generation of talented local surf photographers.

Left Peter Crawford.
Courtesy of the Crawford family.

Above Ray Leighton.
Courtesy Betty Leighton.

EVOLUTION

surf filmmakers

Pioneer surf filmmaker Bob Evans inspired later generations of northern beaches filmmakers including Albe Falzon, David Sumpter, Paul Witzig and David Elfick.

Paul Witzig (b.1940)

Paul Witzig, brother of John, began film work with Bruce Brown in Australia 1963 and contributed Australian footage to *The Endless Summer*. His first feature, *A Day in the Life*, was re-edited for *Hot Generation*, and between 1966 and 1970 he made several more high-performance surf films, including *Evolution*, *Sea of Joy* and *Rolling Home*.

Albe Falzon (b.1945)

Albert Falzon's career in filmmaking was a natural progression from his still photography and magazine publishing. His inaugural feature film *Morning of the Earth* (1972) was hugely successful, and it was also

the first Australian film to receive a gold record for album sales. The 'lefts' at the beginning of the film with Nat, Michael Petersen, Kim 'The Fly' Bradley and Mark Warren were filmed at the Wedge at Whale Beach. *Crystal Voyager,* his entry in the Cannes Film Festival, featured music from Pink Floyd, Talking Heads and Brian Eno, and would hold box-office records for decades. Falzon's travel lust, particularly to remote and spectacular regions of the world, excited the

imaginations of many young Australians. He now calls the north coast of New South Wales home.

David Elfick (b.1944)

David Elfick is a noted Australian film and television writer, director and producer. One of the co-founders of *Tracks* magazine, Elfick began his film career as the producer of the 1971 surf movie *Morning of the Earth*, directed by Albe Falzon. In 1973 Elfick collaborated with surfer, writer and cinematographer George Greenough as producer-director of *Crystal Voyager*, which became one of the most successful Australian surf movies ever made. Elfick later formed an association with writer-director Phillip Noyce, with whom he has collaborated on films including *Newsfront* (1978) and *Rabbit-Proof Fence* (2002).

Above Evolution poster.
Courtesy Mick Mock.

Left Deeper Shade of Blue Poster.
Courtesy Jack McCoy.

(1974), as well as several short films. Usher was first published in *Surfing World* in early 1964 and continues to contribute to this magazine. He has also consistently written features for the *Australian Longboarding* magazine.

Tim Bonython (b.1958)

Big Bells Beach 1981 provided some memorable waves for Bonython's first gig as a filmmaker, which he screened in pubs and clubs up and down the east coast. After leaving Adelaide, Tim and his family made Avalon their home. His early videos include *Surfing into Summer—Filthy Habits*, *Water Slaughter* and *Strike Force* created with Guy Finlay, the *Gorilla Grip* video series with Bill McCausland and Jason Muir, *Biggest Wednesday* (1998) and *Blackwater—The Story of a Place Called Teahupo'o*. Tim's feature documentary *Immersion* was released in 2012. He has worked on many pro events in G-Land, Fiji, Japan, France and California.

Andrew Kidman (b.1970)

Hailing from the northern beaches, surfer and artist Andrew Kidman works in many mediums, including music, writing, painting, photography, surfboard shaping and films. His work is born from his connection to the ocean, and his patience and dedication is remarkably rare in the modern-day commercial arena. The surfing film and book, *Into the Ether,* was released in 2010.

Avalon beachfront office. McCoy is regarded as one of the best and most innovative water cameramen on the planet, and his work was recognised with the Media Award in the 2000 Australian Surfing Hall of Fame.

David Sumpter (b.1943)

David Sumpter (a.k.a. 'the Mex') started his career as a surf-filmmaker in 1974 with *On Any Morning*. This film is etched into surfing history not only for its shoestring budget, but for its ability to capture the early 1970s' surf stoke. Today, the Mex has teamed up with Dick Hoole and lives on the north coast of New South Wales.

Bruce Usher (b.1946) and the Sheppard Brothers

Photographer Bruce Usher grew up next to Mona Vale Beach, while the Sheppard Brothers (Phil and Russell) have lived there since the 1960s. They joined forces to make *Our Day in the Sun* (1972) and *A Winter's Tale*

Jack McCoy (b.1948)

Hawaiian-born Jack McCoy came down to Australia for the 1970 world contest at Bells Beach and stayed. He teamed up with Byron Bay-based Dick Hoole to make surf-film classics such as *Tubular Swells* (1976) and *Storm Riders* (1982). After going solo he has gone on to make over twenty surf films including *Bunyip Dreaming* (1990), *Occy the Documentary* (1998), *TO'* and *Blue Horizon.* Jack's latest film, *A Deeper Shade of Blue* (2011), was a four-year project co-ordinated and edited from his

Above Albe Falzon.

Above David Elphick.

tracks
in 1970

Above First *Tracks* cover, October 1971.
Top *Tracks* Whale Beach office.

The thing that no one who's reading *Tracks* in 2010 can truly understand, is just HOW different the world was 40 years ago. We had a conservative government that'd been in power for 23 years—most of our entire lives. We had a prime minister (Billy McMahon) who was ridiculous. We felt it our duty to point this out, and it wasn't just us. The '60s had *really* only arrived in Australia at around 1970, so there were a lot of people searching for an opportunity to tell authority in its many forms to stick it. Our adolescent and rebellious editorial attitude touched a rich vein in some readers and seriously offended others. We were equally delighted by both.

It did no harm that surfers were intuitively anti-authoritarian, and our (both surfers' and *Tracks*') reputations were (in part anyway) pretty appalling. Years later when he was editor, Phil Jarratt invented a group—Fathers Unite against the

Corruption of Kids (FUCK for short)—to picket the Tracks post office box in Avalon. I wish that we'd thought of that.

We (that was Albe and I) did the layout of the first issue at a ratty old house that I was living in next door to the shop at Whale Beach on Sydney's northern beaches. We started one day and just worked through until we finished on the next. That set a pattern of all-night layout sessions. These were pre-computer days when typesetting was done by typesetters and we'd have endless columns of words that we'd stick down (mostly in the right order) onto cardboard layout sheets. We'd draw boxes where the pictures were to go. David was working for a pop music magazine called *Go Set* and on that first issue he bought down a copy of the latest (first?) Crosby Stills Nash and Young album and we played it all night. Later we migrated up the hill to an 'office' under the house where Albe was living.

There were crowds at the best breaks on the best days, but without the aggression in the water. There were uncrowded waves at maybe most of the country's great surf spots. Hopping into a panel van or a kombi to travel the coast to find them was a realistic dream. By the end of 1970, Albe and I were alternating issues—he was using the free time to

make *Morning of the Earth* (*MOTE*), and I was mostly playing and partly studying. I went to the south-west coast of WA twice in those first two years and they were wonderful surf trips—and all for 'work'.

Like any magazine, we were dealing in dreams. Many of the things that we portrayed were not quite as accessible to the average surfer as we might've suggested. But they were attainable. Tracks ran stills from *MOTE* of the first known (at the time anyway) surfing of Uluwatu in Bali. Albe had a superb talent for the romantic—who can forget the silhouetted figures of Rusty Miller and an elfin Steven Cooney preparing to jump into those unknown waves. It was an invitation to join them.

With no training at all in anything, David, Albe and I created what Tracks became. We were not without some experience, but with no training we did everything—writing, taking pictures, selling the advertising and coming up with the ideas for it, and doing the layout. I enjoyed the turn-about responsibilities with Albe, and finally I left when he and David wanted me to do it full-time. Faced with the success of *MOTE*, they wanted to concentrate on movies.

John Witzig

Edited version of article in *Tracks* 40th Anniversary issue in 2010

courtesy in the surf

Surfing is very much an individual experience, but the shared love of the ocean and the thrill of riding waves binds surfers together as a loose tribe. The surfing industry promoted the surfing dream so efficiently that surfing has become mainstream, with the tribe wearing the same uniform and treating wave riding as if it were one great contest. Glen Henning writes that *"for whatever reason—ego, low self-esteem, selfishness or professional greed—it becomes all too easy for surfers to ruin our heaven on earth."*[1]

Population pressure is having an impact in the surf with more people to share the waves. Older surfers are being edged out of the water by a growing aggressiveness. It becomes increasingly difficult to just go out and have some fun. Even the design of modern surfboards with unnecessarily dangerous pointed tips is more about an aggro aesthetic than function.

Skills and equipment have developed to such an extent that surf breaks once considered too dangerous are now ridden by a growing band of extreme surfers, and even these breaks are protected with fierce territorialism. With surfboards remaining relatively inexpensive for a cashed-up society, breaking a board is not the financial burden it once was.

Surf Rage, the book edited by Nat Young back in 2000, was in response to the increased quantity and frequency of wave rage events. Nat himself was involved in a well-publicised and particularly vicious attack on the northern New South Wales coast. Derek Reilly writes: *"Alpha males dominate surf spots and locals are, and always have been, mostly reactionary hillbillies. And the rules of surfing are complex and fluid."*[2] Put another way, the rules that govern Australian lineups are extremely flexible … if you're a local. That maxim didn't seem to apply to Hawaiian pro surfer Sunny Garcia who was witnessed allegedly ganging up with ASP World Title contender Jeremy Flores from France to bash a local surfer on the Gold Coast in February 2011. This behaviour is no longer tolerated in other sports, but the ASP seems reluctant to seriously discipline the pro surfers who use violence.

It is worth noting that the size of the surfing population of a country does not always reflect the attitude of the surfers that live there. The machismo culture of Brazil means, for example, that although it has a relatively small number of surfers compared to Australia, it has a reputation for having the most aggressive wave riders, particularly when travelling. Unfortunately, the commercialisation of the sport is realising substantial annual growth in people taking to the waves, so the problem of wave sharing is set to increase. Groms (very young surfers) will always be groms and express an element of disrespect for those who don't conform to their spoon fed vision of the way things should be. I recently had a 13-year-old yell out to me in the surf, *"Get air granddad!"* … but then he may have actually said *"Get hair"*, because this grandfather's hearing isn't as good as it once was.

In his later years, Duke Kahanamoku noticed a breakdown in surf etiquette due to increasing crowds. He told *Surfer* magazine in 1965:

I think we have to teach a lot of these kids to first be gentlemen … Try to help each other and not hog the doggone waves. You know, there are so many waves coming in all the time, you don't have to worry about that. Just take your time—wave comes. Let the other guys go, catch another one. And that's what we used to do. We'd see some other fella there first, and we'd say, "You're here first, you take the first wave."

"The best surfer in the water is the one having the most fun." Phil Edwards

global impact

problems and solutions

The Saltwater People represent the embodiment of resource management and sustainability for long-term survival. There was great respect for mother earth, and lore was determined by the seven seasons. Their progression in life is seen as a *"journey through the seven seasons or stages."*[1] The natural laws of water determined the land, consequently shaping the lore of the Saltwater People. Fresh water was respected as indispensable to life and responsible for the very existence of life on earth. Food sources, including ocean and estuary marine life, were cared for and allowed to regenerate.

Misconceptions of how the Aborigines used land and water resources meant that the English settlers were ignorant to the consequences of their occupation and oblivious to the devastating impact on Aboriginal culture. Professor Dennis Foley believes that the Saltwater People and

> most of the eastern seaboard clans that we are related to, are not hunter gatherers in the nomadic sense or in the accepted connotations of what constitutes a hunter-gatherer. We practised land use, horticultural and animal management, in addition to aquaculture. This we practised for thousands of years before these forms of land and sea management evolved on the European continent.[2]

Photo oggy.

The main environmental issue in the modern world is sustainability. Modern economics rely on continual growth and this in itself is not sustainable. Environmental damage is caused by three main driving forces: population, consumption and technological impact. Population growth is particularly problematic in Australia, which currently has one of the highest rates of growth and the highest per capita greenhouse gas emissions in the developed world. Unless population numbers are stabilised, issues such as climate change, the supply of food and fresh water, biodiversity protection and supply of infrastructure will become increasingly difficult to address. The reliance of the food industry on shipping and fossil fuels will see ever-increasing food prices and shortages.

There was never an accurate census made of the Saltwater People's population on the northern beaches around the time of European contact, but it is conservatively estimated to be somewhere of the area of 2,000–3,000. This was an environmentally stable number for the resources and left a small footprint. Population pressure was immediately apparent when

Above Dee Why steps.
Photo Ian Bird.

the First Fleet disgorged over a thousand interlopers into Eora territory, and the effect on the local ecosystem was traumatic within a few years of settlement.

Every saltwater person would be given a totem name, taken from nature, that became part of their identity. It also brought a responsibility to protect that totem, whether it be a bird, fish, insect or object. Anthropologist A.P. Elkin describes totemism as a relationship between a person, or group of people, and a natural species or object.[3] Totems were part of the custodial duties of every saltwater person and sacred to Aboriginal life. The person took the name of the species with which he or she was associated and, according to anthropologists Ronald and Catherine Berndt, shared the same life essence, with this bond going back to a mythical age when the world was forming.[4] Bennelong's totem was the stingray, and so he could not kill or eat this creature. This explains why he declined to eat its flesh when it was offered to him by the Europeans.

Unfortunately, these traditional methods of preserving food supplies have been swamped over the last couple of centuries by wealthy countries protected by powerful navies. These countries have ravaged the resources of less developed, less powerful countries. Humanity seems to be waging a war against nature by poisoning or overexploiting the earth's finite resources. The ocean was once thought of as an inexhaustible resource, but we now know that it is vulnerable. Conservation of the oceans lags alarmingly behind land conservation, and the world's oceans are in trouble. The fate of the oceans will become of the utmost concern this century. Pollution and irresponsible coastal development continue to destroy breeding habitats, while fishing methods such as trawling remain the single biggest threat to the marine environment. If the current unsustainable fishing practices continue it is estimated that there will

be no commercial supplies of wild fish after 2040.[5]

We have done damage to the planet that even our best science cannot fix, but there are organisations and individuals fighting back. William Eugene Smith, an early campaigner, paid a high personal price for his work, but his haunting photographs still stand as a warning against unregulated industry. Using his camera as a weapon, Smith documented the devastating effects of industrial pollution in Minimata, Japan, to bring about awareness and change. In perhaps the most poignant image, a mother cradles her child, Tomoko, while bathing her at her home in Minamata in the early 1970s. Tomoko was born blind, mute and paraplegic, deformed by mercury poisoning after the Chisso Corporation released heavily contaminated effluents into the sea. During Japan's rapid economic growth following World War II, pollution was not taken seriously, and organometallic mercury entered the food chain through fish, causing a tragedy as alarming as that caused by thalidomide. Smith himself wrote: *"The morality that pollution is criminal only after legal conviction is the morality that causes pollution."*[6]

"You are something the whole universe is doing in the same way that a wave is something the whole ocean is doing."

Alan Watts

There are many unsung individuals and community groups all along the northern beaches battling to conserve the lagoons, dunes, wildlife and sea creatures. This work, combined with enlightened regulation, has produced results. In the 1990s water testing showed that the Hawkesbury River was more polluted than India's Ganges, but the situation has now improved. In 2010 Sydney beaches were rated cleaner than they were a decade ago, but that was before deep ocean outfalls began pushing the 'faecal pollution' further out to sea. Only eight of Sydney's beaches were graded *"very good"* and rated as *"almost always suitable for swimming"* by the 2010 Beachwatch program at the Department of Environment, Climate Change and Water. These eight included Whale Beach, Avalon, Bilgola, Bungan, Mona Vale and Shelly Beach, with Whale Beach rated the cleanest.

The natural beauty of the northern beaches is under threat from population growth. For the moment, residents and visitors still hear the call of whipbirds, the crash of the surf and the lapping of the tides. We can still watch sea eagles as they soar above magnificent Pacific Ocean beaches, and peregrine falcons as they scan the last reserves of rainforests, mangroves and drier open woodlands. The first people protected this country for many millennia before the new settlers arrived, and we now need to preserve the area for future generations. If we can suppress our Eurocentric view of Australian history with its smug sense of supremacy and self-importance, we can learn much about sustainability from the original custodians of the land.

"The morality that pollution is criminal only after legal conviction is the morality that causes pollution."

W. Eugene Smith, 1975

the future of surfing

It is in the vested interest of the surf industry to build its market base and encourage consumption. Unfortunately, many of the products offered by this approximately $10 billion per year industry use unsustainable materials or practices. There is no governing body or oversight committee keeping statistics on the global surf economy, and with no reliable figures it is impossible to estimate the full scale of the industry's environmental impact. The encouraging news is that many Australian businesses now conduct regular internal audits of their global carbon footprints and set goals to reduce them. A few visionary companies have made sustainability issues their core concern since the outset.

Commercial surfboard manufacturing in Australia began right here on the northern beaches, but like almost all the manufacturing sector in this country much has changed since those early days. Traditionally, the big companies have had a share in surfboard manufacturing, but this has been the domain of smaller groups of dedicated and hardworking craftsmen. With the advent of computerised shaping machines and cheap offshore manufacturing the dynamic is changing. So too is the way surfers regard their equipment. Today, sponsored pros surfing on the world competition circuit ride boards with minimal layers of fibreglass on thin foam cores. This makes the board lighter but also more fragile, especially in an era of aggressive surfing and aerial maneouvres.

Encouraged by the surfing industry and related media, today's recreational surfers are keen to emulate the pros and ride the same equipment. The standard shortboard has become a disposable item that soon

ends up as waste, and with approximately 8–10 million surfers around the globe it doesn't take much thought to realise how many of the conservatively estimated one million polystyrene and resin boards made each year end up at the tip.

It is also important to note that the resins and foam used to make surfboards are petrochemical derivatives. So too is polychloroprene used in the manufacture of wetsuits. There is not space here to go into the associated environmental issues concerning petroleum acquisition and refinement, but it should be remembered that the huge oil spill in the Gulf of Mexico in 2010 was largely the result of technology being pushed to the limit in the search for fossil fuels. The resins needed for surfboard manufacture are clear resins, requiring an extensive amount of refining, using large amounts of energy and thereby creating a large carbon footprint.

The core of modern surfboards, the blank, has traditionally been made from polyurethane foam (PU).[7] The creation of these blanks utilises processes that are known to give off CO_2, a greenhouse gas, and often employs the use of hydrofluorocarbons, which are known to deplete the ozone. Encouragingly, the numbers of boards produced using polyurethane foam has shrunk dramatically to probably less than 60 percent of the overall figure in the five years since 2006. The rest are made up mostly of polystyrene/epoxy moulds. The fibreglass cloth that covers the blank is often treated with heavy metals, and when fibreglass is sanded the dust given off is toxic. The three main types of resins used in surfboard construction consist of a combination

Andrew Kidman.
Photo Peter Crawford.

of anhydride or isothalic acid, phathalic, makeic and hydride propylene or ethylene glycol and styrene (a benzene derivative). This chemical cocktail is turned into the hard plastic coating on your board by adding methyl ethyl ketone peroxide (commonly known as a 'catalyst') to the resin.

When surfboard blank manufacturing giant Clark Foam shut its doors in 2005, reportedly due to a mass of workers compensation lawsuits and strict EPA regulations, it should have acted as a warning shot to the industry. For a while it did seem to open the door for new innovations in environmentally friendly surfboard construction, but then large-scale production began taking place in places such as China, Taiwan and Thailand, churning out more boards than ever before, and pumping Volatile Organic Compounds (VOCs) into the atmosphere. The emission of VOCs does not stop with construction—as the resins break down they continue to emit VOCs. Offshore textile and chemical factories are not usually subjected to the same environmental regulations in place in the west, and there are well-documented accounts of major environmental pollution caused through lack of regulation.

Many of the dodgier operators have slowly been weeded out by the surf industry's monitoring of efficiency and labour abuses in their factories. In America and Europe the Surf Industry Manufacturers Association (SIMA) is taking a proactive stance, supporting environmental projects and the humanitarian work conducted in remote areas by Surfaid and others. Some new technologies, such

as bamboo boards, BioFoam, Eco Boards, bio-plastic leash plugs and removable fin systems represent a step in the right direction, but research needs to be stepped up. In the end, however, it is the buying habits of the aware consumer that will drive change.

When researching data on the surf industry's environmental credentials I heard a common complaint voiced (usually from brand managers dressed up as so-called 'environmental spokesmen') that it is unfairly singled out for criticism for not spending more on environmental issues, usually citing sports such as golf, tennis or Formula 1 for comparisons. This disingenuous defence by pointing the finger at others fails to acknowledge the fact that the surfing industry does not invest in infrastructure. It does not build or maintain stadiums, courts, pools, ski runs or fields to support its activities. It merely sells the surfing lifestyle 'dream' and exploits our ocean and beach reserves with rising numbers of users. The environment in general is affected through the continued use of petrochemical derivative materials and the production of textiles.

For many years now there has been discussion about the development of wave pools and artificial reefs. Legendary Dee Why surfer and photographer Peter Crawford led a push to build an artificial reef at Freshwater in the mid-1990s. This effort to realise the potential of the north point was ultimately unsuccessful due largely to ecological concerns and cost. Wave pools

also raise environmental issues due to their carbon footprint, but if the growth of the sport continues at its current pace then we will see the commercial development of these forms of 'surf parks' in a very short time. Notable figures such as Kelly Slater and Greg Webber are in the vanguard of designing pools with improved efficiency and promoting them as commercially viable. In these more controlled environments, board design will also evolve with smaller pods made from sustainable materials being developed. It will be a very different experience, but it may be the only way around the growing rule-of-the-jungle mentality where the fittest and most aggressive take all the waves on the crowded beach breaks.

In the meantime, the beaches need to be safeguarded. Surfing in Australia grew out of the life saving movement, but board riders by and large rejected the regimentation of the life saving clubs about the same time that the sport began to be commercialised. Despite this, many surfers respect the work that the 'clubbies' do and are grateful that there is support available when things go wrong in the surf. Unfortunately, the surf life saving movement is in distress itself, and is being forced to look at ways of commercialising its clubhouses to balance the books. This development of the foreshore is, in the main, not favoured by local residents and regular beachgoers. Perhaps it is time for the surf industry to contribute by adding a small surcharge to the price of their products as a way of helping the surf clubs and various environmental groups working to protect

"The forest is not a resource for us, it is life itself. It is the only place for us to live."

Evaristo Nugkuag Ikanan, Peru

and conserve the beaches. Few would be upset at adding a dollar or so to every board or wetsuit purchased to keep their beaches pristine and safe.

For further information on environmental and humanitarian issues related to surfing please refer to:

Surfrider Foundation Australia www.surfrider.org.au
The Surfrider Foundation has become a visible presence in politics and has active branches whose purpose is *"protecting waves and beaches"* through CARE (Conservation Activism Research Education).

Coastalwatch www.coastalwatch.com

SurfAid International www.surfaidinternational.org

Sumba Foundation www.sumbafoundation.org

Misfit Aid www.misfitshapes.com/misfitaid

Surfers Against Sewage www.sas.org.uk

Substainable Surfing Coalition sustainablesurfcoalition.org

Save the Waves Coalition www.savethewaves.org

Surfers' Environmental Alliance (SEA) www.seasurfer.org

Ocean Revolution www.oceanrevolution.org

Waterkeeper Alliance www.waterkeeper.org

Bush Scene, Brisbane Water, NSW, 1848.
Oil on canvas by Conrad Martens. Cedar tree.
Brisbane Waters, near the Hawkesbury River
was once famous for its temperate rainforest.
Dixson Galleries. DG 165.

saltwater
descendants

Contrary to common belief, there are many descendants of the Saltwater People still living in the area. At the beginning of the twentieth century Aboriginal families were still living together in secluded areas behind the Manly Lagoon, at Beauty Point (near the Spit), and near Narrabeen Lagoon. Despite dispossession of land and hounding by police, descendants lived in and around the Narrabeen area long into the late1950s.[1] They survived with odd jobs and collecting food, like oysters, to sell by the Narrabeen tramstop. The shacks of about twenty people were destroyed in 1959 to make way for the New South Wales Academy of Sport at the head of Narrabeen Lagoon.[2]

In the nineteenth and early twentieth centuries, Saltwater People still lived along the cliffs and hunted wallaby, long-necked tortoise, eels and fish. Dennis Foley, a Gai-mariagal man, has fond memories of the special places visited throughout his life and the stories told to him by his elders. Many of these stories are recounted in his book *Repossession of Our Spirit*. There is also a strong connection with the country north of the Hawkesbury River, where "Tracey Howie and the Guringai Tribal Link are representatives of the Guringai people on the Central Coast." [3] Mingaletta Aboriginal & Torres Strait Islander Corporation in Woy Woy operates "a community centre for Indigenous people of the Central Coast peninsula."[4] The Metropolitan Aboriginal Land Council in Redfern has responsibility for land and

Left Rock Art. *Photo oggy.*
Right Outback Meets the Beach. *Photo oggy.*

"Let no one say the past is dead.
The past is all about us and within.
Haunted by tribal memories, I know
This little now, this accidental present
Is not all of me, whose long making
Is so much of the past.

a thousand thousand campfires in the forest
Are in my blood.
Let none tell me the past is wholly gone.
Now is so small a part of time, so small a part
Of all the race years that have moulded me."

OODGEROO NOONUCCAL (1920–1993), *THE PAST*

people in a large part of Sydney and also assists in maintaining sites.

Long-time Brookvale resident Bob Waterer only uncovered his Aboriginal heritage at the age of 81 following the discovery of documents after the death of his sister Joan in 2006. These documents revealed that Mr Waterer's great-great-grandmother was Biddy, also known as Sarah Wallace (1803–1880), believed to be the daughter of Matora, Bungaree's first wife, and half-brother to Bowen Bungaree. Uncle Bob is a great symbol of reconciliation in that late in his life he has embraced his Aboriginal ancestry, a heritage denied to him previously because some of his family viewed it as a stigma. Bob has four children and (at last count) five grandchildren who can now also claim Aboriginal heritage. *The Story of Bob Waterer and his Family 1803–2010*, by Nan Bosler, was launched in July 2011.[5]

Many others claim direct descent from either Matora or Bungaree, including Lynn Stewart, Hanna Matilda Ashby, Margaret Robinson, Reta Smith, Tracey Howie and Trudy Smith[6]. Biddy (Sarah Wallace) set up home on the Hawkesbury River with a Prussian-born pardoned convict, John Ferdinand Lewis, and had ten children. The family flourished on their land grant on the Hawkesbury River, and their descendants included Elizabeth, Mary Anne, James, Thomas and Catherine. Catherine Lewis married Joseph Bens, a Belgian, and settled on Scotland Island. At one stage the family were granted the whole island, and Catherine Bens became known as the 'Queen of Scotland Island'. The descendants of Thomas Lewis lived on Scotland Island for many generations and others still live on the northern beaches.

In 1999 the North Sydney Council, with Aboriginal site officer David Watts, drew up an Aboriginal site management plan for the north side of the Harbour.

Above left Catherine Bens c.1900. 'The Queen of Scotland Island' and Bob's great grandmother. *Photo courtesy of Bob Waterer.*

Above right Bob Waterer. *Bungaree bust sculpture by Laurie Wilson, a Murri man. This bust is located outside the Mosman Civic Centre. Photo Oggy.*

In 2000 the Northside Aboriginal Heritage Office was established with the support of Lane Cove, North Sydney, Manly, Kuringai, Pittwater, Warringah and Willoughby. The centre carries out protection of sites, school heritage talks and visits, and maintains close co-operation with eight local councils to protect and manage the conservation of Aboriginal sites[7]. In 2002 the Guringai Festival was established by a committee including Susan Moylan Coombs and Caroline Glass-Pattison. The Festival celebrates Aboriginal culture and heritage honouring the traditional homelands of Guringai people. Meetings of the Guringai Aboriginal Education Consultative Group and the Aboriginal Support Group—Manly Warringah Pittwater occur each month, and details can be found on their websites.[8]

Aboriginal culture has affected the Australian character and psyche in many, largely unrecognised, ways. Jakelin Troy notes that the Aboriginal language from the Sydney area

still exists in a shadowy form as part of the vocabulary of Australian English. A number of words in modern Australian English were borrowed into early Australian English from the Sydney Language within the first few years of English settlement.[9]

The ultimate testimony to the Saltwater People will be the continuing Indigenous presence in Sydney and an acknowledgement of their culture. In recognising that they are part of us, we will then value that this heritage

accounts for many of *"our most deeply held values, much of our own identity—and even our own humanity."*[10]

One powerful symbol of reconciliation acknowledging the Saltwater People would be to dedicate a site in their honour. The $600,000-plus upgrade of Governor Phillip Park at North Palm Beach in 2010–2011, complete with sandstone walls carved with a likeness of the colonial figure who spent only a brief time in the area, was an opportunity lost. Governor Phillip enjoys many memorials throughout Sydney, while Bungaree and the Saltwater People who lived here for millennia before the arrival of the Europeans are scarcely acknowledged on the northern beaches. This book attempts to raise awareness of Aboriginal spirituality and explain the connection with land and with sea.

There are many suggestions that need to be discussed with various local Aboriginal groups. Perhaps a site of recognition at the base of the new track leading to the Palm Beach lighthouse, a place where Bowen Bungaree once camped, would be a good start in honouring his ancestors. Another concept put forward is a small nature reserve, restored to its native state, where people can escape the pressures of modern life for a moment and just be still. Aside from this, important rock art sites on the northern beaches—such as the whale carving under threat from the widening of Mona

"To live in the hearts we leave behind is to never die."
CARL SAGAN (1934–1996)

Vale Road—need to be preserved before it is too late.

The descendants of the European settlers along Sydney's northern beaches are now reaching their seventh generation, so it is timely to hear the words of Oren R. Lyons, Faithkeeper, Onondaga Nation, a revered Native American elder and scholar who helped draft the 2010 UN resolution on Indigenous Rights:

A thousand years ago or more, the Great Peace Maker came among our people. He introduced the principles of peace, health, equity, justice, and the power of the good minds, which is to say, to be united in thought, body and spirit. He brought peace to our warring nations and he raised new leaders, clan mothers and chiefs, instructing us on our conduct and our responsibilities. Among those many instructions, one continues to resonate around the world today. He said to us, "When you sit in council for the welfare of the people, think not of yourself, nor of your family, or even your generation. Make your decisions for the seventh generation coming so that they may enjoy what you have here today. If you do this, there will be peace."[11]

"Treat the earth well.

It was not given to you by your parents, it was loaned to you by your children.

We do not inherit the Earth from our Ancestors, we borrow it from our Children."

ANCIENT INDIAN PROVERB

supporters

Manly Council
Dick Smith

Warringah Council

Fujifilm Australia

Catholic Schools Office – Diocese of Broken Bay

The Boathouse Palm Beach

The Raymond Family

Blenkhorn & Associates

Mac & Me

Above *Photo Alex Marks.*
Left *Photo oggy.*

Saltwater People of the Broken Bays

Published and distributed in Australia in 2011
by Cyclops Press, ABN 65 054 744 339

First published 2011

Written by **John Ogden**

Designed by **Mark Thacker**

Files by **Vasili Vasiliadis**

Edited by **Fiona Upward**

Print management by **Tony Gordon**

Printed and bound in China

First Edition, 2011.
Cataloguing-in-Publication Data:
A catalogue record of this book is available
from the National Library of Australia.
National Library of Australia Cataloguing-in-Publication entry
Author: Ogden, John.
Title: Saltwater people of the Broken Bays : a history of Sydney's
northern beaches / John Ogden; editor, Fiona Upward.
Edition: 1st ed.
ISBN: 9780980561913 (hbk.)
Series: Saltwater people ; Vol. 1, no. 1.
Notes: Includes bibliographical references.
Subjects: Beaches--New South Wales--Manly Region--History.
Beaches--New South Wales--Manly Region--Social life
and customs.
Beaches--New South Wales--Warringah Region--History.
Beaches--New South Wales--Warringah Region--Social life
and customs.
Manly Region (N.S.W.)--History.
Manly Region (N.S.W.)--Social Life and customs.
Warringah Region (N.S.W.)--History.
Warringah Region (N.S.W.)--Social life and customs.

Other Authors/Contributors:
Upward, Fiona.
McMullen, Jeff.

Dewey Number: 919.441

Environmental Standards

Cyclops Press makes every effort to ensure that the papers used
in its books are made from trees that have been legally sourced
from well-managed and credibly certified forests. This book
is printed using soy-based inks.

Dust jacket: Surf Zone. Photo oggy.

Front endpaper: Drawing Michael Glasheen.
A Kayimai fisherman leaves the surf near Fairy Bower.

Back endpaper: Drawing Michael Glasheen.
A Garigal man watches over Barrenjoey near Palm Beach. Based
on original drawings by Pavel Mikhailov and François Péron.

Other publications by Cyclops Press can be
viewed and purchased online at:
www.cyclopspress.com.au
email: oggy@oggy.com.au

special thanks

The story of the northern beaches is a compilation of many voices, and the author thanks all those organisations and individuals who have generously given permission to reproduce their words, photographs and creative works.

In particular, I want to acknowledge the work and generosity of Jeff McMullen, Dr Keith Vincent Smith, Shelagh Champion OAM and George Champion OAM, Val Attenbrow and Phil Gordon (the Australia Museum), Prof. Dennis Foley, Julie Janson and Prof. Peter Read.

acknowledgements

Rob Stokes MP; Mayor Harvey Rose and Lindsay Godfrey, Pittwater Council; Mayor Jean Hay, Manly Council; Mayor Michael Regan, Warringah Council; Sarah Johnson and Tanya Graf, Manly Art Gallery; Department of Environment, Climate Change & Water, NSW Government; Jakelin Troy; Peter Turbet; Keith Wiley; Emma Lee; Guy Jennings; Pauline Curby; Jan Roberts; Joan Lawrence; Ian Jacobs; Peter Stanbury; John Clegg; Yolanda Borel; Matt Graham; Saxon Duke; Graeme Davey; Ken Israel; Barry Bennett; Denny Keogh; Midget Farrelly; Richard Leplastrier; Bruce Raymond; Nick Carroll; John Witzig; Drew Kampion; Kirk Willcox; Luke Kennedy and *Tracks* magazine; Doug Miesel and *Surfing World*; Doug Lees, Coastal Watch; Swellnet; Jill White; Lisa Jasprizza; Sally Garrett; Jack and Dawn Eden; John Pennings; Bob Weeks; Ron Saggers; Peter Solness; Hugh McLeod; Bruce Channon; Bruce Usher; Nathan Smith; Tom Carroll; Steve Killelea; Stephen Baccon; Ian Bird; Mark Onorati; Sean Davey; Robbie Luscombe-Newman; Justin Crawford; Jedd and Steve Cooney; Guy Finlay; Jules Phillips, Oceaneye; Scott Needham; Alex Marks; Tim Hixson; Roger Scott; John Ware; Wayne Osborn; Dave Fairbairn; Andrew Kidman; Murray Close; Jon Frank; Toby Player; Louise Whelan; Murray Vanderveer; Mandy Zieren; Stuart 'Stretch' Cooper; Mick Glasheen; Ian Faulkner; Bruce Goold; Jacqui Williams; Dougall Walker; Greg Webber; Glen Casey, Patagonia; Gary Dunne, Rip Curl; John Mossop, Billabong; Brendan Donohoe, Surfrider Foundation; Living Ocean; Mick Mock; Andrew Hunter; Teresa Charchalis, artsConnect; Leigh Purcell; Albe Falzon; Barton Lynch; Dougall Walker; Dale Egan; Murray Walding; Geoff Searl and the Avalon Historical Society; Jim Macken; Richard Leplastrier; Ria Murch; Betty Baily; Betty Leighton; Enid Taylor; Nicholina Ralston (Kuner); Marita McRae; Maria Ellers; Jeff McMullen; Reconciliation Australia; Reconciliation NSW; Brian Johnstone, NSW Aboriginal Lands Council; The Metropolitan Local Aboriginal Land Council; Bob Waterer; Nan Bosler; the Aboriginal Education Consultative Group (AECG); Prof. Peter Read, University of Sydney; Eddie Goodall; David Watts, Northside Aboriginal Heritage Office; the Manly, Warringah, Pittwater Aboriginal Support Group; the Grafton Ngerrie Aboriginal Land Council; the Birpai Land Council; ANTaR; David Jeffery and Kylie Simpson, AIATSIS audio visual archive; Lea Gardnam and Mark Pharaoh, South Australian Museum; Dr Heather Gaunt, Museum Victoria; James Wilson-Miller and Kathleen Hackett, Powerhouse Museum; Charley Myers, Bishop Museum, Hawai'i; Jennie Maloney, NGV; the Australian War Memorial; Penny Cuthbert, National Maritime Museum; Gary Crocker, Historic Houses Trust; Di Jackson and Elise Edmonds, the State Library of New South Wales; Tina Graham, Local Studies librarian, Warringah Library; John MacRitchie, Local Studies librarian, Manly Library; Sarah Thompson and Sharelle Ravenscroft, Local Studies librarians, Pittwater Library; Eleanor Galvin, AIATSIS library; Steve Martin; Steve McInnes, SLSNSW; Ray Moran and Ray Peterson, Manly Life Saving Club; Marc Maddox, North Steyne SLSC; George Webster, Freshwater SLSC; Brian Russell and Charlie Kuhn, South Curl Curl SLSC; Richie Burke, Dee Why SLSC; Col McLean and Michael King, Newport SLSC; Richard Stewart and Paul Hughes, Whale Beach SLSC; Johnny Carter, Palm Beach SLSC; and Graham Howard, North Palm Beach SLSC.

'Australian Aborigine'.
Photo by Henry King, 1890s.
Courtesy Powerhouse Museum.

notes

INTRODUCTION

1. Keith Willey, *When the Sky Fell Down*, Collins, Sydney, 1979, p. 9.

2. James Cook, *Captain Cook's Journal during his first voyage round the world made in H.M. Bark "Endeavour" 1768–71*, Sir W.J.L. Wharton (ed.), Elliot Stock, London, 1893.

3. Bill Barnett, Ken Brown & Bob Parkhill, *The Beach Comes First 1912–2003*, North Narrabeen SLSC, 2007, p. 15. The story of the North Narrabeen Surf Life Saving Club.

4. Jules Verne, *Twenty Thousand Leagues Under the Seas*, 1869, part i, chapter 10.

5. Ashley Jones-Evans, Linda Gregoriou & Dale Jones-Evans, *Sea Gods. Australian Surfers*, FTB Group Pty Ltd, Sydney, 2000.

THE FIRST PEOPLE, THE SALTWATER PEOPLE

1. Ian Jacobs, *A Fascinating Heritage of Sydney's Northern Beaches*, Ian Jacobs, Bayview NSW, 2008, p. 18.

2. Dennis Foley & Ricky Maynard, *Repossession of Our Spirit: Traditional Owners of Northern Sydney*, Aboriginal History Inc., Canberra, 2001. pp. 7–12.

3. Emma Lee, Warringah (NSW) Council & Metropolitan Local Aboriginal Land Council (Redfern NSW), *The Tale of a Whale: Significant Aboriginal Landscapes of the Northern Beaches*, Warringah Council, Dee Why NSW, 2002, p. 8.

4. City of Sydney website, *Barani: Indigenous History of Sydney City*, www.cityofsydney. nsw.gov.au/barani/

5. Lee, *The Tale of a Whale*, p. 9.

6. A History of Aboriginal Australia website, www.historyofaboriginalsydney.edu.au/ timeline

7. Anthropologist Ronald Berndt, in Valerie Attenbrow, *Sydney's Aboriginal Past: Investigating the Archaeological and Historical Records*, UNSW Press, Sydney, 2002, p. 129.

8. A.P. Elkin, *Aboriginal Men of High Degree: Initiation and Sorcery in the World's Oldest Tradition*, Queensland University Press, St Lucia Qld, 1977, p. 14.

9. David Collins & B.H. Fletcher (ed.), *An Account of the English Colony in NSW*, Vol. 1, A.H. & A.W. Reid, Sydney, 1975, p. 453.

10. John Hunter, *An Historical Journal of Events at Sydney and at Sea, 1787–1792*, Angus & Robertson in association with the Royal Australian Historical Society, Sydney, 1968, p. 37.

11. G.B. Worgan, *Journal of a First Fleet Surgeon (1788)*, Library Council of NSW, Sydney, 1978, p. 19.

12. G. Paterson, *The History of New South Wales*, McKenzie & Dent, Newcastle upon Tyne, 1811, p. 497.

13. W.R. Govett, A. Potts & G. Renard, *Sketches of New South Wales Written and Illustrated for the Saturday Magazine in 1836–37 by William Romaine Govett, together with an Essay on the Saturday Magazine by Gaston Renard and an Account of His Life by Annette Potts*, Gaston Renard, Melbourne, 1977, p. 54.

14. Govett, *Sketches of NSW*, p. 68.

15. Peter Turbet, *The Aborigines of the Sydney District before 1788*, Kangaroo Press, East Roseville NSW, 2001, pp. 13–15.

16. Sandra Bowdler, 'Hook, line and dilly bag: an interpretation of an Australian coastal shell midden', *Mankind*, 10(4), 1976, pp. 254–256.

17. William Bradley & Public Library of New South Wales, William Dixson Foundation, *A Voyage to New South Wales: The Journal of Lieutenant William Bradley RN of HMS Sirius, 1786-1792*. Trustees of the Public

Library of New South Wales in association with Ure Smith, Sydney, 1969, p. 92.

18. Val Attenbrow, *Sydney's Aboriginal Past*, p. 98.

19. John White, *Journal of a Voyage to New South Wales*, 1912 (1790): 2000.

20. William Scott, *The Port Stephens Blacks: Recollections of William Scott*, Chronicle Office, Dungog NSW, 1929, p. 18.

21. Scott, *The Port Stephens Blacks*, p. 18.

22. Mahroot (Boatswain), 'Report from the Select Committee on the condition of Aborigines', NSW Legislative Council Votes and Proceedings, Sydney (1845: 5).

23. Keith Vincent Smith, *King Bungaree: A Sydney Aborigine Meets the Great South Pacific Explorers, 1799–1830*. Kangaroo Press, Kenthurst NSW, 1992, p. 18.

Malgun

1. John Turnbull, *A voyage round the world in the years 1800, 1801, 1802 and 1804: in which the author visited the principal islands in the Pacific Ocean, and the English settlements of Port Jackson and Norfolk Island*, printed for Richard Phillips by T. Gillet, London, 1805, pp. 84–5.

2. William Scott, *The Port Stephens Blacks: Recollections of William Scott*, Chronicle, Dungog NSW, 1929, p. 5

3. Scott, *The Port Stephens Blacks*, pp. 7–8.

4. Scott, *The Port Stephens Blacks*, p. 8.

5. Scott, *The Port Stephens Blacks*, p. 8.

THE ARRIVAL OF THE FIRST BOAT PEOPLE

1. James Cook, *Captain Cook's Journal during his first voyage round the world made in H.M. Bark "Endeavour" 1768–71*, Sir W.J.L. Wharton (ed.), Elliot Stock, London, 1893.

2. *Captain Cook's Journals*, Lieutenant James King, 1779.

3. Augustin Kramer, *The Samoa Islands,*

Vols I & II, University of Hawai'i Press, Honolulu, 1994–1995.

4. William Bradley & Public Library of New South Wales, William Dixson Foundation. *A Voyage to New South Wales: The Journal of Lieutenant William Bradley RN of HMS Sirius, 1786–1792*, Trustees of the Public Library of New South Wales in association with Ure Smith, Sydney, 1969, p. 100.

5. Matt Warshaw, *The History of Surfing*, Chronicle Books, San Francisco, 2010, p. 21.

6. Warshaw, *The History of Surfing*, p. 22.

7. Arthur Phillip & Viscount Thomas Townshend Sydney 1733–1800, G.R. Tipping (ed.), *The Official Account Through Governor Phillip's Letters to Lord Sydney*, G.R. Tipping, Beecroft NSW, 1988, p. 47.

8. *An Authentic and interesting narrative of the late expedition to Botany Bay: as performed by Commodore Phillips and the fleet of the seven transport ships under his command ... / written by an officer*, printed by W. Bailey, H. Lemoine and J. Parsons, London, 1789, p. 28.

9. Bradley, *Voyage to NSW*, p. 68.

10. Pauline Curby, *Seven Miles from Sydney: A History of Manly*, Manly Council, Manly NSW, 2001, p. 19.

11. See David Collins & B.H. Fletcher (ed.), *An Account of the English Colony in NSW*, Vol. 1, A.H. & A.W. Reid, Sydney, 1975, pp. 466–485, for a detailed account of these ceremonies.

12. Watkin Tench, *1789–1793 Sydney's First Four Years: A Complete Account of the Settlement at Port Jackson*, Angus & Robertson, Sydney, 1961, p. 37.

13. Virginia MacLeod, *Pictorial History: Manly*, Kingsclear Books, Alexandria NSW, 2008, p. 3.

14. MacLeod, *Pictorial History: Manly*, p. 5.

15. Arthur Phillip, in John Hunter, *An Historical Journal of Events at Sydney and*

at Sea, 1787–1792, Angus & Robertson in association with the Royal Australian Historical Society, Sydney, 1968, p. 312.

16. Tench, *Sydney's First Four Years*, p. 151.

17. Phillip, in Hunter, *An Historical Journal*, p. 93.

18. Collins, *An Account of the English Colony in NSW*, Vol. 1, Appendix VIII, Diseases.

19. Collins, *An Account of the English Colony in NSW*, Vol. 1, p. 71.

20. Hunter, *An Historical Journal*, p. 139.

21. Tench, *Sydney's First Four Years*, pp. 125–126.

22. Emma Lee, Warringah (NSW) Council & Metropolitan Local Aboriginal Land Council (Redfern NSW), *The Tale of a Whale: Significant Aboriginal Landscapes of the Northern Beaches*, Warringah Council, Dee Why NSW, 2002, p. 55.

23. Southwell, D. 1787–93, extract from the Southwell Papers, *Historic Records of NSW*, reprinted in Tim F. Flannery, *The Birth of Sydney*, Text Publishing, Melbourne, 1999, p. 104.

24. Tench, *Sydney's First Four Years*, p. 134.

25. Lee, *The Tale of a Whale*, p. 55.

26. Lee, *The Tale of a Whale*, p. 50.

27. Curby, *Seven Miles from Sydney*, p. 52.

28. Lee, *The Tale of a Whale*, p. 51.

29. Lee, *The Tale of a Whale*, p. 56.

30. Waterhouse, in William Bradley & Public Library of New South Wales, William Dixson Foundation. *A Voyage to New South Wales: The Journal of Lieutenant William Bradley RN of HMS Sirius, 1786–1792*, Trustees of the Public Library of New South Wales in association with Ure Smith, Sydney, 1969, pp. 22–30.

31. Phillip, in Hunter, *An Historical Journal*, p. 309.

32. Thomas Keneally, *The Commonwealth of Thieves*, Random House Australia,

Melbourne, 2007, pp. 249–304.

33. Lee, *The Tale of a Whale*, p. 58.

34. Thompson, 1791, in Keith Willey, *When the Sky Fell Down,* Collins, Sydney, 1979, p. 118.

35. Alexander Strachan, *Remarkable Incidents in the Life of the Rev. Samuel Leigh: Missionary to the Settlers and Savages of Australia and New Zealand: With a Succinct History of the Origin and Progress of the Missions in Those Colonies*, James Nicholls, London, 1855, p. 117.

CETACEANS

1. Heathcote Williams, *Whale Nation*, Jonathon Cape, London, 1988. pp. 10–11.

2. Dennis Foley & Ricky Maynard, *Repossession of Our Spirit: Traditional Owners of Northern Sydney*, Aboriginal History Inc., Canberra, 2001, p. 79.

3. Foley, *Repossession of Our Spirit*, p. 79.

4. Dennis Foley, 'A Living Harbour', *Hindsight*, Radio National broadcast, 20 June 2010, mpegmedia.abc.net.au/rn/podcast/extra/2010/hht_20100620_foley.mp3

5. Foley, *Repossession of Our Spirit*, p. 80,

6. Alex Roberts with Kath Schilling, *Aboriginal Women's Fishing in New South Wales: A Thematic History*, Department of Environment, Climate Change & Water NSW, Sydney, 2010, p. 5.

7. Williams, *Whale Nation*, pp. 30–31.

SALTWATER SEAFARERS

1. Pauline Curby, *Seven Miles from Sydney: A History of Manly*, Manly Council, Manly NSW, 2001, p. 172.

2. 'Mari Nawi: Aboriginal Odysseys 1790–1850' exhibition, presented at the State Library of New South Wales from 20 September to 12 December 2010.

3. Keith Vincent Smith, *Mari Nawi: Aboriginal Odysseys*, Rosenberg Publishing, Kenthurst NSW, 2010, p. 89.

4. Smith, *Mari Nawi*, p. 93.

5. Smith, *Mari Nawi*, p. 93.

6. Smith, *Mari Nawi*, p. 96.

7. Smith, *Mari Nawi*, p. 114.

8. Portia Fitzsimmons, *Eastern Suburbs Album: pictorial memories of Darling Point, Double Bay, Rose Bay, Vaucluse, Watsons Bay, Bellevue Hill, Bondi, Waver-*

ley and Bronte, Atrand Pty Ltd, Sydney, 1985, pp. 8–9.

9. Dr John Harris to Governor P.G. King, 25 June 1801, King Family Papers, vol. 8, Further Papers, 1775–1806, MS A10980-2, State Library of NSW, Mitchell Library.

10. Lieutenant C.F.N. Menzies to Governor P.G. King, Kings Town, Newcastle, 1 July 1804, *Historical Records of Australia*, Series 1, Vol. 5, pp. 415–416.

11. Menzies to King, 5 October 1804, *Historical Records of Australia*, Vol. 5, p. 423.

12. Smith, *Mari Nawi*, p. 135.

13. 'Death of King Boongarie', *Sydney Gazette*, 27 November 1830, p. 3.

14. 'Donations to the Australia Museum', *Sydney Morning Herald*, 9 December 1857, p. 8.

15. The Dictionary of Sydney website, www.dictionaryofsydney.org/entry/bungaree?zoom_highlightsub=bungaree

16. Maybanke Anderson, 'The Story of Pittwater', *Journal of the Royal Australian Historical Society (JRAHS)*, Vol. VI, Part IV, 1920.

17. Guy Jennings & Charles De Boos, *My Holiday and Other Early Travels from Manly to Palm Beach 1861*, Aramo, Newport Beach, 1991, p. 54. Articles by Charles de Boos reprinted from the *Sunday Mail* on successive Sundays from 22 June 1861 and successive Sundays.

18. Jennings & De Boos, *My Holiday and Other Early Travels*. Recounted by Smith in *Mari Nawi*, p. 138.

19. Jennings & De Boos, *My Holiday and Other Early Travels*, p. 54.

OUTLAWS

Saltwater outlaws

1. Ian Jacobs, *A Fascinating Heritage of Sydney's Northern Beaches*, Ian Jacobs, Bayview NSW, 2008, p. 25.

2. David Collins & B.H. Fletcher (ed.), *An Account of the English Colony in NSW*, Vol. 2, A.H. & A.W. Reid, Sydney, 1975, p. 4.

3. Shelagh Champion & George Champion, *Manly, Warringah and Pittwater, Vol. 1 1788–1850*, S. & G. Champion, Killarney Heights, 1997, p. 18.

4. *Sydney Gazette*, 28 April 1805.

5. James Macken, *Early Pittwater: A Nostal-*

gic Look at its Soldiers, Seamen, Smugglers and Settlers, Anchor Publications, Cammeray NSW, 2004, p. 2.

6. Macken, *Early Pittwater*, p. 2.

7. Jim Boyce, *Pictorial History: Warringah*. Kingsclear Books, Alexandria NSW, 2006, p. 2.

8. Richard Atkins, *Opinion on Treatment to be Adopted Towards the Natives'*, 20 July 1805, *Historical Records of Australia*, Series 1, Vol. 5, p. 502.

9. Keith Vincent Smith, *Mari Nawi: Aboriginal Odysseys*, Rosenberg Publishing, Kenthurst NSW, 2010, p. 62.

10. Naomi Parry, 'Musquito (c.1780–1825)', *Australian Directory of Biography*, Supplementary Volume, Melbourne University Press, Melbourne, 2005, p. 299.

11. Rev. William Horton, Letter to the Wesleyan Missionary Society, Hobart Town, Van Diemen's Land, 3 June 1823, BT Box 52:1269-74, ML.

12. *Hobart Town Gazette*, 25 February 1825; *Sydney Gazette*, 17 March 1825.

Bushrangers

13. Shelagh Champion & George Champion, *Lieutenant James Grant's Journey to Manly, Warringah and Pittwater, 25th and 26th February, 1801*, S. & G. Champion, Killarney Heights NSW, 1991, p. 4.

14. Bill Barnett, Ken Brown & Bob Parkhill, *The Beach Comes First 1912–2003*, North Narrabeen SLSC, 2007, p. 19. The story of the North Narrabeen Surf Life Saving Club.

15. Pauline Curby, *Seven Miles from Sydney: A History of Manly*, Manly Council, Manly NSW, 2001, p. 128.

16. Curby, *Seven Miles from Sydney*, p. 129.

17. Curby, *Seven Miles from Sydney*, p. 35.

18. Champion & Champion, *Manly, Warringah and Pittwater, Vol. 1 1788–1850*, p. 49.

19. Correspondence with Shelagh Champion, 4 June 2011.

20. Shelagh Champion & George Champion, *Manly, Warringah and Pittwater, Vol. 2 1850–1880*, S. & G. Champion, Killarney Heights, 1998, pp. 121–125.

21. Expression used in chapter 2 of Champion & Champion, *Manly, Warringah and*

Pittwater, Vol. 1 1788–1850, pp. 17–28.

22. Champion & Champion, *Manly, Warringah and Pittwater, Vol. 1 1788–1850*, p. 25.

23. Alan Sharpe, *Manly to Palm Beach: Pictorial Memories*, Atrand, Sydney, 1983, p. 107.

24. Julie Janson, *Black Mary & Gunjies: two plays by Julie Janson*, Aboriginal Studies Press, Canberra, 1996, p. 2.

25. Neil Mercer, *Sydney Morning Herald*, 15 Feb. 2003.

26. Arthur Stanley Smith & Tom Noble, *Neddy: The Life and Crimes of Arthur Stanley Smith: An Autobiography with Tom Noble*, Kerr, Chippendale NSW, 1998.

The ocean's outlaws

27. Ashley Jones-Evans, Linda Gregoriou & Dale Jones-Evans, *Sea Gods. Australian Surfers*, FTB Group Pty Ltd, Sydney, 2000.

28. C. Bede Maxwell, *Surf: Australians Against the Sea*, Angus & Robertson, Sydney, 1949, p. 12.

29. Maxwell, *Surf*, p. 14.

30. Curby, *Seven Miles from Sydney*, p. 121.

31. Curby, *Seven Miles from Sydney*, p. 123.

32. Matt Warshaw, *The History of Surfing*, Chronicle Books, San Francisco, 2010.

The Australian crawl

1. John Leonard, *The New York Times Guide to Essential Knowledge: A Desk Reference for the Curious Mind*, St Martin's Press, New York, 2007, p. 942.

2. Greenwich Baths website, www.greenwichbaths.com.au

THE BROKEN BAYS

1. Matt Warshaw, *The History of Surfing*, Chronicle Books, San Francisco, 2010, p. 67.

2. Mark Warren, *Mark Warren's Atlas of Australian Surfing* (2nd edn), Harper Sports, Sydney, 1998.

Manly and Queenscliff

1. Arthur Phillip & Viscount Thomas Townshend Sydney 1733–1800, G.R. Tipping (ed.), *The Official Account Through Governor Phillip's Letters to Lord Sydney*, G.R. Tipping, Beecroft NSW, 1988, p. 47.

2. Shelagh Champion & George Champion, *Manly, Warringah and Pittwater, Vol. 1 1788–1850*, S. & G. Champion, Killarney Heights, 1997, p. 3.

3. Emma Lee, Warringah (NSW) Council & Metropolitan Local Aboriginal Land Council (Redfern NSW), *The Tale of a Whale: Significant Aboriginal Landscapes of the Northern Beaches*, Warringah Council, Dee Why NSW, 2002, p. 50.

4. W.R. Govett, A. Potts & G. Renard, *Sketches of New South Wales Written and Illustrated for the Saturday Magazine in 1836–37 by William Romaine Govett, together with an Essay on the Saturday Magazine by Gaston Renard and an Account of His Life by Annette Potts*, Gaston Renard, Melbourne, 1977, p. 55.

5. Dennis Foley & Ricky Maynard, *Repossession of Our Spirit: Traditional Owners of Northern Sydney*, Aboriginal History Inc., Canberra, 2001, p. 80.

6. NSW Ocean Baths website, www.nsw-oceanbaths.com

7. Alan Sharpe, *Manly to Palm Beach: Pictorial Memories*, Atrand, Sydney, 1983, p. 9.

8. Sharpe, *Manly to Palm Beach*, p. 7.

9. The Dictionary of Sydney website, www.dictionaryofsydney.org/entry/fairy_bower

10. Kent Pearson, 'Origins and Development of Pacific Seaboard Surfing', in *Surfing Subcultures of Australia and New Zealand*, University of Queensland Press, St Lucia Qld, 1979, p. 34.

11. C. Bede Maxwell, *Surf: Australians Against the Sea*, Angus & Robertson, Sydney, 1949, p. 7.

12. Arthur Lowe, quoted in Matt Warshaw, *The History of Surfing*, Chronicle Books, San Francisco, 2010, p. 57.

13. Jean McGlynn & Charles A. McDonald, *Manly*. Currawong Press, Milsons Point NSW, 1976, pp. 39–40.

14. Sharpe, *Manly to Palm Beach*, p. 44.

15. Shelagh Champion, in correspondence to John Ogden, 2 June 2011.

16. Joan Lawrence, *Pictorial History: Pittwater*, Kingsclear Books, Alexandria NSW, 2006, p. 14.

17. Matthew Benns. *100 Years—A Celebration of Surf Life Saving at North Steyne 1907–2007*, North Steyne SLSC, 2007.

18. Warshaw, *The History of Surfing*, p. 58.
19. Murray Walding, *Blue Heaven, The Story of Australian Surfing*, Hardie Grant Books, South Yarra Vic., 2006, p. 17.
20. Warshaw, *The History of Surfing*, p. 87.
21. Our Manly website, www.ourmanly.com. au/Sports/Manly_Surf_Legends.aspx
22. Manly and Sydney's Northern Beaches website, members.ozemail.com. au/~russo/oceanbeach/nh.html
23. Ian Jacobs, *A Fascinating Heritage of Sydney's Northern Beaches*, Ian Jacobs, Bayview NSW, 2008, p. 71.
24. Our Manly website, www.ourmanly.com. au/Sports/Manly_Surf_Legends.aspx

The Queenscliff bombie

1. Surf Research website, www.surfresearch. com.au/1959_Foam.html
2. Beachnet website, 'Bombora', members. ozemail.com.au/~russo/oceanbeach/ bombora.html
3. Farrelly Surfboards website, 'Midget's Shaping History', farrellysurfboards.com/ index.php/shaping
4. Beachnet website, 'Bombora', members. ozemail.com.au/~russo/oceanbeach/ bombora.html

Freshwater and Curl Curl

1. Freshwater Amateur Swimming Club website, www.fasc.asn.au/history. html#HistorySuburb
2. Alan Sharpe, *Manly to Palm Beach: Pictorial Memories*, Atrand, Sydney, 1983, p. 7.
3. C. Bede Maxwell, *Surf: Australians Against the Sea*, Angus & Robertson, Sydney, 1949, p. 12.
4. *Sydney Morning Herald*, 8 February 1915, p. 13, cited in Gwen Gordon, *Harbord, Queenscliff and South Curl Curl, 1788–2000*, Warringah Council, Harbord 2000, p. 40.
5. Sharpe, *Manly to Palm Beach*, p. 77.
6. Nick Carroll, 'Surfing Life', *Pittwater Life*, March 2011.
7. Nat Young & Craig McGregor, *The History of Surfing*, Palm Beach Press, Sydney, 1983, p. 49-50.
8. *Ellimatta*, Winter 2007, p. 1, accessed at www.asgmwp.net/ElimattaWinter2007. pdf

9. Interview with Richard Leplastrier, Lovett Bay, February 2011.
10. Brenton Cherry, *Manly Daily*, 17 May 2011, p. 6.
11. Cherry, 17 May 2011, p. 6.
12. Brenton Cherry, *Manly Daily*, 25 May 2011, p. 5.
13. Cherry, 25 May 2011, p. 5.

Brookvale: the genesis of the surfboard industry

1. Matthew Benns, *100 Years—A Celebration of Surf Life Saving at North Steyne 1907–2007*, North Steyne SLSC, 2007.
2. Warshaw, Matt, *The History of Surfing*, Chronicle Books, San Francisco, 2010, p. 134.
3. Nick Carroll, December 2000, 'Terry Fitzgerald (April 2, 1950–), Surfline website, www.surfline.com/surfing-a-to-z/terry-fitzgerald-biography-and-photos_804/
4. Nick Carroll, October 2000, 'Damien Hardman (January 23, 1966–)', Surfline website, www.surfline.com/surfing-a-to-z/simon-anderson-biography-and-photos_745/
5. Nick Carroll, October 2000, 'Simon Anderson (July 7, 1954–)', Surfline website, www.surfline.com/surfing-a-to-z/damien-hardman-biography-and-photos_827/

For more information see 'Evolution of the Surfboard' in Murray Walding, *Blue Heaven: The Story of Australian Surfing*, Hardie Grant Books, South Yarra Vic., 2006, p. 11.

Dee Why and Long Reef

1. David Messent, *Sydney's Northern Beaches*, David Messent Photography, Balgowlah NSW, 1999, p. 48.
2. Jim Boyce, *Pictorial History: Warringah*, Kingsclear Books, Alexandria NSW, 2006, p. 130.
3. Alan Sharpe, *Manly to Palm Beach: Pictorial Memories*, Atrand, Sydney, 1983, p. 80.
4. Charles Swancott, *Dee Why to Barrenjoey and Pittwater*, the author, Woy Woy NSW, 1967, p. 62.

Collaroy, Narrabeen and Turimetta

1. Dennis Foley & Ricky Maynard, *Repossession of Our Spirit: Traditional Owners of*

Northern Sydney, Aboriginal History Inc., Canberra, 2001, p. 65.
2. Bill Barnett, Ken Brown & Bob Parkhill, *The Beach Comes First 1912–2003*, North Narrabeen SLSC, 2007, p. 17. The story of the North Narrabeen Surf Life Saving Club.
3. Foley, *Repossession of Our Spirit*, p. 42.
4. Foley, *Repossession of Our Spirit*, p. 49.
5. Stuart 'Stretch' Cooper, correspondence, Avalon, 2010.
6. Foley, *Repossession of Our Spirit*, p. 42.

Warriewood, Mona Vale And Bongin Bongin Bay

1. Joan Lawrence, *Pictorial History: Pittwater*, Kingsclear Books, Alexandria NSW, 2006, p. 97.
2. Maybanke Anderson, *Maybanke Anderson's Story of Pittwater: 1770 to 1920*, Ruskin Rowe Press, Avalon Beach, 1996, pp. 35–36.
3. Charles Swancott, *Dee Why to Barrenjoey and Pittwater*, the author, Woy Woy NSW, 1967, pp. 73–74.
4. Swancott, *Dee Why to Barrenjoey and Pittwater*, p. 77.
5. Ian Jacobs, *A Fascinating Heritage of Sydney's Northern Beaches*, Ian Jacobs, Bayview NSW, 2008, p. 72.
6. Pittwater Council website, www.pittwater. nsw.gov.au/recreation/parks_and_reserves/find_a_park/parks/mona_vale/ mona_vale_head
7. Lawrence, *Pictorial History: Pittwater*, p. 98.
8. Damien Hardman biography on Surfline website, www.surfline.com/surfing-a-to-z/damien-hardman-biography-and-photos_827/

Bungan Beach

1. Shelagh Champion & George Champion, *Manly, Warringah and Pittwater, Vol. 1 1788–1850*, S. & G. Champion, Killarney Heights, 1997, p. 39.
2. Maybanke Anderson, *Maybanke Anderson's Story of Pittwater: 1770 to 1920*, Ruskin Rowe Press, Avalon Beach, 1996, p. 52.
3. www.pittwater.nsw.gov.au
4. Guy Jennings, *The Newport Story, 1788–1988*, Aramo, Newport Beach, 1987, p. 59.

5. National Parks website, www.pittwater. nsw.gov.au/recreation/parks_and_reserves/find_a_park/parks/newport/bungan

Newport Beach

1. Maybanke Anderson, *Maybanke Anderson's Story of Pittwater: 1770 to 1920*, Ruskin Rowe Press, Avalon Beach, 1996, p. 22.
2. Guy Jennings & Charles De Boos, *My Holiday and Other Early Travels from Manly to Palm Beach 1861*, Aramo, Newport Beach, 1991, p. 48.
3. Guy Jennings, *Newport Surf Life Saving Club, 1909–2009: The First Century*, Newport Surf Life Saving Club, Newport, 2009, p. 10.
4. Jennings, *Newport Surf Life Saving Club*, p. 27.
5. Jennings, *Newport Surf Life Saving Club*, p. 10.
6. Guy Jennings, *The Newport Story, 1788–1988*, Aramo, Newport Beach 1987 p. 59.
7. Jennings, *The Newport Story*, p. 59.
8. Matthew Cawood, in Jill White, *Dupain's Beaches*, Chapter & Verse, Neutral Bay NSW, 2000, p. 14.

Bilgola Beach

1. National Parks website, environment.nsw. gov.au/NationalParks/
2. Pittwater Council website, www.pittwater. nsw.gov.au/recreation/parks_and_reserves/find_a_park/parks/bilgola/bilgola_ south_head

Avalon Beach

1. H.A. Guerber, *Myths and Legends of the Middle Ages: Their Origin and Influence on Literature and Art*. G.G. Harrap & Company, London, 1909, p. 309.
2. Shelagh Champion & George Champion, *Manly, Warringah and Pittwater, Vol. 1 1788–1850*, S. & G. Champion, Killarney Heights, 1997, p. 64.
3. *Sydney Morning Herald*, 22 March 1861.
4. Jan Roberts, *Avalon: Landscape & Harmony: Walter Burley Griffin, Alexander Stewart Jolly & Harry Ruskin Rowe*, Ruskin Rowe Press, Avalon Beach NSW, 1999, p. 18.
5. Joan Lawrence, *Pictorial History:*

Pittwater, Kingsclear Books, Alexandria NSW, 2006, p. 14.
6. Information supplied by Friends of Avalon Dunes (FOAD).

Whale Beach

1. Joan Lawrence, *Pictorial History: Pittwater*, Kingsclear Books, Alexandria NSW, 2006, p. 35.
2. Maybanke Anderson, *Maybanke Anderson's Story of Pittwater: 1770 to 1920*, Ruskin Rowe Press, Avalon Beach, 1996, pp. 40–41.
3. Mona Vale Library website, www.pittwater.nsw.gov.au/library/local_history
4. Jan Roberts, *Avalon: Landscape & Harmony: Walter Burley Griffin, Alexander Stewart Jolly & Harry Ruskin Rowe*, Ruskin Rowe Press, Avalon Beach NSW, 1999, pp. 23–24.

Palm Beach

1. Maybanke Anderson, *Maybanke Anderson's Story of Pittwater: 1770 to 1920*, Ruskin Rowe Press, Avalon Beach, 1996, p. 36.
2. Dennis Foley & Ricky Maynard, *Repossession of Our Spirit: Traditional Owners of Northern Sydney*, Aboriginal History Inc., Canberra, 2001, p. 38.
3. Denis Byrne, *Aboriginal Sites on the Palm Beach Barrier*, a report to Warringah Shire, 1984, p. 1.
4. Anderson, *Maybanke Anderson's Story of Pittwater*, p. 30.
5. Foley, *Repossession of Our Spirit*, p. 38.
6. Joan Steege, *Palm Beach 1788–1988*, Palm Beach Association, Sydney, 1984, p. 24.
7. Alan Sharpe, *Manly to Palm Beach: Pictorial Memories*, Atrand, Sydney, 1983, p. 107.
8. Geoff Searl, 'Times Past', *Pittwater Life*, March 2011.
9. Jervis Sparks, *The Red Light of Palm Beach*, Jervis Sparks, Maleny Qld, 2005.
10. Anderson, *Maybanke Anderson's Story of Pittwater*, p. 35.
11. Interview with Terry Kirkpatrick, 11 April 2011.
12. C. Bede Maxwell, *Surf: Australians Against the Sea*, Angus & Robertson, Sydney, 1949, p. 129
13. Maxwell, *Surf*, p. 129

14. *Honolulu Star Bulletin*, 18 Jan. 1939; *Daily Telegraph*, 6 Feb. 1995.

15. Maxwell, *Surf*, p. 241.

16. Sean Brawley, *Beach Beyond: A History of the Palm Beach Surf Club 1921–1996*, UNSW Press, Sydney, 1996, pp. 63–66.

BOHEMIANS AND BLUE BLOODS

1. Living Ocean (part).

Writers

2. Richard Edwards & Roderick Shaw, *Warringah 1988: A Celebration by its Artists and Writers*, Shire of Warringah, NSW, 1989.

3. *Sydney Morning Herald* article, Edwards & Shaw, *Warringah 1988*.

Town planners and architects

4. Jan Roberts, *Avalon: Landscape & Harmony: Walter Burley Griffin, Alexander Stewart Jolly & Harry Ruskin Rowe*, Ruskin Rowe Press, Avalon Beach NSW, 1999.

5. Roberts, *Avalon*, p. 7.

6. Roberts, *Avalon*, p. 20.

7. Roberts, *Avalon*, p. 11.

8. Philip Drew, *Peter Stutchbury: Of People and Places: Between the Bush and the Beach*, Pesaro Publishing, Balmain NSW, 2000, p. 681.

9. Julie Collins, Architects of South Australia website, http://www.architectsdatabase.unisa.edu.au/arch_full.asp?Arch_ID=48

10. Roberts, *Avalon*, p. 83.

11. www.architecture.about.com

12. www.ozetecture.org/oze

13. Glenn Mercutt, interview by Geraldine O'Brien, Architecture Writer, *Sydney Morning Herald*, 15 April 2002.

FUTURE PLANNING

1. Jan Roberts, *Avalon: Landscape & Harmony: Walter Burley Griffin, Alexander Stewart Jolly & Harry Ruskin Rowe*, Ruskin Rowe Press, Avalon Beach NSW, 1999, p. 19.

2. Robin Boyd, *Australia's Home*, Melbourne University Press, Carlton Vic., 1952, preface.

3. Interview with Richard Leplastrier, Lovett Bay, February 2011.

THE SURFING TRIBE

1. Steve Hawk, *Waves*, Chronicle Books, San Francisco, 2005, p. 13.

2. Hawk, *Waves*, p. 9.

3. Ashley Jones-Evans, Linda Gregoriou & Dale Jones-Evans, *Sea Gods. Australian Surfers*, FTB Group Pty Ltd, Sydney, 2000.

4. Jones-Evans, Gregoriou & Jones-Evans, *Sea Gods*.

World champions

1. Ashley Jones-Evans, Linda Gregoriou & Dale Jones-Evans, *Sea Gods: Australian Surfers*, FTB Group Pty Ltd, Sydney, 2000.

2. Tim Baker, *High Surf: The World's Most Inspiring Surfers, Waveriding as a Way of Life, the Ocean as Teacher*, Harper Sports, Pymble NSW, 2007, p. 145.

3. Nick Carroll, October 2000, Surfline website. 'Bernard "Midget" Farrelly (September 13, 1944–)', www.surfline.com/surfing-a-to-z/bernard-midget-farrelly-biography-and-photos_801/

4. Matt Warshaw, *The History of Surfing*, Chronicle Books, San Francisco, 2010, p. 365.

5. Corroborated by correspondence.

6. 'Layne Beachley', Focus Series website , www.focusseries.com.au/biography/layne-beachley

7. 'Chelsea Hedges, Australia', ASP website, www.aspworldtour.com/surfers/womens-profiles/chelsea-hedges/

8. Stuart 'Stretch' Cooper, in correspondence to John Ogden, January 2011.

9. 'Wendy Botha', Girls Who Surf website, www.girls-who-surf.com/wendy-botha.html

Surfers' surfers

1. C. Bede Maxwell, *Surf: Australians Against the Sea*, Angus & Robertson, Sydney, 1949, p. 10.

2. Maxwell, *Surf*, p. 12.

3. Nick Carroll, August 2000, 'Bob Pike (1940–May 20, 1999)', Surfline website, www.surfline.com/surfing-a-to-z/bob-pike-biography-and-photos_882/

4. Dave Keogh interview with Ken Gray, 'Manly Surfing History—45 Years On and Ken's Still Amped', Our Manly website, www.ourmanly.com.au/Sports/Manly_Surf_Legends.aspx

5. Tim Baker, Words by Tim Baker website, www.bytimbaker.com/recent_works/australia-day-with-herro/

6. Shane Herring, on Words by Tim Baker website, www.bytimbaker.com/recent_works/australia-day-with-herro/

NORTHSIDE SURF MEDIA

Surfing magazines

1. Drew Kampion, *Stoked! A History of Surf Culture*. General Publishing Group, Santa Monica CA, 1997, and Gibbs Smith, Layton UT, 1997, chap. 3.

2. Steve Pezman, interview in Cyrus Sutton's film *Under the Sun*.

3. Kampion, *Stoked!*, chap. 3.

COURTESY IN THE SURF

1. Glen Henning, in Nat Young, *Surf Rage: A Surfer's Guide to Turning Negatives into Positives*, Nymboida Press, Sydney, 2000, p. 135.

2. Henning, in Young, *Surf Rage*, p. 35.

GLOBAL IMPACT

Problems and Solutions

1. Dennis Foley & Ricky Maynard, *Repossession of Our Spirit: Traditional Owners of Northern Sydney*, Aboriginal History Inc., Canberra, 2001, p. 12.

2. Foley, *Repossession of Our Spirit*, p. 47.

3. A.P. Elkin, *Aboriginal Men of High Degree: Initiation and Sorcery in the World's Oldest Tradition*, Queensland University Press, St Lucia Qld, 1977, p. 166.

4. Ronald M. Berndt & Catherine H. Berndt, *The World of the First Australians*, Ure Smith, Sydney, 1977, p. 231.

5. Ray Grigg, 'From Tuna to Squid, Jellyfish or Algae', Sierra Club BC website, www.sierraclub.bc.ca/local-groups/Quadra-Island/publications/from-tuna-to-squid-jellyfish-or-algae

6. W. Eugene Smith & Aileen M. Smith, *Minamata: the Story of the Poisoning of a City, and of the People Who Chose to Carry the Burden of Courage*, Holt, Rinehart & Winston, New York, 1975, p. 170.

The future of surfing

7. Nat Young, personal communication, 17 April 2007. Dahlberg, personal communication, 27 April 2007.

SALTWATER DESCENDANTS

1. Dennis Foley & Ricky Maynard, *Repossession of Our Spirit: Traditional Owners of Northern Sydney*, Aboriginal History Inc., Canberra, 2001, p. 57.

2. Julie Janson & Peter Read, *People of the Guringai Language*, information sheet, Department of History, University of Sydney, 2011.

3. Julie Janson & Peter Read, *People of the Guringai Language*, information sheet, Department of History, University of Sydney, 2011.

4. Julie Janson & Peter Read, *People of the Guringai Language*, information sheet, Department of History, University of Sydney, 2011.

5. Nan Bosler, Pat Frater (ed.) & Paul McCarthy (illustrator) & Aboriginal Support Group (NSW) 2011, *The Story of Bob Waterer and his Family 1803–2011*, Aboriginal Support Group—Manly Warringah Pittwater, Collaroy NSW, 2011.

6. Julie Janson & Peter Read, *People of the Guringai Language*, information sheet, Department of History, University of Sydney, 2011.

7. Julie Janson & Peter Read, *People of the Guringai Language*, information sheet, Department of History, University of Sydney, 2011.

8. For more information, go to www.historyofaboriginalsydney.edu.au, www.asgmwp.net and www.aecg.nsw.edu.au.

9. Jakelin Troy, *The Sydney Language*, J. Troy, Flynn ACT, 1994, preface.

10. Paul Keating. *Redfern Speech (Year for the World's Indigenous People)—10 December 1992*. The Hon. Paul Keating Official Website, www.keating.org.au/main.cfm

11. Oren R. Lyons, Faithkeeper, Turtle Clan, Onondaga Nation Council of Chiefs Haudenosaunee, in Dana Gluckstein, *Dignity: In Honor of the Rights of Indigenous Peoples*, powerHouse Books, Brooklyn NY, 2010, p. 13.

Photo Ray Leighton. Courtesy Betty Leighton.

bibliography

Aboriginal Support Group—Manly Warringah Pittwater. *A Story To Tell … On a Road Toward Reconciliation*. ASG-MWP, Narrabeen NSW, 2002.

An Authentic and interesting narrative of the late expedition to Botany Bay: as performed by Commodore Phillips and the fleet of the seven transport ships under his command … / written by an officer. W. Bailey, H. Lemoine and J. Parsons, London, 1789.

Anderson, Maybanke. 'The Story of Pittwater', *Journal of the Royal Australian Historical Society (JRAHS)*, Vol. VI, Part IV, 1920.

Anderson, Maybanke. *Maybanke Anderson's Story of Pittwater: 1770 to 1920*. Ruskin Rowe Press, Avalon Beach, 1996.

Architects of South Australia website, www.architectsdatabase.unisa.edu.au

Atkins, Richard. '*Opinion on Treatment to be Adopted Towards the Natives*'. 20 July 1805. *Historical Records of Australia*, Series 1, Vol. 5, p. 502.

Attenbrow, Valerie. *Sydney's Aboriginal Past: Investigating the Archaeological and Historical Records*. UNSW Press, Sydney, 2002.

Australian Directory of Biography, Supplementary Volume. Melbourne University Press, Melbourne, 2005.

Baker, Tim. *High Surf: The World's Most Inspiring Surfers, Waveriding as a Way of Life, the Ocean as Teacher*. Harper Sports, Pymble NSW, 2007.

Baker, Tim. Words by Tim Baker website. www.bytimbaker.com

Barnett, Bill, Brown, Ken & Parkhill, Bob. *The Beach Comes First 1912–2003*. North Narrabeen SLSC, 2007.

Benns, Matthew. *100 Years—A Celebration of Surf Life Saving at North Steyne 1907–2007*. North Steyne SLSC, 2007.

Berndt, Ronald M. & Berndt, Catherine H. *The World of the First Australians*. Ure Smith, Sydney, 1977.

Booth, Douglas. 'Clubbies: Managing Pleasure and Discipline', *Between the Flags: One Hundred Summers of Australian Surf Lifesaving*, Edwin Jaggard (ed.). UNSW Press, Sydney, 2006.

Bosler, Nan, Frater, Pat (ed.) & McCarthy, Paul (illustrator) & Aboriginal Support Group (NSW) 2011. *The Story of Bob Waterer and his Family 1803–2011*. Aboriginal Support

Group—Manly Warringah Pittwater, Collaroy NSW, 2011.

Bowdler, Sandra. 'Hook, line and dilly bag: an interpretation of an Australian coastal shell midden', *Mankind*, 10(4), 1976.

Boyce, Jim. *Pictorial History: Warringah*. Kingsclear Books, Alexandria NSW, 2006.

Boyd, Robin. *Australia's Home*. Melbourne University Press, Carlton Vic., 1952.

Bradley, William & Public Library of New South Wales. William Dixson Foundation. *A Voyage to New South Wales: The Journal of Lieutenant William Bradley RN of HMS Sirius, 1786–1792*. Trustees of the Public Library of New South Wales in association with Ure Smith, Sydney, 1969.

Brawley, Sean. *Beach Beyond: A History of the Palm Beach Surf Club 1921–1996*. UNSW Press, Sydney, 1996.

Brook, Jack. *Shut Out from the World: the Hawkesbury Aborigines Reserve and Mission 1889–1946*. Deerubbin Press, Berowra Heights NSW, 1999 (2nd edn).

Broome, Richard. *Aboriginal Australians: A History Since 1788*. Allen & Unwin, Sydney, 2010.

Byrne, Denis. *Aboriginal Sites on the Palm Beach Barrier*. A report to Warringah Shire, 1984.

Calado, Jorge. *Waterproof: Water in Photography Since 1852*. Edition Stemmle, Zurich, 1998.

Carroll, Nick. *The Last Wave*. Angus & Robertson, Sydney, 1999.

Carroll, Nick. *Visions of the Breaking Wave*. Morrison Media, North Burleigh Qld, 1991.

Carter, Jeff. *Surf Beaches of Australia's East Coast*. Angus & Robertson, Sydney, 1986.

Cato, John. *The Story of the Camera in Australia*. Georgian House, Melbourne, 1955.

Champion, George & Champion, Shelagh. *Did the Aborigines of Manly, Warringah and Pittwater Peninsula Really Belong to the Kuring-gai Tribe?* Unpublished paper, 2003 (revised 2011).

Champion, George & Champion, Shelagh. *Journey to Broken Bay by Land: 22nd to 25th August, 1788*. S. & G. Champion, Killarney Heights, 1990.

Champion, Shelagh & Champion, George. *Bathing, Drowning and Life Saving in Manly, Warringah and Pittwater to 1915*. Book House, Glebe, 2000.

Champion, Shelagh & Champion, George. *Lieutenant James Grant's Journey to Manly, Warringah and Pittwater, 25th and 26th February, 1801*. S. & G. Champion, Killarney Heights, NSW, 1991.

Champion, Shelagh & Champion, George. *Manly, Warringah and Pittwater, Vol. 1 1788–1850*. S. & G. Champion, Killarney Heights, 1997.

Champion, Shelagh & Champion, George. *Manly, Warringah and Pittwater, Vol. 2 1850–1880*. S. & G. Champion, Killarney Heights, 1998.

City of Sydney website. *Barani: Indigenous History of Sydney City*. www.cityofsydney.nsw.gov.au/barani

Cliff, Stafford. *The Way We Live: By the Sea*. Thames & Hudson, London, 2006.

Cobley, John. *Sydney Cove, 1788*. Hodder & Stoughton, London, 1962.

Collins, David, B.H. Fletcher (ed.), *An Account of the English Colony in NSW*, Vols 1 & 2. A.H. & A.W. Reid, Sydney, 1975.

Cook, James. *Captain Cook's Journal during his first voyage round the world made in H.M. Bark "Endeavour" 1768–71*. Sir W.J.L. Wharton (ed.). Elliot Stock, London, 1893. Accessed at http://www.gutenberg.org/files/8106/8106-h/8106-h.htm

Curby, Pauline. *Freshie: Freshwater Surf Life Saving Club—The First 100 Years*. UNSW Press, Sydney, 2007.

Curby, Pauline. *Pittwater Rising: The Making of Pittwater Council*. Pittwater Council, Mona Vale NSW, 2002.

Curby, Pauline. *Seven Miles from Sydney: A History of Manly*. Manly Council, Manly NSW, 2001.

Curlewis, Jean & Cazneaux, Harold. *Sydney Surfing*. Art in Australia, Sydney, 1929.

Currie, Jessica. *Bo-ra-ne Ya-goo-na Par-ry-boo-go (Yesterday Today Tomorrow)*. Willoughby Council, 2008.

Danson, Ted & D'Orso, Michael. *Oceana: Our Endangered Oceans and What We Can Do to Save Them*. Rodale Books, Emmaus PA, 2011.

Day, David. *Smugglers and Sailors: The Customs History of Australia 1788–1901*. AGPS Press for Australian Customs Service, Canberra, 1992.

Drew, Philip. *Peter Stutchbury: Of People and Places: Between the Bush and the Beach*. Pesaro Publishing, Balmain NSW, 2000.

Dutton, Geoffrey. *Sun, Sea, Surf and Sand—The Myth of the Beach*. Oxford University Press, Melbourne, 1985.

Edwards, Richard & Shaw, Roderick. *Warringah 1988: A Celebration by its Artists and Writers*. Shire of Warringah NSW, 1989.

Elkin, A.P. *Aboriginal Men of High Degree: Initia-*

tion and Sorcery in the World's Oldest Tradition. Queensland University Press, St Lucia Qld, 1977.

Finlay, Jack. *Caught Inside: Surf Writings and Photographs*. Stormy Weather Productions, Geelong, 1992.

Fitzsimmons, Portia. *Eastern Suburbs Album: Pictorial Memories of Darling Point, Double Bay, Rose Bay, Vaucluse, Watsons Bay, Bellevue Hill, Bondi, Waverley and Bronte*. Atrand Pty Ltd, Sydney, 1985.

Flannery, Tim F. *The Birth of Sydney*. Text Publishing, Melbourne, 1999.

Fletcher, Patrick. *The Story of Bungaree*. Sydney Harbour Federation Trust, 2009.

Foley, Dennis & Maynard, Ricky. *Repossession of Our Spirit: Traditional Owners of Northern Sydney*. Aboriginal History Inc., Canberra, 2001.

Freshwater Amateur Swimming Club website, www.fasc.asn.au/history.html

Galton, Barry. *Gladiators of the Surf: The Australian Surf Life Saving Championships, a History*. A.H. & A.W. Reed Pty Ltd, Frenchs Forest NSW, 1984.

Gluckstein, Dana. *Dignity: In Honor of the Rights of Indigenous Peoples*. powerHouse Books, Brooklyn NY, 2010.

Govett, W.R., Potts, A. & Renard, G. *Sketches of New South Wales Written and Illustrated for the Saturday Magazine in 1836–37 by William Romaine Govett, together with an Essay on the Saturday Magazine by Gaston Renard and an Account of His Life by Annette Potts*. Gaston Renard, Melbourne, 1977.

Guerber, H.A. *Myths and Legends of the Middle*

Photo Ray Leighton. Courtesy Betty Leighton.

Ages: Their Origin and Influence on Literature and Art. G.G. Harrap & Company, London, 1909.

Hall, Lincoln. *Douglas Mawson: The Life of an Explorer*. New Holland Publishers, Sydney, 2011.

Hawk, Steve. *Waves*. Chronicle Books, San Francisco, 2005.

Hickson, Melinda. *Aboriginal Sydney*. Aboriginal Studies Press, Canberra, 2001.

A History of Aboriginal Australia website. www.historyofaboriginalsydney.edu.au/timeline

Hixson, Tim. *Beach*. Bangalley Press, Avalon NSW, 1998.

Horton, Rev. William. *Letter to the Wesleyan Missionary Society, Hobart Town, Van Diemen's Land, 3 June 1823*, BT Box 52:1269-74, ML.

Hunter, John. *An Historical Journal of Events at Sydney and at Sea, 1787–1792*. Angus & Robertson in association with the Royal Australian Historical Society, Sydney, 1968.

Isobel & Watling, Thomas (b. 1762). *Nanbaree*. Isobel, West Perth, 1994.

Jacobs, Ian & Vosper, James. *A History of the Aboriginal Clans of Sydney's Northern Beaches*. Northside Printing, Brookvale NSW, 2003.

Jacobs, Ian. *A Fascinating Heritage of Sydney's Northern Beaches*, Ian Jacobs, Bayview NSW, 2008.

Jaggard, Ed. 'Australian surf lifesaving and the "forgotten members"', *Australian Historical Studies*. 29(112), 1999, pp. 23–43.

Jaggard, Ed. 'Tempering the testosterone: masculinity, women and Australian surf lifesaving', *The International Journal of the History of Sport*, 18(4) 2001, pp. 16–36.

Janson, Julie. *Black Mary & Gunjies: Two Plays by Julie Janson*. Aboriginal Studies Press, Canberra, 1996.

Jennings, Guy & Jennings, Joan. *Mona Vale Stories*. Arcadia Publishing, Newport Beach, 2007.

Jennings, Guy. *The Newport Story, 1788–1988*. Aramo, Newport Beach, 1987.

Jennings, Guy. *Newport Surf Life Saving Club, 1909–2009: The First Century*. Newport Surf Life Saving Club, Newport, 2009.

Jennings, Guy & De Boos, Charles. *My Holiday and Other Early Travels from Manly to Palm Beach 1861*. Aramo, Newport Beach, 1991.

Johnson, Pamela (ed.). *Evolution of an Icon: 100 Years of Surf Lifesaving in New South Wales*. UNSW Press, Sydney, 2008.

Jones-Evans, Ashley, Gregoriou, Linda & Jones-Evans, Dale. *Sea Gods: Australian Surfers*. FTB Group Pty Ltd, Sydney, 2000.

Kampion, Drew. *Stoked! A History of Surf Culture*. General Publishing Group, Santa Monica CA, 1997, and Gibbs Smith, Layton UT, 1997.

Keating, P.J. *Redfern Speech (Year for the World's Indigenous People)—10 December 1992*. The Hon. Paul Keating Official Website, www.keating.org.au/main.cfm

Keneally, Thomas. *The Commonwealth of Thieves*. Random House Australia, Melbourne, 2007.

King, Lieutenant. James *Captain Cook's Journals*, 1779.

Kohen, James & Blacktown and District Historical Society. *The Darug and their Neighbours: the traditional Aboriginal owners of the Sydney region*, Darug Link in association with the Blacktown and District Historical Society, Blacktown NSW, 1993.

Kramer, Augustin. *The Samoa Islands*. Vols I & II. University of Hawai'i Press, Honolulu, 1994–1995.

Lawrence, Joan. *Pictorial History: Pittwater*. Kingsclear Books, Alexandria NSW, 2006.

Lee, Emma, Warringah (NSW) Council & Metropolitan Local Aboriginal Land Council (Redfern NSW). *The Tale of a Whale: Significant Aboriginal Landscapes of the Northern Beaches*. Warringah Council, Dee Why NSW, 2002.

Leonard, John. *The New York Times Guide to Essential Knowledge: A Desk Reference for the Curious Mind*. St Martin's Press, New York, 2007.

McDonald, Charles. *Stories of the Peninsula: Manly-Warringah*. Child & Henry Publishing, Brookvale NSW, 1980.

McDonald, Charles E. & Henderson, Clive W.T. *The Manly-Warringah Story*. Hamlyn, Sydney, 1975.

McGlynn, Jean & McDonald, Charles A. *Manly*. Currawong Press, Milsons Point NSW, 1976.

Macken, James. *Early Pittwater: A Nostalgic Look at its Soldiers, Seamen, Smugglers and Settlers*. Anchor Publications, Cammeray NSW, 2004.

Macken, Jim. *Martin Burke: Father of Pittwater*. J.J. Macken, Sydney, 1994.

MacLeod, Virginia. *Pictorial History: Manly*. Kingsclear Books, Alexandria NSW, 2008.

McMillan, James. *Blue Yonder: A Journey to the Heart of Surf Culture*. Macmillan, Sydney, 2005.

Maxwell, C. Bede. *Surf: Australians Against the Sea*. Angus & Robertson, Sydney, 1949.

Messent, David. *Sydney's Northern Beaches*. David Messent Photography, Balgowlah NSW, 1999.

Newbury, Paul W. (ed.). *Aboriginal Heroes of the Resistance: From Pemulwuy to Mabo*. Action for

World Development, Surry Hills NSW, 1999.

Ogden, John. *Australienation: Portrait of a Bi-cultural Country*. Cyclops Press, Sydney, 2000.

Ogden, John. *Portraits from a Land Without People: A Pictorial Anthology of Indigenous Australia 1847–2008*. Cyclops Press, Sydney, 2009.

Oliver, Douglas L. *Native Cultures of the Pacific Islands*. University of Hawai'i Press, Honolulu, 1989.

Osmond, Frederick Gary. *Nimble Savages: Myth, Race, Social Memory and Australian Aquatic Sport*. University of Queensland, St Lucia Qld, 2006.

Parbury, Nigel. *Survival A History of Aboriginal Life in NSW*. NSW Department of Aboriginal Affairs, 1991.

Parke, Trent & Autio, Narelle. *The Seventh Wave*. Hot Chilli Press, Kirribilli NSW, 2000.

Paterson, G. *The History of New South Wales*. McKenzie & Dent, Newcastle upon Tyne, 1811.

Pearson, Kent. *Surfing Subcultures of Australia and New Zealand*. University of Queensland Press, St Lucia Qld, 1979.

Phillip, Arthur & Sydney, Thomas Townshend Viscount 1733–1800, Tipping, G.R. (ed.), *The Official Account Through Governor Phillip's Letters to Lord Sydney*. G.R. Tipping, Beecroft NSW, 1988.

Pittwater Natural Heritage Association. *Birds of Warriewood Wetland Irrawong Reserve*, Pittwater Natural Heritage Association, 2004.

Pollon, Frances & Healy, Gerald. *The Book of Sydney Suburbs*. Angus & Robertson, North Ryde, 1988.

Popp, T. & N., & Walker, Bill. *Footprints on Rock: Aboriginal Art of the Sydney Region*. Metropolitan Local Aboriginal Land Council, Redfern NSW, 1997.

Read, Peter & Janson, Julie. *People of Guringai Language Country: 1900–2010*. Poster by Peter Read and Julie Janson. Poster design and layout by MacDonald Hamilton. Department of History, University of Sydney, Sydney, 2010.

Reid, Christo. *Cactus: Surfing Journals from Solitude*. Strangelove Press, Sydney, 2010.

Roberts, Alex, with Schilling, Kath. *Aboriginal Women's Fishing in New South Wales: A thematic history*. Department of Environment, Climate Change & Water NSW, Sydney, 2010. Accessed at www.environment.nsw.gov.au/resources/cultureheritage/10131abwfish.pdf

Roberts, Jan. *Avalon: Landscape & Harmony: Walter Burley Griffin, Alexander Stewart Jolly & Harry Ruskin Rowe*. Ruskin Rowe Press, Avalon Beach NSW, 1999.

Searl, Geoff. *ABSLSC 75 Years Saving Lives*, Publisher, City, 2000.

Scott, William, *The Port Stephens Blacks: Recollections of William Scott*. Chronicle, Dungog NSW, 1929.

Sharpe, Alan. *Manly to Palm Beach: Pictorial Memories*, Atrand, Sydney, 1983.

Slater, Kelly & Jarratt, Phil. *Kelly Slater: For the Love*. Chronicle Books, San Francisco, 2008.

Smith, Keith Vincent. *King Bungaree: A Sydney Aborigine Meets the Great South Pacific Explorers, 1799–1830*. Kangaroo Press, Kenthurst NSW, 1992.

Smith, Keith Vincent. *Mari Nawi: Aboriginal Odysseys*. Rosenberg Publishing, Kenthurst NSW, 2010.

Smith, W. Eugene & Smith, Aileen M. *Minamata: The Story of the Poisoning of a City, and of the People Who Chose to Carry the Burden of Courage*. Holt, Rinehart & Winston, New York, 1975.

Somerville, Margaret & Perkins, Tony. *Singing the Coast*. Aboriginal Studies Press, Canberra, 2010.

Sparks, Jervis. *The Red Light of Palm Beach*. Jervis Sparks, Maleny Qld, 2005.

Sparks, Jervis. *Tales from Barrenjoey*. Forest Publications, Newport Beach NSW, 1992.

Stanbury, Peter & Clegg, John. *A Field Guide to Aboriginal Rock Paintings*. Sydney University Press, Sydney, 1990.

Steege, Joan. *Palm Beach 1788–1988*. Palm Beach Association, Sydney, 1984.

Strachan, Alexander. *Remarkable Incidents in the Life of the Rev. Samuel Leigh: Missionary to the Settlers and Savages of Australia and New Zealand: With a Succinct History of the Origin and Progress of the Missions in Those Colonies*. James Nicholls, London, 1855.

Surfline website. www.surfline.com

Swancott, Charles. *Dee Why to Barrenjoey and Pittwater*. The author, Woy Woy NSW, 1967.

Tench, Watkin. *1789–1793 Sydney's First Four Years: A Complete Account of the Settlement at Port Jackson*. Angus & Robertson, Sydney, 1961.

Troy, Jakelin. *The Sydney Language*. J. Troy, Flynn ACT, 1994.

Turbet, Peter. *The Aborigines of the Sydney District Before 1788*. Kangaroo Press, East Roseville NSW, 2001.

Turnbull, John. *A Voyage Round the World in the Years 1800, 1801, 1802 and 1804: In Which the Author Visited the Principal Islands in the Pacific Ocean, and the English settlements of Port Jackson*

and Norfolk Island. Printed for Richard Phillips by T. Gillet, London, 1805.

Walding, Murray. *Blue Heaven: The Story of Australian Surfing*. Hardie Grant Books, South Yarra Vic., 2006.

Warren, Mark. *Mark Warren's Atlas of Australian Surfing* (2nd edn). Harper Sports, Sydney, 1998.

Warringah History, Malcolm D. Prentis (ed.). Warringah Shire Council. 1988.

Warshaw, Matt. *Above the Roar: 50 Surfer Interviews*. Waterhouse, Santa Cruz, 1997.

Warshaw, Matt. *The History of Surfing*. Chronicle Books, San Francisco, 2010.

White, Jill. *Dupain's Beaches*. Chapter & Verse, Neutral Bay NSW, 2000.

White, John. *Journal of a Voyage to New South Wales*. A.H. Chisholm (ed.), Angus & Robertson, Sydney, 1962.

Willey, Keith. *When the Sky Fell Down*. Collins, Sydney, 1979.

Williams, Heathcote. *Whale Nation*. Jonathon Cape, London, 1988.

Winton, Tim. *Land's Edge: A Coastal Memoir*. Penguin, Camberwell Vic, 1993.

Woodriff, Jim. *Riding the Waves of Change*. University of the Sunshine Coast, Qld, 2003.

Worgan, G.B. *Journal of a First Fleet Surgeon (1788)*. Library Council of NSW, Sydney, 1978.

Young, Nat & McGregor, Craig. *The History of Surfing*. Palm Beach Press, Sydney, 1983.

Young, Nat. *Surf Rage: A Surfer's Guide to Turning Negatives into Positives*. Nymboida Press, Sydney, 2000.

Zahn, Kara. *Whales*. Gallery Books, New York, 1988.

contributing writers

CARROLL, Nick (b.1959)
Nick Carroll is a lifelong surfer who grew up at Newport Beach and co-founded the somewhat notorious Newport Plus Boardriders in the mid-seventies. He is one of the few surfers to have board-paddled the entire length of the Sydney northern beaches non-stop. Nick still lives and surfs at Newport despite many years of travelling to all sorts of apparently far more glamorous places. He is married to Wendy with two almost-adult children.

FOLEY, Dennis (b. 1951)
Professor Dennis Foley is of the Gai-mariagal Aboriginal people of Northern Sydney. His

people on his father's side are Wiradjuri. As Professor of Indigenous Research at the University of Newcastle, he is interested in academic research into the area of Indigenous entrepreneurship within Australia and the Pacific, publishing in the fields of history, cultural studies, management/entrepreneurship and education. Dennis is also a practitioner in the visual arts and author of Repossession of Our Spirit (2001).

WILLCOX, Kirk (b.1957)
Kirk Willcox is a former editor of *Tracks* magazine, who co-founded STOP (Stop The Ocean Pollution) in 1981 to help protect Australian beaches. With Tom Carroll, he co-wrote the two-time world champion's biography *The Wave Within*. A former marketing/communications manager with Quiksilver International, based on the northern beaches, Willcox is currently marketing/communications director with humanitarian organisation SurfAid International. He is most proud that his two children, Simon and Ashley, grew up with a love of the ocean.

WITZIG, John (b.1944)
Photographer and journalist John Witzig had his first piece of surf journalism published in 1963 for *Surfing World*. He wrote the *"splendidly inflammatory"* article 'We're Tops Now' for the American publication *Surfer* following Nat Young's win at the World Championships in San Diego in 1967. Witzig went on to edit *Surf International*, and in 1970 co-founded *Tracks* with Albe Falzon and David Elfick, working from an office based at Whale Beach. Witzig founded *Sea Notes* in 1977 and has published several books on Australian photography.

picture credits

ARTISTS

BARAK, William (King Billy) (1824–1903)
William Barak was an early Aboriginal artist in the colonial period. His work reflected the duality of his *"strong tribal identity and his status as an important intermediary in the cultural dialogue that took place between the black and white inhabitants of the early Victorian settlement."* (From Aboriginal Art Resource website, www.aboriginalartresource.com/aboriginal-artists/william-king-billy-barak)

EARLE, Augustus (1793–1838)
Born in London, Earle was a professional painter who travelled widely. He reached Australia in 1825 and published his *Views of Australia* the following year. Apart from his work in Sydney he journeyed from the Port Macquarie area across to the Wellington Valley

and down to the Illawarra to sketch landscapes and portraits of Aborigines. Following further voyages around the globe accompanied by dissolute living, described by Charles Darwin as *"open licentiousness"*, Earle died of *"asthma and debility"* in London.

FAULKNER, Ian (b.1959)
Ian Faulkner has spent most of his life in the Pittwater area, and over the last 25 years he has worked in all genres of illustration. Faulkner is fascinated by natural and Indigenous history, and has illustrated the oldest artefacts yet found in Australia and Melanesia, as well as illustrating the 'Iceman' from Northern Italy's artefacts, and skulls from Java over 130,000 years old. More of his work can be found at www.ianfaulkneril-lustrator.com.

GLASHEEN, Michael (b.1942)
Mick Glasheen is a filmmaker and artist who lives on the northern beaches. His films include *Teleologic Telecast from Spaceship Earth: On Board with Buckminster Fuller* (1970), *Uluru* (1977), *River Time* (1983) and *Aboriginal Memorial* (1988). At present Glasheen is working on a series of panoramic paintings titled *Singing the Land—Guringai Country*.

GOOLD, Bruce (b.1948)
Bruce Goold was born in Newcastle, NSW. His father was an artist, Spitfire pilot and furniture retailer. Goold studied art as a boarder at Sydney Grammar School, the National Art School, Sydney, and in Newcastle. He was a member of the Yellow House before travelling to Bali and Southeast Asia, and then settling on the northern beaches in 1976. He works mainly in linocut and woodcut prints, and has designed popular loud rayon shirts for Mambo as well as an extensive range of hand-printed tropical furnishing fabrics. Goold has had large solo exhibitions in Sydney, Melbourne and London.

LESUEUR, Charles-Alexandre (1778–1846)
Born in Le Havre, France, Charles-Alexandre Lesueur became a natural history artist, naturalist and explorer. In 1800, the French government commissioned two corvettes, the *Géographe* and the *Naturaliste*, under the command of Post-Captain Nicholas Baudin to undertake a scientific voyage of discovery to the Australian continent, still known as New Holland. Lesueur was taken on, not as an artist or scientist, but as an assistant gunner. During the journey François Péron, a brilliant young medical botanist and anthropologist, was appointed chief zoologist and endorsed Lesueur to work with him as an illustrator. His drawings and etchings of local flora and fauna are regarded as having major significance. (From 'The Naturalists' website, www.abc.net.au/naviga-tors/naturalists/lesueur.htm)

LYCETT, Joseph (1774–1828)
Born in Staffordshire, England, Lycett was by profession a portrait and miniature painter before being convicted of forgery and transported to Sydney in 1814. Life improved for Lycett after Wallis became commandant in 1816 and he received a pardon. According to Commissioner John Thomas Bigge, Lycett's *"habits of intoxication"* were *"fixed and incurable"*, but he managed to produce a large body of work, including the printing of twelve sets of drawings bound together and sold as *Views in Australia* (London, 1825).

MIKHAILOV, Pavel Nikolaivich (1786–1840)
Pavel Mikhailov was born in St Petersburg, Russia. He graduated from the Russian Imperial Academy School around 1807, and was honoured with the title of Academician in 1815. Mikhailov was made the official artist on the F. Bellingshausen and M. Lazarev expedition to the Antarctic and the Pacific (1819–1821). He was a marine artist who drew natural history and ethnographic subjects as well as views of Sydney Harbour.

PETIT, Nicolas-Martin (1777–1805)
Petit was was just entering his teens at the start of the French Revolution and studied graphic arts. He was taught by Napoleon's portrait painter, Jacques Louis David, the greatest of neoclassical artists. In 1800, Petit joined Post-Captain Nicholas Baudin on a scientific voyage of discovery to the Australian continent. Among the scientists, botanists and artists were the young artists François Péron, Charles-Alexandre Lesueur and Petit. As the journey progressed Petit began to specialise in the drawing of portraits of indigenous peoples the expedition encountered. Petit returned to France in 1804 and died at just twenty-eight. (From 'The Naturalists' website, www.abc.net.au/navigators/naturalists/petit.htm)

PRATTENT, Thomas
A London engraver and printmaker active in the late eighteenth century.

RHODES, Mark (b.1969)
Mark Rhodes' paintings deal with the relationships between the forces of nature and their effect on our psyche. Growing up on the northern beaches and becoming a keen surfer, he expresses his physical experiences and observations in his work. *"When the elements shape our world there is an infinite source of inspiration and personal experience to be embraced."* Rhodes' career spans more than twenty years, and in June 2011 he exhibited a solo show at Manly Art Gallery and Museum.

RODIUS, Charles (1802–1860)
German-born Charles Rodius, who had worked as a draughtsman and engraver in Paris, was sent to New South Wales in 1829 for theft. He was assigned, without salary, to the Department of Public Works. Rodius frequented the nearby Domain, where he made many sketches of Aboriginal people, including the *View from the Government Domain, Sydney, 1833*, in which fishermen at Woolloomooloo Bay (Walla-mulla) wear cut-off trousers, but still use the traditional *mooting* or pronged fishing spear.

WATLING, Thomas (1762–c.1814)
Born in Scotland, Thomas Watling was transported to Australia for possessing forged banknotes. Arriving in Sydney in 1792, he was quickly was assigned to Surgeon John White, an ardent naturalist, who employed Watling's artistic skill. In addition to picturesque landscapes, Watling drew the Cadigal leader Colebee (White-breasted Sea Eagle), his wife 'Da-ring-ha' or Daringa (Stingray), his nephew Nanbarry (Parrot Mouth) and his kinsman Caruey (White Cockatoo). These works are on loan from the Natural History Museum, South Kensington, London. (From SLNSW Eora catalogue.)

WILLIAMS, Jacqui
Jacqui Williams is a Bundjalung artist from the North Coast of New South Wales whose lino prints depict the native animals and plants found in her country. Among her subjects are the pippies found scattered from the beaches in Bundjalung country, and the whales that follow that coast as they migrate to and from their breeding grounds. Williams' bold prints render animal and plant forms within a background of rhythmic patterns, creating a strong sense of movement within the frame. She has also achieved different textural effects within her works by employing materials such as sand and gesso. (From Design & Art Australia Online, www.daao.org.au/bio/jacqui-williams/#artist_biography)

PHOTOGRAPHERS

BACCON, Steve (b.1971)
Stephen Baccon currently specialises in portraiture, people and fashion, coming from a background in news and sport.

BIRD, Ian (b.1985)
At the age of 19, Bird was offered a job as an assistant with a professional photographer. Before long he had bought his first camera equipment and, following three or four years' mentoring, started up his own business in 2009. Corporate work and sports photography pay the bills, but being a northern beaches local all his spare time goes into surfing photography.

CALE, Robin (c.1890–1971)
President of the Newport SLSC from 1932 for 36 years and a respected professional photographer, Robin Cale started his career in 1908 and by 1920 had his own studio in Neutral Bay. During the 1920s he purchased a weekender in Newport, joining the vibrant artistic community found there, and was conferred Life Membership of the Newport SLSC in 1947. Cale once said that *"while there was light on the beach … that's where I would like to spend the day."*

CAZNEAUX, Harold (1878–1953)
Born in New Zealand, Cazneaux returned with his family to Sydney around 1887. He followed his father into Hammer & Co. studio in Adelaide as an artist retoucher, but joined Freeman's studio in Sydney in 1904, also as a retoucher. He became a freelancer and opened his own studio in 1919. Cazneaux's stature is based on the extraordinary diversity of his work—landscapes and portraits. He died at his Roseville home on 19 June 1953.

COONEY, Jedd (b.1982)
With the ability and eye to capture the beauty and rawness of everyday life, Cooney's love of photography proves that for him it is more than just a job. Growing up on Sydney's northern beaches has played a major role in his ability to capture the earthiness of the beach and urban lifestyle, which in turn permeates through his work as a portrait and fashion photographer. Jedd Cooney's father, Steve, was one of the intrepid travellers exploring the possibilities of Indonesia in Albe Falzon's 1972 classic surf film *Morning of the Earth*.

CRAWFORD, Justin (b.1977)
Justin was born into Dee Why and the world of photography as the son of the late and great Peter Crawford. Being exposed so early to the way photography captures 'moments in time' triggered Justin's mind. Currently his work can be seen through campaigns for many major surfing/fashion labels.

CRAWFORD, Peter (1952–1999)
Like many others, Dee Why surfer Peter Crawford began his career in the surf media at *Surfing World* magazine. He became a masthead photographer for *Surfer* from 1977 to 1994 and co-founded *Waves* magazine in 1980 while remaining a regular contributor to virtually all Australian surf magazines. Crawford's work was recognised posthumously with the Media Award in the 2001 Australian Surfing Hall of Fame.

DAVEY, Sean (b.1961)
From the island State of Tasmania, Sean Davey entered the world as a rather famous (at the time!) triplet. He took his first picture—of an ocean wave—at the age of 16, and has been actively involved at all levels of surf publishing and advertising, resulting in more than 140 magazine covers worldwide. Woody Woodworth, Warren Bolster, Jeff Hornbaker, Bruce Channon and Peter Crawford were all major influences. Davey is a 'hired gun', specialising in water photography.

DUPAIN, Max (1911–1992)
Maxwell Spencer Dupain was born in Ashfield, Sydney. He grew up spending his weekends at Newport Beach where his family had a holiday house. In 1928 he met Harold Cazneaux, but abandoned the pictorialist style and became Australia's leading modernist photographer in the 1930s. After a long career specialising in architectural photography, Dupain was awarded an OBE in 1982 and Companion of Australia, the country's highest honour, in 1992.

EDEN, Jack (b.1931)
Described as *"the photographic biographer"* of Australian surfing history, Eden shot the majority his images of the Australian surf scene between the late fifties through to the late sixties for use in his magazine, *Surfabout*. Eden diligently recorded this golden period of surfing history, and his work displays a good grasp of photography craft, learnt in part through correspondence with legendary American photographer Ansel Adams. This was a time of great growth and development in surfing, and after the war years the nation was ready to embrace the relaxed and carefree lifestyle. The name for *Surfabout* was adapted from the Aboriginal concept of 'walkabout', and the debut issue was emblazoned with Aboriginal motifs.

FAIRBAIRN, David (b.1985)
Born in Manly hospital, David Fairbairn is a qualified electrician but currently works for O'Neill wetsuits. Fairbairn says: *"I only shoot for with mates, either bodysurfing shoreys, or just pulling into closeouts, haha, so I never would have expected something like this."*

FRANK, Jon (b.1971)
Jon Frank's twenty-year career has seen him work as a photographer and cinematographer across the globe. Frank photographed and directed the surf films *Litmus, Super Computer* and *Mick, Myself & Eugene*. For the past twelve years he has worked as senior photographer for *Surfing World* magazine (Australia). His images have been featured in various magazines and books, including his own *Waves of the Sea* (1999), and his photography has been exhibited in Slovenia, Portugal, USA and Australia. In 2009 Jon collaborated with Richard Tognetti, Artistic Director of the Australian Chamber Orchestra, and select members from the Slovene Philharmonic for 'The Glide', a concert of ocean-related imagery set to classical music.

HIXSON, Tim (b.1950)
Tim Hixson first began photography while a student at Southern Illinois University. In 1969 he hitchhiked to California on Route 66 with an Instamatic camera, and in 1970 began using plastic Diana cameras, completing his degree in Cinema and Photography in 1972. After returning home to Australia he lived in Byron Bay, then moved to Avalon, working out of his studio in North Sydney, shooting commercially and developing his personal photography. In 1998 he revived his interest in plastic camera photography, producing the exhibition and book *Beach*. Hixson continues to explore the ocean and beach culture using traditional and alternative photography.

HURLEY, Frank (1885–1962)
James Francis 'Frank' Hurley, OBE was a photographer, filmmaker and adventurer. Born in Sydney, Hurley ran away from home at the age of 14 to work on the docks. He bought his first camera as a 17-year-old and taught himself photography. He joined Douglas Mawson as photographer on the 1911–1914 Australian Antarctic Expedition, and was also later the official photographer on Ernest Shackleton's Imperial Trans-Antarctic Expedition 1914–1916. In 1917, he joined the AIF as an honorary captain and captured battlefield scenes during the Battle of Passchendaele. For much of the 1930s Hurley worked in Sydney for Cinesound, but in 1940 he resumed war photography with the AIF in the Middle East. He died in Sydney, at Collaroy Plateau, in 1962. (From John Cato, *The Story of the Camera in Australia*, and *Australian Dictionary of Biography*.)

KIDMAN, Andrew (b.1970)
Hailing from the northern beaches, surfer and artist Andrew Kidman works in many mediums, including music, writing, painting, photography, surfboard shaping and films. His work is born from his connection to the ocean, and his patience and dedication are remarkably rare in the modern-day commercial arena. The surfing film and book, *Into the Ether,* was released in 2010.

LEIGHTON, Ray (1917–2002)
Sydney fashion photographer Ray Leighton was born in Sydney. He left school at 14 and took a job at the *Herald,* finding work as a darkroom assistant. Here he met photographer Damien Parer and learnt the trade which became his career. At the outbreak of World War II, Leighton joined the RAAF as a pilot, and also had a stint as a military photographer. After the war he opened his own studio, specialising in fashion (especially swimsuits). In 1992 he wrote his memoirs, *The Escapades of a Professional Photographer.* In his later years, despite having Parkinson's disease, Leighton still made his daily morning visits to the Manly Life Saving Club.

MARKS, Alex (b.1982)
Starting back in the days of film, Super 8 and VHS videos, Alex Marks was always drawn into the world of photography and video. He remembers *"dubbing music tracks over VHS surf footage for entire weekends as a 15-year-old kid"*, and finds it *"amazing how quickly things have changed and I'm only 29."* Simply put, in his own words, *"Capturing the world around me through cameras makes me happy. I will continue to make pictures, experiment and document the waves and everything else around me for my entire life."* (Bio provided.)

McLEOD, Hugh (b.1951)
Off the body, onto the board early '64 with a first shorebreak pitch onto Pavilion sands at Palm Beach. Gremmie-hood at Freshie, then usual stoked boomer surf trajectory. Left school at 15, first job in advertising, then art studios and book design before *Surfing World* magazine involvement. Photography gradually replaced illustration as his primary creative tool.

MOORE, David (1927–2003)
By 1947 Moore had abandoned his intention to study architecture and went to work in the photographic studio of Russell Roberts. He found the fashion and commercial work there too artificial, and left to work with Max Dupain the following year. Inspired by Dupain and the work of American photographers like Walker Evans and Dorothea Lange, Moore spent his spare time photographing different aspects of Sydney, concentrating on the urban poor. During the 1950s he pursued a career as a photojournalist and worked in the UK before joining New York photo-agency Black Star and returning to Australia in 1958. Moore was involved in the foundation of the Australian Centre for Photography.

NEEDHAM, Scott (b.1969)
Scott Needham has spent most of his life on the northern beaches, minus twenty years or so of navigating the world. He loves surfing, family, ocean and mountains, food and design. Needham is a little disillusioned with photography post-digital, so goes surfing instead and lets Banksy (the modern Shakespeare) do the commentary on this fractured planet … so there.

OGDEN, John (b.1952)
Ogden grew up in South Australia, where he worked briefly as a psychiatric nurse and tuna fisherman before becoming a photographer for seminal Australian magazines such as *Tracks, Ram* and *Matilda* during the 1970s. While working as a photojournalist in Southeast Asia during the last days of the Vietnam War he had a chance meeting with the legendary Australian cameraman Neil Davis and decided to turn his attention to cinematography. Since 1980 he has worked as a director of photography, filming documentaries, drama, MTV and advertising around the world. Ogden produced his first book *Australienation* in 2000, followed by *Portraits from a Land Without People* in 2009. Claims that he invented the left eye monocle and that he once worked as a bareback rider at Bullen's Circus could not be confirmed at the time of printing.

ONORATI, Mark (b.1962)
Sydney-born Mark Onorati was given his first surfboard, a Barry Bennett twin fin, when he was 5 years old and never looked back. After surfing as much as possible for the next four decades, a back injury forced him from the water. This setback had its rewards in that Onorati borrowed a camera to shoot surf pics on a reef close to his Narrabeen home, and a new obsession was born.

PENNINGS, John (b.1939)
John Pennings grew up in Newport and learnt to surf at the Neptune Street break—now known as the Peak. In 1956 he watched visiting American lifeguards career across the waves at a surf carnival at Avalon Beach on balsa boards and really got stoked on surfing. His surf photography got going with a 1962 article and photos about the Whale Beach Wedge in *Surfing World.* The following year he was on hand to photograph a classic North Narrabeen day, and captured a memorable image of local surfer Jim Fordham that was made into a mural and hung in the Narrabeen Surf Club hall for the Saturday night stomps. Pennings' photograph of Wayne Lynch taken at the 1968 Australian Titles at Palm Beach is one of the iconic photos of that era.

PERROTT, Ron (1935–1991)
Ron Perrott was born in Sydney and took to surfing in the early days. He made his own Malibu boards in his dad's carpentry factory at Harbord before focusing on his love of photography. His images became well known in Australian surfing in the 1960s in the then pre-eminent surfing magazine *American Surfer* as well as the original Australian surfing magazines. In the mid 1960s he adventured to and surfed in Europe, then settled and photographed in South Africa for many years. Subsequently, he travelled to New Zealand and away from surf photography, returning to Australia at the end of 1988.

PHILLIPS, Jules (b.1970)
Growing up in central North Island New Zealand is where Phillips would often find the fossilised remains of an ancient ocean in his own back yard—shells and fishes carved free from the limestone cliffs—and it was there his affinity with the unknown was born, 500 miles from the sea. Decades later, his coastal view of the world now continues to emerge as a thought-provoking process through the lens: *"The more we see, the more we realise there is to know, and the more we wish to learn and know."*

PLAYER, Toby (b.1977)
Hailing from Avalon and still residing on the beaches. Runs the Bodyboard King shop. Still surfs as much as he can and gets on the lens when he's surfed out.

SCOTT, Roger (b.1944)
Roger Scott was born in North Sydney and began work as a photographic printer for Leicagraph in 1961. He started taking photographs in 1969 and travelled widely throughout the 1970s, working as a freelance photographer since 1978. Scott's photographs are held in major Australian and international collections, and have been selected for several books. His own book, *From the Street*, was published by Chapter & Verse in 2001.

SMITH, Nathan (b.1972)
If you've flipped through a *Tracks* magazine in the last five to six years then you're bound to have come across some of Nathan Smith's work. Although primarily known for his amazing surf photography, he also shoots fashion, lifestyle and portraiture. Once a pro surfer himself, Smith opted to pack his board away and start photographing his peers. Today, Smith is one of the most respected and sought-after photographers in the surfing world.

SOLNESS, Peter (b.1958)
Since his early years as a surfing photographer for *Tracks* and *Surfing World* magazines in the 1970s, Peter Solness has maintained a dialogue with the Australian landscape. These include books such as *Tree Stories*, published by Chapter & Verse in 1999, and his current photographic series, 'Illuminated Landscape', that explores the other-worldly beauty of the Australian bush at night, lit by moonlight and simple hand torches. Samples of these recent works can be seen at www.illuminated-landscape.com.

USHER, Bruce (b.1946)
Bruce grew up in a house next to the reserve on Mona Vale Headland. Life revolved around the headland, the track down to the beach and surfing. In the early sixties Usher's father built a darkroom under the house and he discovered black-and-white photographic printing. He graduated from using an old box Brownie to borrowing his father's 35mm SLR camera with a Tamron telephoto lens. In the August 1964 issue of *Surfing World* his first words and photos were published. A decade later he co-produced and filmed the classic surfing film *A Winter's Tale* with Phil and Russell Sheppard. Since the mid-seventies, Usher has been a Sydney-based professional photographer.

WARE, John (b.1948)
John Ware was born Scotland and immigrated to Australia with his family in 1964. Living in Wollongong, Ware began an electrical apprenticeship at Port Kembla Steelworks and also learnt how to swim and surf. He moved to Sydney, where he opened Friar Tuck Kneeboards in Brookvale with brother Peter. Taking up photography, Ware freelanced for *Surfing World, Tracks* and *Sea Notes* magazines, becoming well known for his water shots taken using the Aquaware water housings he designed and built. Cinematography was his next step, and he worked as a director/cinematographer for Oasis Films, shooting TV commercials for many years before retiring.

WEEKS, Bob (b.1940)
Growing up in Sydney, Weeks began taking, developing and printing photographs back in the fifties when he was just 10 years old. Surfing with his mates up and down Sydney's beaches, he captured 1960s surfing history. Weeks moved to northern New South Wales in 1971, where he still works full time as a professional photographer.

WHELAN, Louise (b.1967)
Louise Whelan's passionate approach to photography has resulted in full and varied bodies of work. Her versatile approach captures many subjects and genres. Whelan is a Moran Photo Prize finalist 2011, Olive Cotton Portrait Prize finalist 2011 and Winner of the The Clerk Of The House Plein Air NSW Parliamentary Photo Prize 2010. At the time of printing, this Avalon-based photographer was working with the State Library of NSW documenting every ethnic community in the State, and had also been selected as one of the ten Australian photographers to work on the the Fuji 10 x10 Project 2011.

ZIEREN, Mandy (b.1978)
Mandy Zieren is an Avalon-based bodyboarder and photographer. As a bodyboarder Mandy was under-18 Australian Junior Champion in 1995, then Australian Pro Tour Champ 2002 and 2003. She won numerous regional and State titles and single events along the way, including the first Pipeline Pro 2006. Her highest World Tour ranking was third in 2005.